# aurora metro press

Founded in 1989 to publish and promote new writing, the press has specialised in new drama and fiction, winning recognition and awards from the industry.

*new drama anthologies*
**Young Blood,** five plays for young performers.
ed. Sally Goldsworthy **ISBN 0-9515877-6-5 £9.95**

**Charles Way: Plays for Young Performers**
**ISBN 0-9536757-1-8 £9.95**

**Black and Asian Plays Anthology,** introduced by Afia Nkrumah **ISBN 0-9536757-4-2 £9.95**

**Six Plays by Black and Asian Women Writers.** ed. Kadija George **ISBN 0-9515877-2-2 £7.50**

**Best of the Fest.** new plays celebrating 10 years of London New Play Festival ed. Phil Setren **ISBN 0-9515877-8-1 £12.99**

**Seven plays by women,** female voices, fighting lives.
ed. Cheryl Robson **ISBN 0-9515877-1-4 £5.95**

*European drama anthologies*
**Balkan Plots,** plays from Central and Eastern Europe, introduced by Gina Landor **ISBN 0-9536757-3-4 £9.95**

**Eastern Promise,** 7 plays from Central and Eastern Europe eds. Sian Evans and Cheryl Robson **ISBN 0-9515877-9-X £11.99**

**Mediterranean plays by women.** ed. Marion Baraitser **ISBN 0-9515877-3-0 £9.95**

**A touch of the Dutch:** plays n
**ISBN 0-9515877-7-3 £9.95**

D1514116

We gratefully acknowledge financial assistance from Channel 4 TV, The Arts Council of England, London Arts and the Association of London Government.

Cover photo from 'Fittings: The Last Freak Show' by Joel Fildes. 0161 773 0070
With thanks to: Jenny Sealey, Roger Nelson, Annette Cumper, Richard Wilson, Jamie Beddard, Patrick Baldwin, Simon Gould, Joel Fildes.

**ISBN 0-9536757-6-9** Printed by Antony Rowe, Chippenham

# GRAE*ae* PLAYS 1

**new plays redefining disability**

selected and introduced by Jenny Sealey
with a foreword by Richard Wilson

**Hound**
by Maria Oshodi

**Soft Vengeance**
by April De Angelis

**Sympathy for the Devil**
by Ray Harrison Graham

**Fittings: The Last Freak Show**
by Mike Kenny

**Into The Mystic**
by Peter Wolf

**peeling**
by Kaite O'Reilly

# AURORA METRO PRESS

LONDON ARTS

Association of
**London** Government

Funded by
THE
**ARTS**
**COUNCIL**
OF ENGLAND

**Grae'ae,** *n.* pl.[L; Gr. *Graiai*, pl. of *graia*, old woman, from *grais*, old; akin to *geron*, old man.] in Greek Mythology, the three daughters of Phorcus, a sea god: they acted as guards for the Gorgons and had but one eye and one tooth to share among them.

# Foreword
## by Richard Wilson

This anthology marks the end of Grae*ae*'s 21<sup>st</sup> year and sees the company gearing up for the premiere of *peeling*; the 34<sup>th</sup> production, and latest inclusion in this publication.

Those twenty-one years have been a long, hard and eventful struggle to keep going and, more importantly, growing. To have become such a respected, creative and occasionally irksome player on the British theatre circuit is a glowing testimony to all those who have invested time and energy into the company.

Many doors have been battered, motorways navigated, theatregoers entertained and enlightened, critics bemused (not difficult!), and not a few disabled people empowered along the way.

This collection of plays confronts an enormous range of issues and perceptions surrounding disability. The six plays are vastly different in their topics and approach, but all share a communality of spirit.

The six plays – *Hound* by Maria Oshodi, *Soft Vengeance* by April De Angelis, *Sympathy for the Devil* by Ray Harrison Graham, *Fittings: The Last Freak Show* by Mike Kenny, *Into The Mystic* by Peter Wolf and *peeling* by Kaite O'Reilly – are taken chronologically, and provide invaluable insights into an artistic journey. They also shed light on the development of the creative processes that have led disability arts out of the ghetto into a wider artistic arena.

Grae*ae* is a company I have been delighted to support for a number of years as patron, audience member and erstwhile workshop leader. I have watched their development with interest, and was only too happy to lend my name to this anthology. It is not only a celebration of past successes, but should also provide a lively springboard as Grae*ae* looks towards the next 21 years.

# Contents

# Introduction
## by Jenny Sealey

Grae*ae* is Britain's premier professional theatre company of disabled people. Founded by Nabil Shaban and Richard Tomlinson in 1980 to address the exclusion of disabled people within theatre, Grae*ae* tours nationally and internationally, and is the only professional theatre company of physically and sensory disabled people in Europe.

The company has become renowned for producing theatre that is pioneering in its aesthetic and content, and is an influential theatrical voice with audiences, theatre workers, critics, the arts establishment and the disabled community. The development of new writing has always been central to Grae*ae*'s work. New writing, as we know, is the life-blood of dynamic theatre and is often 'the research and development laboratory' for the film and television industry. Consequently, it is even more important for Grae*ae* to nurture new work in a field fraught with the politics of representation.

In 1995, a research project supported by the Paul Hamlyn Foundation identified existing opportunities and initiatives to encourage the development of disabled people writing for the theatre. This highlighted dramatic gaps in provision of opportunities for disabled people and pinpointed the isolation of aspiring writers trying to navigate their way through the writing process; from initial ideas, to commission. This anthology starts with the new writing developed under the artistic directorship of Ewan Marshall. He set up a series of writing initiatives, and his debut was *Hound,* a new play by Maria Oshodi. A play by a black, disabled writer for a disabled theatre company, about hard-core disability issues. This marked an important breakthrough for Grae*ae*, as it established a new voice of disabled artists in British theatre, and challenged the assumption that disability theatre was either 'worthy' or appealing to the sympathy of its audiences.

Previously, the failing of much new writing in disability theatre was that it left its audiences feeling browbeaten by a 'message.' Here there are clear parallels with some black, gay and lesbian and feminist theatre writing, which – at its worst – had also become mundane and stereotypical. Important though these experiments were in developing the confidence of theatre artists, the result was often counter-productive ghettoisation. Despite this, there remained the relentless necessity to have a voice, and a determination to tell the hidden stories of disabled people. This meant that Grae*ae* had to rediscover its audience and to find genuinely engaging theatrical material that would both challenge and inspire.

Ewan continued to work closely with writers to develop scripts that tackled difficult issues which would challenge both actors and audiences. Perhaps it's no coincidence that in developing this writing, he so often looked to explore the overlap between disability and racial issues. He brought together the creative force of April De Angelis – herself non-disabled – and Albie Sachs, to adapt Albie's life story of the fallout from a political bombing in South Africa – *Soft Vengeance*. The sheer political intensity of the play and Albie's determination not to be viewed as a victim worked to offer a new range of nuances to disability theatre.

*Sympathy for the Devil* by Ray Harrison Graham, a collaboration between Basic Theatre Company and Grae*ae,* looked at the double impact of being both black and disabled. The play asked crucial questions of identity; is a person black or disabled first? Is discrimination compounded by this dual identity? What is the emotional impact of experiencing two contrasting forms of prejudice?

Following Ewan in 1997, I took up the reigns as Artistic Director of the company, and took on a mission to ensure that all our new work was nurtured within a collaborative ethos. Wherever possible, our teams were exclusively disabled, but often – where other skills and experience were sought – we welcomed non-disabled colleagues. In a sense, this collaborative sensibility has helped disabled artists to gain confidence as theatre-makers. It's no coincidence that some of our most promising performers are now stretching their theatrical wings as directors and writers. Our strand of major new writing initiatives has been solidly underpinned by this growing sense of ensemble.

In 2000 we saw the successful culmination of the Grae*ae*/ Writernet *Disabled Writers' Mentoring Scheme* at Soho Theatre. Nine 'mentees' worked with established writers – Alan Plater, Lucinda Coxon, Patrick Marber, Mark Ravenhill, Kaite O'Reilly, Philip Osment, Anne Coburn, Elizabeth Melville and Sarah Woods. As with all Grae*ae*'s work, practical concerns were placed alongside artistic considerations and all our developing writers had their access requirements met so they could focus on their writing. All nine have now completed their first draft of a full-length play. It was through this scheme that Grae*ae* nurtured the work of Peter Wolf and commissioned *Into The Mystic* with Mark Ravenhill working as Peter's mentor.

Over the last four years Grae*ae* has been redefining and pushing at the notion of 'access,' to encompass an aesthetic as well as practical and political vision. We have received enormous encouragement and positive feedback from blind and visually impaired audience members for weaving live audio description into the fabric of our plays. Our deaf, BSL (British Sign Language) using audience has also consistently seen BSL employed imaginatively on the stage. We are currently embracing the challenge to make our plays as access-ible as possible to the non-BSL using element within the deaf community. Each new play is now developed through intensive alliances between writers, directors, actors and deaf and blind advisors. Perhaps uniquely in theatre, 'access' has become integral to dramaturgy. Maybe one day all plays will be made this way.

The next four plays mark the journey of the company's commit-ment to explore artistic accessibility through new narratives. *Fittings: The Last Freak Show* was a collaboration between Fittings Multi Media Arts and Grae*ae*. Garry Robson, myself and the actors, worked with the writer Mike Kenny, to ensure the structure of text worked with the actors' particular delivery of speech. The text was written in such a way as to enable a character to sign and speak at the same time (Sign Supported English, or SSE). Issues of access therefore influenced the script and became part of an artistic and character approach.

*Fittings* toured in a tent and was a truly wild affair playing at an eclectic number of venues from Glastonbury, to the undercroft in The Roundhouse in Camden. People were horrified to hear the word 'Freaks' reclaimed but once the rogue character of Gustav Drool, the ringmaster gave the audience the permission to look at the freaks, people sat back to be entertained in the style of the old carnivals.

*Into The Mystic* by Peter Wolf was a commission born out of the mentoring scheme described above. A passion play pitching the cold logic of medical science against the mystery of being human, *Into The Mystic* asks new questions about our identity in a world of junk food and genetic engineering.

The force behind the meticulous research was Peter's own battle – his auto-immune disease; his isolation and years in the darkness when his past came back to overwhelm his present. Peter and I worked to ensure the text carried a linear visual narrative to enable blind audiences to hear what was happening physically on stage. This process developed especially through the role of the doctor by having him recording everything about the protagonist Jade into a dictaphone. It became both a medical and obsessional tool for the character to relay the visual and physical disintegration of Jade. This in turn worked as Audio Description (AD). In production week it became clear that additional audio description was needed to locate scenes and costume changes. The sign language interpreter took on the role of vocalising additional AD. I have deliberately kept all AD as part of the final draft to emphasise our aim to create a wholly accessible production.

*peeling* by Kaite O'Reilly is a new commission which has created a tight relationship between a writer who is formerly visually impaired and a director who is deaf. *peeling* wholly addresses new narratives through the inclusion of Audio Description as a starting point and now an integral part of the text. We have challenged new ways of incorporating sign language, through the use of BSL and SSE, believing in the theatricality of signed language being written, voiced over and signed in its own grammatical form. *peeling* has strengthened our resolve in the potential of everyone in the audience receiving the same information, but not necessarily at the same time.

*peeling* examines the issues of sex and pregnancy through the stories of three disabled women. Such issues are hidden from the mainstream and gross assumptions will continue to be made because people dare not ask and few artists have explored the subject. Each character has differing opinions on sex /abortion /motherhood /adoption and this works to demystify the issues, enabling us to broker the gap between the disabled and non-disabled experience and think more globally about being women.

We are at present collaborating on the **disPlay 4** project with Writernet, Soho Theatre and Writers' Centre (in association with the BBC and Channel 4). Four new writers have received first draft commissions. Also we are engaged in a series of **Wild Lunches**, with Paines Plough Theatre Company, culminating in their infamous 'lock in' enabling the writer to pen their first draft for a lunchtime reading. We have young disabled people on writing courses with the Royal Court Young People's Theatre. In all this work, we are trying to raise our script development from the isolation so often experienced by companies concerned with the politics of representation and to engage with a range of both innovative and proven dramaturgical practices.

This anthology is all about the visibility and the inclusion of disabled artists within society. All Grae*ae*'s work aims to promote the excellence of its artists, but it can never shirk from the responsibility to educate its audience by the very virtue of being disabled professionals in a world of barriers and a lack of positive role models. Only when disabled artists have a fair and representative degree of exposure will exclusion and discriminatory attitudes start to shift.

This anthology is also intended as a resource for those working both educationally and as practitioners in the field of disability and the arts. It can be used practically with students to explore the texts and the issues they raise through workshops, drama and readings. It can be used as a study aid by those interested in researching the ways disabled artists have increasingly come to the fore in the last ten years and hopefully, it may be used to develop future courses for the training of actors, directors, technicians etc. or more generally to enable people to gain awareness and understanding of disability.

I hope this anthology is the first of many, (there are so many more stories to be told), and that it charts Grae*ae*'s (accessible) journey into new theatrical landscapes.

# <u>Hound</u>

# Hound

Writing well for me means that something critical has to be at stake, something for which I am prepared to raise myself above the parapet. This play was my first public examination of my own disability. Furthermore, I took the risk of confronting the sometimes-negative effects of a charity system, on which I knew, I would still need to depend.

Despite the play being boycotted in some parts of the country to which it toured, I do not regret the risk I took. Audiences told me they recognized their own experiences portrayed, and I was glad to have used the opportunity to include the accounts of the many people who I interviewed during my research.

On a personal level, I developed artistically. Casting the production exposed Britain's lack of visually impaired trained actors and the limited way they were accustomed to work on stage. Having worked as an actor with sighted directors myself, I understood how frustrating this could be as a performer, and so began to put some thought into how to address this state of affairs.

Over the past several years I have created an arts company, *Extant*, dedicated to the development of blind actors and the production of innovative work from our rich visually impaired culture. Initially, we were funded to research the uncharted relationship between visual impairment, spatial awareness, movement and the stage, with a group of blind professional actors. Now we are developing creative material with which we can test some of the findings from the research project. *Extant* has also built international links with a network of blind theatre companies who come together at the Blind in Theatre Festival, which is held every two years, hosted by a company called *New Life* in Zagreb, Croatia. Where there is a neglect of visual impaired performers in Britain, these festivals offer a forum for cultural exchange and identification with up to nine companies travelling across the globe to present their work. *Extant* is currently planning to bring the 50 year old company, *New Life*, to England on tour and present them in their dynamic, absurdist and highly physical production of *Zeros and Nils*.

**Maria Oshodi**

# Hound

## Maria Oshodi

This play was first performed on 12th February, 1992 at Oval House Theatre, London with the following cast.

| CHARACTERS | CAST |
| --- | --- |
| **Vince** | David Bowen |
| **Nazma** | Veronique Christie |
| **Joe** | Dave Kent |
| **Aysha** | Marvel Opara |
| **Desirée** | Kate Portal |
| **Compere** | David Bowen |
| Live dog | Giles |
| | |
| Director | Ewan Marshall |
| Designer | Sue Mayes |
| Lighting designer | Ace McCarron |

*Characters:*

**Vince Stevens** *A sighted, attractive, white man in his mid-thirties. Fully dedicated to his job and fully affected by it.*

**Nazma Zabic** *A sighted attractive, Asian woman in her early thirties. Confident, and trying to make progress with issues important to her.*

**Joe Tilson** *A congenitally, blind, white man in his early thirties. He has defined himself through the success of his career.*

**Aysha Kharno** *A congenitally blind, black woman in her late twenties. Confident and trying to define herself on her own terms.*

**Desiree Langholm** *A newly blind, attractive, white woman in her early twenties, caught between old and new expectations of herself.*

**Compere** *A sighted white man, thirty to forty with all the energy and effort of a minor celebrity.*

**ACT ONE**
**SCENE 1**
*A music mosaic, combining elements of sound, later featured in the*
*play, but now super imposed with an assortment of other influences.*
*Perhaps, a jamboree theme tune, an emotive, sentimental melody, the*
*sound of numerous telephones ringing, of cash rolling, morse code*
*beeps, the hyped cheering from crowds, snatches of fund raising, pop*
*records, etc. After some time the sounds fade and a spot light down*
*stage snaps on. In this light, the Compere stands, holding a*
*microphone, and wearing a jazzy suit.*

**COMPERE** *(to the audience, and laughing)* Thanks Chris! Right,
okay. Well we've got a personal appeal coming up right now.

*Nazma leads Joe and a dog on stage.*

**COMPERE** I'd like to introduce you to Mr Joe Tilson and his
wonderful pal. Come on people, let's give them a big hand!

*Nazma stands with Joe and his dog, by the Compere.*

**COMPERE** Thanks Naz.
**JOE** *(to the dog)* Sit!
**COMPERE** Only if I can't lie down. Oh the dog. Oh look, *(To*
*the audience)* isn't he a clever boy?! Delightful, delightful.
**NAZMA** *(into a microphone as she exits)* Nice close shots on both
of them, camera two.
**COMPERE** Now Joe, thank you very much for coming into the
studio, live tonight. It's very brave of you, I must admit, and I
should know. They offered me danger money to do this show.
**JOE** Not at all, it's my pleasure.
**COMPERE** So you've come in to tell us about this very special
friend of yours, haven't you?
**JOE** Yes indeed, good old Charles.
**COMPERE** *(to the audience)* And Charles, ladies and gentlemen, is
of course a seeing eye dog. What's he like Joe?
**JOE** Terrific.
**COMPERE** Your best friend?
**JOE** With out a doubt, because he's the most–

**COMPERE** *(raising his hand to his ear)* Hold on, hold on. I think we're getting our next total through.
*(A high frequency squeal sounds)*
*(Holding his head)* God, our audience might be legless tonight, but the last thing they want to do is go home deaf as well. Right, let's see how cheque book and credit card crazy you are. There it is! Flashing on your screens now.
*(Nazma walks behind the two carrying a huge cheque displaying the figure, and exits)*
The fabulously staggering £249,607 and 51 pence! And we've only just started. That magic figure shows how big your hearts are, but that amount is nowhere near enough. We'll be showing you soon some very hungry hard working organisations out there. We can feed the most salivating of them, with any wonga you could kindly spare, so, please, please, please, dig deep and pledge, pledge, pledge, and keep those phone lines burning.
*(Turning back to Joe)* Joe, what d'you say?

**JOE** Oh yes, most definitely.

**COMPERE** Joe, you were telling us about your trusty friend. Now, however much we would want them to, they don't last for ever, do they?

**JOE** No. After years of hard and loyal work, they get ill and, well, pass on, or just grow old.

**COMPERE** *(Stroking the dog's head)* How old is this feller?

**JOE** Eleven, and he's reached the ripe old age for retirement now.

**COMPERE** *(clocks a doleful look at the audience)* But, you've come on tonight to tell us how everyone, through their generosity, can help.

**JOE** It only takes five pence from everyone out there, to buy and train three dogs, that could help me and three others, just like me.

**COMPERE** Did you hear that? Just five pence, that's all it takes and we can get Joe's problems solved. *(He pats Joe's shoulder)* Good Joe, thanks. *(He pats the dog)* And thanks Charles, good boy.

**JOE** Er...

**COMPERE** Yeah Joe, something else?

**JOE**             I'd just like to add that the Royal Bank of Britain, where I work, have told me to mention that if anyone makes a cheque out to the appeal, then automatically their account with us gets free bank charges for six months.

**COMPERE**     How about that then? What a gesture. Thank you, Royal Bank of Britain. Now, you lot out there have got no excuse, come on, let's buy Joe a new pair of eyes. Remember, you could so easily be him. Now back to our evening of sheer, mental, wackiness. We're going to take you over to the auction rooms, right now, where you can join with our celebrities in imagining yourselves behind the wheel of that spanking, sparkling, two seater, Cheetah. *(Pause. A look of confusion passes over his face. The spot light begins to dim)* No? Er, right, we're going into a break, or is it up to the sponsored slug chew in Liverpool? *(Laughing)* Not there either! Well any-way, that's a taste of the rip-roaring fun we've got in store for you tonight... and ladies and gentlemen, this is just to prove that it's all live.

*The spotlight fades to blackout.*

**SCENE 2**
*A chorus of barking dogs, that fade into distant sounds.*

**VOICEOVER** This is the class. You are the students. Welcome to the Centre.

*Lights come up on stage. To stage left: the students lounge area, carpeted, and with comfortable sofas, arm chairs, and polished tables in between. These are arranged, squarely around the edge of the carpet. The stage left wall has a door which leads out of the student lounge. Down stage, behind the lounge, runs a corridor. The down stage wall from left to right has, an office door, a pay telephone, double swing doors with glass panels at the top, which lead off-stage, a fire extinguisher and a small bar with two stools that are turned up-side down on the counter. Stage right is bare, and should remain unlit, except for room and street scenes etc.*

*Enter Vince, through office door, into the corridor. He walks briskly along, towards stage right, whistling.*

**VINCE** *(seeing Joe, off stage right)* Hey Joe, my man! Great to see you.

*He exits right and enters again, moments later, leading Joe who is carrying a suitcase.*

**VINCE** *(reaching for the case)* I'll take that.

**JOE**        That's alright Vince.

**VINCE**      Fine by me. Save these old shoulders the strain.

**JOE**        But you don't save the old elbow from any straining in the bar, I bet?

**VINCE** *(laughing)* That's right. The only place worth doing any straining, eh Joe?

**JOE**        Good to know that some things stay the same.

**VINCE**      So, when was it that you were last here then?

**JOE**        Eight years in March.

**VINCE**      Yeah?

**JOE**        Yep. I was twenty-two when I got Champ.

**VINCE**      I must have been in the kennels then. Phew! That seems like some time back in the last century now.

**JOE**        Not to me. Coming through those doors again, brings it all back. Feels like yesterday.

**VINCE**      Okay then Joe, let's see if your memory stands up to the test of time. You've come in the main doors, so where are you now?

**JOE**        In the main corridor.

**VINCE**      Okay, an' what's on your left?

**JOE**        The bar, a set of double swing doors and an office door at the top.

**VINCE**      And what's on the other side of the double doors?

**JOE**        Student bedrooms, and beyond them the grooming room, and beyond that a set of doors leading out to the car park, kennels, obstacle walk and fields.

**VINCE**      That's fantastic.

**JOE**        And what's the number of my room please?

**VINCE**      Yours is , em, number five.

**JOE**        Well that's through these doors and down on the left if I'm not mistaken.

**VINCE**      You're not. God, I don't know how you do it.

**JOE**            Training Vince, you should know all about that.

**VINCE**            It looks like I can leave the next three weeks up to
you then Joe. I expect smooth sailing from beginning to end.

**JOE**            I certainly hope so, and not for my sake, but for the
programme as well.

**VINCE** *(knocking on the right of the double doors and guiding Joe
through)* Yes, we must have a little chat about that...

*Blackout.*

**VOICEOVER** For the next three weeks, our main concern is to
train you and your dog, and that should be your first and foremost
concern too. If being trained is not your main priority, then you
should reconsider, as this is unfortunately not the place for you.

*Lights come up on corridor, where Aysha is at the telephone. She
dials and Vince enters the corridor, stage left.*

**VINCE**            Oh good, you found the phone then Aysha?

**AYSHA**            Yeah, no problem.

**VINCE** *(going into his office)* Good, lovely.

*He exits through the door, leaving it open.*

**AYSHA** *(on phone.)* Hello, this is a message for Stephanie, it's
Aysha Karno. My number at the Centre is, *(She feels the Braille
numbers on the phone)* 0243-336-950. You've already got the
address and can you please remember not to forward any letters to
me here, in print? I don't want to have to get anyone here to read
them for me. Thanks. I'll be in contact soon. Bye. *(She hangs up)*

**VINCE** *(comes out of his office)* Gonna be expecting lots of calls
then Aysha?

**AYSHA** *(starts)* Eh?

**VINCE**            Oh I just overheard you then, giving out the
telephone number. It's good to know that our Braille labels are
clear and easy to locate on the box.

**AYSHA** *(relaxing)* Oh yeah, right. Well, seeing as you mention it.
That label is okay, but the one on my door with my name on, isn't.

**VINCE**            Oh why's that? Is Aysha Kharno wrong?

AYSHA      That's not, but the Mrs is.

VINCE      Mrs? Oh I see!

AYSHA      I wonder why you thought that? I wouldn't have put that on any of your forms.

VINCE      Well, probably because you've got a little boy, haven't you?

AYSHA      Hmm?

VINCE      Most likely why it was thought that you were, well you know. But, if it's a problem, then no problem. Nothing simpler. It can be changed. We'll knock out the middle letter of Mrs, and we hide a multitude of sins, don't we?

*Blackout.*

VOICEOVER There are only a handful of you, the students, here, but there are many times your number, of staff. We are all attempting to operate successfully, so to ensure we all function safely and sanely at our different levels there are some important rules that we must adhere to.

*Lights come up on the student lounge. A knock on the student lounge door, off stage. Vince enters, leading Desirée in.*

VINCE      And when you want to leave again, knock on the door. It's just in case there's someone else on the other side. Then they know the door's about to be opened, and it'll save us any unnecessary bumps or bruises.

DESIREE    Right, okay.

VINCE      You'll get used to it. Now in here, this is the student lounge, an' you can basically, whenever you've got any free time, come in here, twenty four hours a day. This is your communal area. You can sit around, chat, make yourself tea or coffee, at any time. It's always there with a supply of biscuits and sandwiches. Now ahead of us there are three doors, leading to a TV room, a games room and a tape library, and there are some patio windows...

DESIREE *(looking right)* Over there.

VINCE      Oh yeah that's right, you've got some residual vision haven't you?

**DESIREE**     Yeah, I have.

**VINCE**        Well that's something that could come in useful
while you're training, or it could work against you, by getting in
the way. We'll have to see. I'll describe the lay-out of the room to
you shall I?

**DESIREE**     Thanks.

**VINCE**        Well on the floor, in the middle, there's a large
rectangular rug, you can feel the edge of it here with your foot.
It's completely bare and it's, *(He walks her forward)* One, two,
three, four, five, six paces in length, and one, two, three, four, say
five paces in width. Have you got that?

**DESIREE**     Yes thanks.

**VINCE** *(completing the circuit of the rug)* There are armchairs and
sofas all round here, and then we're back to the door, okay?

**DESIREE**     Yeah, got it.

**VINCE**        Right, Desirée... rather nice name you've got there.

**DESIREE**     Oh, do you like it?

**VINCE**        Don't you?

**DESIREE**     Well, it's alright.

**VINCE**        Suits you. *(Pause)* Now the people you came with,
are they still here?

**DESIREE**     No, I told them I... well they've gone.

**VINCE**        Right, well if I leave you here, do you think you
could find your own way back to your room?

**DESIREE**     Out of this room, turn left, left again, down the
corridor to the swing doors, through them, and I'm on the right.

**VINCE**        Good, lovely. Now, how do we walk in the
corridors?

**DESIREE**     Always on the right hand side.

**VINCE**        Ah, pretty bright as well. I see we'll have no trouble
with your orientation, will we?

*He leaves. For a moment Desirée looks in the direction of the door.
A faint, hollow, musical sound stirs. She turns and begins to move
about the room.*

**DESIREE** *(half aloud)* Up on the right, grope the wall, down on the
left, knock at the door. Six paces, four paces, three blind mice.

*She collapses, resigned, into a chair and exhales a long sigh. The musical vibration lingers as lights go down on the lounge.*

**VOICEOVER** In this confined space, we will all have to come into contact with each other. You have not been chosen because you have compatible personalities. You have been chosen because of your common need. If we were all angels, then this could be heaven. But we are not. We are human, and there are bound to be some of us who do not get on. If this is the case, then it is strongly urged that you do not resort to in-fighting or back-biting. Instead, go to your room, roll up a sock, place it in your mouth, and scream.

## SCENE 3
*Lights up on student lounge. Desirée hauls herself up out of the chair and goes to the door. As she knocks on it, there is a knock on the other side. She steps back and Joe enters.*

**JOE** *(more to himself)* And if I'm right, then is this the lounge?
**DESIREE** Yes, it is. *(Aside)* Another wall-groper.
**JOE** Oh, someone's here. *(Aside)* Kennel girl or student,?
**DESIREE** Yes, I'm just going.
**JOE** *(closing the door)* Who have I the pleasure of?
**DESIREE** *(aside)* Oh God. *(To Joe)* I'm Desirée.
**JOE** *(holds his hand out)* Pleased to meet you. I'm Joe. *(Aside)* Hasn't shaken my hand... she's a student.
**DESIREE** Well I must finish my unpacking. *(She knocks on the door)*
**JOE** Oh, leaving already?

*Another knock comes from the other side of the door.*

**DESIREE** *(aside)* Doesn't look like it.
**AYSHA** *(opening the door and coming in)* Hi!

*The others reply.*

**AYSHA** We've all got to meet in here, haven't we?
**DESIREE** *(aside)* A black girl.

**JOE** *(aside)*   Sure she's black.

**DESIREE**      Oh, I thought it was later.

**JOE**          No, it's now. They're going to take us out and go through some basic training.

**DESIREE**      Basic training?

**AYSHA**        You know, all that stuff they did with us on the streets, when they came to our homes to interview us.

**JOE**          We'll more than likely go out one by one with our instructor, to polish up the preliminaries.

**AYSHA** *(to Joe)* You been through all this before, as well then?

**JOE**          Yeah, had a Lab-cross, called Charles. Worked for eight years, retired him two months ago.

**AYSHA** *(aside)* This guy is white and about thirty.

**DESIREE**      Might as well sit down again.

*The three move across the room.*

**DESIREE** *(aside)* Those two are replacements. Am I the only applicant?

**JOE** *(sitting and patting a seat next to him)* There's a seat here Desirée.

**DESIREE**      That's alright Joe, I've got one here.

*The three sit with plenty of room between them. There is a brief silence.*

**AYSHA**        I'm Aysha.

**DESIREE** *(aside)* The extravert.

**JOE**          I'm Joe, and Desirée and I have already been acquainted.

**DESIREE**      That's me.

**AYSHA** *(aside)* White, twenty three, grew up in the home counties.

*There is a short silence.*

**DESIREE** *(aside)* It seems that the stream of conversation amongst the head hangers has run out already.

**AYSHA** *(aside)* Don't need the weather man to tell me that I'm in for the driest three weeks on record.

**JOE** *(aside)* I wonder if there are any other men in class.

*More silence.*

**AYSHA** *(aside)* The maternity ward was like this. Baby sounds,
   baby smells, things around for the baby, and waiting for the stork
   to bring the bundle.
**JOE** *(aside)* No visits for the first ten days. Hope Denise won't miss
   me too much.
**DESIREE** *(aside)* Well this is it. Officially squeezed into the
   sausage machine. Maybe I'll even get a Datsun.

*Knock at the door and Vince enters.*

**VINCE**          Right now, who shall I have first?... Er, Desirée?

*Blackout.*

**SCENE 4**
*Lights come up on stage right. In the background, a faint military
drill plays. Vince enters on the edge of the stage, holding a harness
handle, between him and Desirée.*

**VINCE**          You're Desirée and who am I?
**DESIREE**        The dog.
**VINCE**          What?
**DESIREE** *(louder)* The dog!
**VINCE**          Better. Fido heard you that time. Okay, what do you
   say?
**DESIREE**        Forward

*Vince walks forward and Desirée follows.*

**VINCE**          S.I.T.
**DESIREE**        Sit.
**VINCE**          Fido's sitting. What am I?
**DESIREE**        A dog.
**VINCE**          No!
**DESIREE**        Oh yes, um... good boy.

**VINCE**          Right, what else? *(Pause)* I'm going. *(He makes a move)*

**DESIREE**     No, stay!

**VINCE**          And what am I?

**DESIREE**     Good boy.

**VINCE**          Right, and again.

**DESIREE**         Forward.

**VINCE** *(not moving)* Fido is not too enthused.

**DESIREE** *(jollier)* Forward.

**VINCE** *(walking and leading Desirée offstage)* And keep that positive re-enforcement coming. *(He re-enters, leading Joe on.)* I'm speeding up.

**JOE**             Steady, good boy.

**VINCE**          I'm slowing down.

**JOE**             Hup up, good boy.

**VINCE**          S.I.T.

**JOE**             Sit.

**VINCE**          And a flick on that handle.

**JOE**             Oh yeah, right. With Charles–

**VINCE**          Forget Charles. You're getting a new dog, who needs his handle flicked. Okay, we want to go left.

**JOE** *(steps back and slaps his thigh)* Left.

**VINCE** *(moving around Joe and leading him offstage)* And lots of praise. *(He returns, leading on Aysha.)* Right, I'm sniffing.

**AYSHA** *(laughing)* Leave it!

**VINCE**          It's a very interesting lamp post. I'm still sniffing.

**AYSHA** *(harder)* Leave it!

**VINCE**          Where do I go?

**AYSHA**         Straight on.

**VINCE**          And what am I?

**AYSHA**         Good dog.

**VINCE**          I'm not wagging my tail.

**AYSHA**         So?

**VINCE**          Make me wag my tail, or I won't do anything for you..

**AYSHA** *(more enthusiastic)* Good boy, good boy.

**VINCE**          Ah, it's wagging now.

*He leads her offstage and the drill music fades out with the lights.*

**SCENE 5**

*Lights come back up on the student lounge. A knock on the door and Joe enters, followed by Aysha and Desirée. They all hold carrier bags.*

**JOE**  No, not today. It'll be some time tomorrow, I imagine.

**DESIREE**  Really! God. Where can I sit?

**AYSHA**  Anywhere. The others are still outside. We've got the place to ourselves.

*They all sit and begin rooting around in their bags.*

**JOE**  Yes, there's a big introduction procedure. What generally happens is that we wait in our rooms, and at some point, our instructors, bring our ones to us. They tell us to sit in our chairs, so we don't look too threatening when they come in with them, don't they Aysha?

**AYSHA**  All I remember them telling us, was we might have to wait, so we musn't forget to go to the toilet. *(Foraging in the bag)* They really should have thrown a couple of spare nappies in here for us as well.

**DESIREE**  I can't remember what half the things in this bag are for.

**JOE**  It's a peculiar moment.

**DESIREE**  Peculiar, what?

**JOE**  Well... they leave the dogs with us, and naturally, we want to make a bit of a fuss of them, and the dogs, on the whole like that, but they don't respond that much to it, not at first.

**AYSHA**  Yeah, that's true. They're well into the instructors aren't they? I was all geared up last time. I'd been waiting so long for it, and then I felt real shock... yeah, it was hard when I realised that the thing didn't even want to be with me.

**JOE**  Well it's pretty understandable that they're going to be attached to the people who've had them for eight months, but it's our job now to reverse that attachment to ourselves. That's what they've got us here for.

**AYSHA** *(sighing)* Yes, for a nice spell of internment, and who'd have it any other way.

**DESIREE** All these bits and pieces, to clean the dog, to put on the dog, to wear ourselves. It's like a Chinese puzzle. What's this belt thing?

**JOE** Probably a Sam Brown, but I've gone one better than that. Vince has shown me the new range of waterproof clothing that they've got on sale here. I've put my order in already.

**DESIREE** What, it's luminous, like a Sam Brown?

**JOE** Yeah, I think I've ordered green, or was it yellow? Anyway, it's an all-in-one suit.

**DESIREE** And all in all that sounds, em, brilliant.

**AYSHA** Gonna get one?

**DESIREE** Let's say I'm contemplating it.

**JOE** There's a limited stock, so I wouldn't take too long.

**DESIREE** With some luck they might run out. *(fumbling with the chain)* I don't get the way this choke chain is meant to go.

**JOE** Check chain.

**AYSHA** Joe's put you in check, so don't forget.

**JOE** It's best to tell her now. You know they don't like slip ups like that.

**DESIREE** It'll all pale into insignificance, once they witness the other cock ups I'll probably perform.

**JOE** Oh you'll be alright. I've never heard of anyone failing. You've got nothing to worry about. I'm not saying it's not going to be hard work, but you'll never look back. They give us great dogs here, and they're worth every bit of effort, eh Aysha?

**AYSHA** Effort? Too right... sometimes, carrying them up escalators, or when they roll in 'odour de fox', or hunting for a restaurant that won't turn you away.

**JOE** *(laughing)* Oh dear, you do look on the black side of things.

**AYSHA** It's inescapable, sometimes Joe.

**JOE** You know, you should meet my fiancée, Denise. You two would get on.

**AYSHA** Is that so?

**JOE** Yeah, she's not much into dogs either.

**AYSHA** If I wasn't into dogs, I wouldn't be here, and without one I wouldn't feel safe coming home from work late at night.

**DESIREE** What do you do?

**AYSHA** I co-ordinate a youth project. So what's your partner's problem, Joe?

**JOE** She says she doesn't want the responsibility, the smell or the dirt.

**AYSHA** But it's a mobility aid for you.

**JOE** I've tried everything to persuade her, but she's so stubborn. She doesn't want anything to do with them.

**AYSHA** That's a bit out of order.

**DESIREE** If she marries into the blind, what does she expect?

**JOE** All I can do, is tell her that when we're married, she'll just have to put up with it, because that's how I come, part and parcel with the dog.

**DESIREE** Maybe she's already thinking of suitable grounds for divorce.

**JOE** Know about divorce then, do you?

**DESIREE** Should do... I'm studying law.

**AYSHA** Isn't married life going to be a bit hard on you, Joe, if that's how she feels?

**JOE** I don't know what else I can do, really. I mean, I would have thought she'd have been convinced by the example I set her. When we're out for instance, I walk twice as fast as her.

**DESIREE** Twice as fast?

**JOE** Yes, she's always tripping people up left, right and centre and getting comments thrown at her like: 'You shouldn't be out'. But no, she will be a stickler for her stick.

**AYSHA** Oh!

**DESIREE** I thought she was –

**AYSHA** So did I. Oh right... so it's her getting the stick from you and Joe Public, because of her stick. Now that *is* out of order.

**JOE** It's just lunacy to me, when she can tell that I just don't get that hassle with a dog.

**DESIREE** Have you ever used a cane, Aysha?

**AYSHA** Yeah.

**JOE** We've found our way around this little problem of ours though. As we both work in the same bank, both our incomes put together can get us quite a good mortgage, for a roomy house where me, her and the dog can all be happy in our own space, so Bob's your uncle – we're getting hitched in October. *(Pause)*

**AYSHA** Have you managed to do the chain?

**DESIREE** Here. *(Giving it to her)*

**AYSHA** *(checking it)* No, that's the wrong way.
**DESIREE**      God, that chain has just about choked my patience.
**JOE**             Check.
**DESIREE**      Choke, check... what does it matter what you call it?
I can't even get the chain right! *(She throws the chain aside on the
floor and flops on a chair.)*

*Blackout.*

## SCENE 6
*Lights up on lounge and corridor. Footsteps are heard offstage.
Nazma bursts through the swing doors and stands in the corridor for
a moment, looking around.*

**NAZMA**        Right, so those were the student's rooms, and what's
down here?
*(She turns towards stage left and walks up the corridor. After
glancing into the staff office, she closes that door and continues
up the corridor, disappearing offstage for a moment. The student
lounge door opens and Nazma enters the room)*
Hmm, cosy and a nice, strong light in here too.
*(Closing the door, she re-enters the corridor. Vince enters from
the other end and hurries up to meet her)*
**VINCE**        Hello?
**NAZMA** *(holding out her hand)* Nazma Zabic. TV West, hi.
**VINCE**        Oh right, yeah, *(shakes her hand)* Vince Stevens. It's
a pleasure to meet you face to face at last.
**NAZMA**        There's only so much one can do by phone. Now, the
real business begins.
**VINCE**        Yeah, well, shall we take a seat somewhere? Let's
grab a pew in the bar. It's closed at the moment. We won't be
disturbed in there.
**NAZMA**        Okay. How are you for office space then? A bit
stretched?
**VINCE** *(removing stools from the bar)* Ah, you could say. The
builders have just started work on a new wing.
**NAZMA**        I had noticed. And what side of the Centre will they
be working? Over there? That's the car park isn't it? *(She starts
scribbling on a pad)*

**VINCE**  Yeah, all the new admin and finance offices, the appeals office, and the residential vet, are all planned for the new building there and one of the fields behind this house hopefully will be turned into our new, bigger car park, if the money lasts.

**NAZMA**  Right, right... so for lawns and flowerbeds out there, now read, cement mixers and pneumatic drills, yeah? Okay. *(thinks)* Well it's expansion to provide an improved service, yeah. *(She scribbles)*

**VINCE**  Most definitely. Let me sort out a drink for you.

**NAZMA**  Orange juice thank you. I must say, I am surprised at how cosy and well catered it is here. Thank you. *(drinks)*

**VINCE**  Well, if we try and get everyone under one roof, to save ourselves organisational headaches, then there has to be a certain amount of facilities here, to suit all needs and because we're in quite a cut off spot.

**NAZMA** *(looking around)* Yes this part is quite old. You can tell from the outside.

**VINCE**  Well, it used to be a Manor House for the surrounding estate, about two hundred years ago.

**NAZMA**  Interesting. Yes, an historical aspect would give the programme a breadth. I'm going to have to discuss the timing of that more with the producer. Might need more information in that area then, if that's alright.

**VINCE**  Yeah.

**NAZMA**  Good. *(scribbles notes)* And with that we can also reflect the solidity, er, the tried and tested nature of your association.

**VINCE**  Oh well yes, the Major's who you want – he's the expert there, and I'm sure he'll be delighted to assist you.

**NAZMA**  Right good. Now, I need to talk about Joe. Am I right in thinking that he won't be training alone?

**VINCE**  No. Even though it's quite a small class this time, the students will be in groups. An apprentice instructor is taking the three elderly students, and I'm training the three younger ones, including Joe.

**NAZMA**  And will they be trained together, or individually?

**VINCE**  Well, they will be doing the same walks, but during that, they'll be getting individual instruction.

**NAZMA**     Okay, so that means that the other two with Joe, will be more than likely appearing in shots as well. I'll need to get their permission. What are their names?

**VINCE**     Aysha and Desirée.

**NAZMA**     Two women, good. Now, interiors. *(looks around)*

**VINCE**     Yes?

**NAZMA**     We're going to have to set up extra lighting here in the corridors, and any bedrooms or offices we use.

**VINCE**     Lights, right. I'd better let the house Keeper know about that.

**NAZMA**     But communal spaces, with lots of windows, letting in natural light, we won't need to set up much there.

**VINCE**     Like the student lounge, or the dining hall.

**NAZMA**     Yes, the dining room should be a good one. Tell me, how does that work?

**VINCE**     Well, there are lots of chairs and tables and we all sit down to eat.

**NAZMA** *(smiles)* No, what I mean is, what's the service? Self, or waited, and will these three be sitting together?

**VINCE**     Oh, I see. No, we bring their food to them at the tables and at the moment, no, these three aren't sitting together.

**NAZMA**     Communal, domestic shots, yeah. Add a feeling of warmth and sharing.

**VINCE**     Oh yeah?

**NAZMA**     Yes, and we can also show the viewer that your association's money also goes on the costs of boarding the students, as well as the training service.

**VINCE**     Yes, I see, that's right.

**NAZMA**     Yes, and I like the idea of bringing the food to them. It illustrates the concept behind the whole programme of help, and also, it'll reflect on the staff here, as of course, caring people.

**VINCE** *(slightly embarrassed)* Yeah well, em, I'll look into getting the students re-arranged on their tables then.

**NAZMA**     If you could. Now, I've got to sort out a shooting schedule for the crew, so, if you could give me some sort of time-table of how Joe's training is going to go in the next three weeks, that will be much appreciated.

**VINCE**     Yes, there's one upstairs where my stuff's been shifted. *(gets up)*

NAZMA     I can already see that this is going to be a tight fit.
VINCE     Is it?
NAZMA     Well, there's all the personal element of Joe as well, and his great achievements in the bank.
VINCE     We've all got a lot of respect for him here. Joe's a good example of diligence and hard work.
NAZMA     Definitely. He's amazing, but it looks like I'm going to have to be, as well. The producer is insisting on at least a seven minute interview with him, and with all the rest of the information... phew!
VINCE     Well, you strike me as very, em, capable. I'm sure you'll find a way, and anything you need from us, you know, we'll do our best. Now, I'll just go and get that timetable for you.
NAZMA *(standing up)* Well, I'll come with you shall I? You could show me around a bit more.
VINCE *(as they move off)* How long have you been doing this job then?
NAZMA     Too long, I think, sometimes. *(laughs)* No! Wouldn't do anything else. It's great, especially when I get a chance to learn about places like this. It's all so new and interesting.

*Blackout.*

**SCENE 7**
*Lights come up stage right. The military drill music is loud. Vince enters wearing a regulation black anorak , which swishes as his arms move back and forth.*

VINCE *(standing and shouting in time to the music)* A Retriever dog called Milton born, 3...12...89... Desirée!

*Desirée enters wearing a dog's head and a Sam Brown belt. She stands in line.*

VINCE     A German Shepherd called Wonder, born 30th...3rd...90... Joe!

*Joe enters wearing a dog's head and an all-in-one, luminous waterproof.*

**VINCE**            A chocolate Lab bitch called Keller, born
    22$^{nd}$...11$^{th}$...89... Aysha!

*Aysha enters, wearing her dog's head and two reflective armbands.*
*She stands in line next to Joe.*

**VINCE**            Now you're off the mini bus, standing in line. You're
    going to do Paxton Lane.

*The three march on the spot.*

**VINCE**            Okay, go!
**ALL THREE**   Forward.
**VINCE**            Straight on!
**ALL THREE**    Straight on.
**VINCE**            And praise!
**ALL THREE**   Good boy/girl
**VINCE**            First down kerb, S.I.T.
**ALL THREE**    Up to the kerb, sit.
**VINCE**            Right!

*All three step back and point right, except for Desirée.*

**ALL THREE**   Right.
**VINCE**            Desirée point! And straight on.
**ALL THREE** *(Now facing right)* Straight on.
**VINCE**            Praise!
**ALL THREE**   Good boy/girl
**VINCE**            Joe, crack that chain and slow him down.
**JOE**             Steady, good boy.
**VINCE**            First down kerb, S.I.T.
**ALL THREE**   Up to the kerb, sit.
**VINCE**            S.I.T. your dog Desirée!
**DESIREE**      Sit!
**VINCE**            Come on Desirée, that dog's taking you to the
    cleaners.
**VINCE**            Okay, right.
**ALL THREE** *(stepping back and pointing right)* Right and straight
    on. Good boy/girl.

*The three march offstage.*

**VINCE** *(following them)* Lengthen your stride Aysha and Desirée. I cannot hear you!

*They exit and music fades.*

## SCENE 8
*Stage right remains lit. Desirée's room. Desirée enters, removing her dog's head. She sighs heavily and sits down, next to the head, stroking it.*

**DESIREE**      Millie, Millie, Milton. *(Sighs again)* In five year's time, will we be sitting beside each other?

*Vince enters.*

**VINCE**        Desirée, it's Vince.
**DESIREE**      Oh, come in.
**VINCE**        Hi, how' re you doing?
**DESIREE** *(quiet)* Alright.
**VINCE** *(coming further in the room)* You made one or two blunders today?
**DESIREE**      Yeah.
**VINCE**        You've basically got to become more positive, Desirée.
**DESIREE**      Yes, I know.
**VINCE**        And it's got to show in your voice. You can do it. You've just got to become a bit more determined with this dog. It's not going to be easy. He's stubborn but once he knows that you're not going to let him get away with thinking he's the boss, that's when you'll have cracked it, and you'll work well together.
**DESIREE**      I don't know. *(Pause)*
**VINCE** *(coming closer)* You know, looking at it, as a sighted person, the cane is the more logical form of mobility to go for, as working with a dog is more harder to learn.
**DESIREE**      Perhaps. There was no one in my area to teach me to use it for a long time, and when there was eventually, I just didn't, well get round to phoning her.

**VINCE**          Canes are not our concern, except that most people
need good training with one before they can get on this course,
other wise their orientation's crap. The only reason that we
accepted you, was because you gave good, intelligent responses
when we walked you at your interview. You've got to use that
intelligence now Desirée, to make it work.

**DESIREE**      Yes I know, because if it doesn't work then...

**VINCE** *(shaking his head)* Uh, uh. You're on the course now and we
don't want to hear talk like that. That's not going to get us
anywhere is it?

**DESIREE**      No.

**VINCE** *(squats down next to her)* Look, the first week is always the
most difficult, take my word for it and there are a lot of people
finding it hard, not only you. Look at the replacements. They
think they know it all and when they get here, their new dog lets
them know they don't. You've got every chance of succeeding, if
you use that pretty head of yours and keep your attitude positive.
There's at least ten grand gone into Milton and it just takes you
now to make it all worth it. Can you do it?

**DESIREE** *(smiling tentatively)* Yeah.

**VINCE**          And then you can leave here, with your independ-
ence and only have to rely on him. Okay?

**DESIREE**      Yeah.

**VINCE** *(stroking her arm)* Great. Any time you want to talk like
this, Desirée... I'm here, right.

**DESIREE**      Right.

**VINCE**          Or a few drinks at the bar works wonders sometimes.

**DESIREE**      Do you go in there?

**VINCE**          All the time. You need to get out of this room and
socialise a bit more.

**DESIREE**      I will.

**VINCE**          Your first drinks on me then.

**DESIREE**      Thanks. *(remembers)* Oh Vince, before I forget,
could you address this letter for me please?

**VINCE**          Sure. *(Taking it)* Who's it to? Your boyfriend?

**DESIREE**      I haven't got one

**VINCE**          I don't believe that.

**DESIREE** *(smiles)* It's to my parents, to let them know I'm here, and
what I'm doing.

**VINCE**  I haven't got a pen. I'll do it in my office. *(goes to exit)*

**DESIREE**  Thanks a lot.

**VINCE**  Any time. *(stops)* By the way, there's something I wanted to ask you. Have you heard about this TV thing that's going on here?.

**DESIREE**  Yes, Joe said something at dinner.

**VINCE**  Well yes, TV West are doing a programme on the charity and are planning to film, mainly Joe, but because you're on the same minibus as him, doing the same walks, there's the likelihood of you getting caught in a few shots. I just thought I'd let you know.

*The hollow and echoing music of the ghost fades in.*

**DESIREE** *(concerned)* Oh.

**VINCE**  This is just the kind of publicity we need.

**DESIREE**  Oh right.

**VINCE**  It'll be your fifteen minutes of fame.

**DESIREE** *(forcing a smile)* Yeah.

**VINCE** *(exiting)* See you on the minibus in fifteen minutes then.

*As soon as he has gone, Desirée jumps up and paces her room.*

**DESIREE**  Yes, smile, right, smile, fine, smile, thanks! *(stops, obviously listening. Then smiling broadly and falsely)* So you're here? Hi, great to see you! Sorry, slightly inappropriate for the both of us but I really must say how much I appreciate you grop-ing and shambling your way through again. Yes, it was you wasn't it? I distinctly remember now. Those icy, crumbled fingers of yours, clutching at each corner of my mouth and dragging it back into that pathetic little smile. Thanks. Due to that, you've made it possible for me to appear on national television now. Fantastic! *(She laughs)* Just what I always wanted. The glamour of the harness, the white symbol cane, reflective armbands and belts; and there's me, captured on film, in all this glorious paraphenalia, part of the pantomime outing, crocodiling the streets. *(She repeatedly whacks the symbol cane into the palm of her hand)* And you're going to be there? Silly, of course you are.

Stumbling along and tap, tap, tapping your staff. *(She reflects as she hits out a rhythm in her hand)* That staff. The long, hard, smooth, white, hot, spear, molten, metal, gleaming, bright. My automatic, frozen, hand, gripped, ridged, pure, heat. On street, white, tentacle, feels, concrete. Me, insect, creeps behind, blind. And my, small, sight, saw, eyes, stare, turn, away, run, away, from, white, hot, searing, stick, that, burned, into, icy, flesh, this icy flesh in the palm of my hand! *(She flinches violently and flings the cane away. After a long pause)* Yes, you'll be there as usual, right there next to me, in your foul, rotting grey rags. *(Pause)* But! Make sure you're wearing your luminous Sam Brown. We don't want you involved in a nasty accident with a car, while the cameras are rolling. Oh right! Yes of course, that wouldn't matter in your case, would it? But, hang on. You know, because of that, you probably won't show up in the film anyway. Well, the dead just don't, do they? And if they don't, will I? Come on, tell me! You're super-sensitive, aren't you, with mystical properties? Foretell me the future then, with your second sight. *(She waits, the musical echo vibrates around then she sighs)* Oh, don't tax yourself. I'm not that worried really. I know that my image can evade exposure, as well, because I also know death, you see. *(Pause)* I wear black for lilac and blue. I wear black for orange blossom on spring trees, and I wear black for all those new faces, gone. *(sitting back down, she strokes the dog's head)* You're a beautiful animal. This just isn't fair on you. Harnessed up. All your dignity and freedom, gone.

*The lights fade to blackout. The music lingers.*

**SCENE 9**
*The sound from the previous scene lingers in the air. The stage is in darkness. Nazma knocks on the student lounge door and opens it into the darkened room.*

**NAZMA**          Hello? Joe? *(She enters from the bright corridor outside and feels for the light switch)* Is there anyone here? *(She takes a step further into the room, still holding onto the open door).*

**VINCE** *(creeping up behind her)* Boo!

**NAZMA** *(jumping)* Oh God. *(He laughs)* Don't do things like that, I'm really scared of the dark.

**VINCE**      Don't worry, I'm here to protect you now.

**NAZMA**     The light will be protection enough, thank you.

**VINCE**      Why didn't you put it on then?

**NAZMA**     I couldn't find it.

**VINCE**      It's out here.

*Vince brings up the lights on the student lounge from outside. The music fades away.*

**NAZMA**     That's better. *(She turns to look at Joe)* God, he can read Braille in the dark

**VINCE**      That's one thing to be said for being like them. You save pounds on the electric.

**NAZMA**     Some consolation.

**VINCE**      Yeah well, we've all got grief.

**NAZMA**     I hope I don't make any, well you know, mistakes, or anything.

**VINCE** *(hesitates, then understands)* Oh yeah, well I was a bit nervous of that when I first came here, but part of our apprenticeship is to do a twenty-four hour blindfold stint. That helps a lot. You then know what it's like, and it's not such a big deal any more. Maybe you should give it a try sometime?

**NAZMA**     There really is only time for priorities, you know?

**VINCE**      Fair enough. By the way, Desirée's given her consent. We just need the coloured woman, Aysha's now.

**NAZMA**     And what colour does she happen to be?

**VINCE**      Sort of black.

**NAZMA**     Well she shouldn't be too hard to identify here then.

**VINCE** *(understanding)* There was a guy from Ghana, Guyana, who used to drive the minibus but he left a few weeks ago.

**NAZMA**     Really? Anyway, I think I ought to get on and talk to Joe.

**VINCE**      Yeah, *(calls)* Yo Joe! Can we have a moment?

**JOE** *(removing his headset)* Yeah, I thought someone had come in.

**VINCE**      Nazma's here. She wants to have that chat with you.

**NAZMA**     What were you listening to Joe?

**JOE**          Oh, some Miles Davis. I like reading and listening to
music together.

**NAZMA**     And the book?

**JOE**          It's a collection of short stories by H.G. Wells.

**VINCE**      I'll be off, okay? Nazma – anything, just shout.

*Knocking on the door, he exits.*

**NAZMA**     Okay Joe. What I basically want to do, is ask you a
few questions, so I know what areas of your life to cover in the
interview.

**JOE**          Fire away.

**NAZMA**     And I hope you'll excuse my ignorance. It's all a bit
new for me because actually, you're the first blind person I've
ever spoken to properly.

**JOE**          I'd better set a good example, so I'm not the last.

*They both laugh and lights dim on them, coming up on the grooming
room. Desirée is behind her dog's head which is on a pole standing
in front of her. She grooms the fur methodically.*

**DESIREE** *(singing)* How much is that doggy in the window? The
one with the waggly tail? How much is that doggy in the
window? I do hope that doggy's for sale. *(Pause)* You're an
advert, brush, brush. Got to make you look good, comb those
knots, and comb out mine, because I'm in the window too.

*Lights dim on grooming room and brighten on the lounge.*

**NAZMA**     And how do you like it here in the centre?

**JOE**          Well, what more could you ask for? Lovely food, lots
of it, and all there, ready and waiting for you three times a day.
Laundry collected every morning, clean, dry and folded on your
bed by lunchtime. And then when you need to relax in the
evening because the work is hard, you'll soon see, there's the bar.
Plenty of staff and students in there, so there's no problem finding
company.

**NAZMA**     Club Mediterranean S.E.D.A?!

**JOE**     Yes, you could say that! I think that was the impression my bank had as well. They were even reluctant to let me have
three weeks off to come here, even when I said I would take it as
unpaid holiday. Then all of a sudden my manager turns around
and says, 'Take the three weeks and an extra one if you want.'
Beats me.

**NAZMA**     Your manager? Ah yes, that's Mr Bailey?

**JOE**     Mr Bailey, that's right.

*The lights dim. Lights come up on stage right. The grooming room.
Aysha rushes in with her dog's head on a pole.*

**DESIREE**     Graham wants you for obedience training.

**AYSHA**     Oh fuck it! He'll just have to wait. I need some time
in the day for other things apart from the dog.

**DESIREE**     . I know, this place is like concentrated orange juice.
We're either grooming the dog–

**AYSHA**     Or out in the run–

**DESIREE**     Or in a lecture.

**AYSHA/DESIREE** Walking the dog, feeding the dog, playing with
the dog–

**DESIREE**     And being, as good as the dog.

**AYSHA**     Everything we do has to be at the same time,

**DESIREE**     And all to the same standard.

**AYSHA**     Well if my present standard is anything to go by,
we're all pretty low.

**DESIREE**     Oh?

**AYSHA**     Well this morning, didn't you hear Vince yelling at
me across the street? Keller walked me right into this lamp post,
and then up someone's drive, straight into their garden.

**DESIREE**     I didn't know that.

**AYSHA**     He made me feel like pure shit.

**DESIREE**     He makes me feel like that all the time.

**AYSHA**     God forbid any of us fail. It'll be, 'Under the minibus
one, two three!'

**DESIREE** *(laughing)* I'll be first in line. God, I didn't know anyone
else was feeling like this.

**AYSHA**     I'm sure everyone's going through it.

**DESIREE** Well, why does everybody just go on about their Sheering that did this and their Huxley that did that, and Wonder's a good boy, he's such a good boy.

**AYSHA** Yeah, is Wonder taller than your dog?

**DESIREE** Is Wonder thinner than your dog?

**AYSHA** Wonder's got the longest fur.

**DESIREE** Wonder's got the biggest paws.

**AYSHA** Wonder's got the baddest breath.

**DESIREE** *(laughing)* It's either all that, or everyone breezing around saying, 'I'm fine, all right, yes, fine thanks.'

**AYSHA** It's because we're all meant to be screaming in our rooms.

*Lights dim on grooming room. Lights brighten on student lounge.*

**NAZMA** What exactly are your duties as Assistant Manager, Joe?

**JOE** I supervise six members of staff in the sales department, organising what they do, and authorising orders and sales.

**NAZMA** And how did you work yourself up to that responsible position?

**JOE** *(sighs)* Well, I started at grade one, in the machine room, doing basic computer work.

**NAZMA** How old were you?

**JOE** Nineteen, and I'd been for thirty eight jobs before I got this one at the bank.

**NAZMA** So, you were pretty determined from the start, and was it that, that got you to grade two?

**JOE** Yes, especially when I was told by my supervisor that all disabled staff usually stayed at grade one. That really got me going. I went and got myself all genned up on an advanced computer course, applied for a grade two and then hit them at the interview with a blow by blow account of how I could handle every aspect of the job. I showed them that with my new computer skills and personal readers, I could get over the obstacles of records, standing orders, enquiries, correspondence etc.

**NAZMA** So you were promoted, and...

**JOE**     After my third application, yes.

**NAZMA**   Right, and when did you get the next?

**JOE**     Not until I had done a good few years at night school to get the bank exams. And then, what happened next? I know, I tried for that grade three at Bradford region, but no luck.

**NAZMA**   Didn't do too well in the exams?

**JOE**     Passed with flying colours!

**NAZMA**   So what was the problem?

**JOE**     It's not the bank's policy really, you know, to let you know.

**NAZMA**   But you do? *(Pause)* What? Come on, just between you and me Joe.

**JOE** *(sighs, after a pause)* The Personnel Officer did say that there were a number of reasons, one being they would have to re-arrange the office to move my desk nearer a plug socket, and the other was using staff time, to show me things like where the bus stop was.

**NAZMA**   What?

**JOE**     And what was it? Inconsistency of appearance.

**NAZMA**   What does that mean?

**JOE**     Hazarding a guess, a combination of a red shirt, green tie and yellow trousers, I think.

**NAZMA**   What did you do?!

**JOE**     I made sure that my punctuality was faultless, and every bit of my paper work was up to date, even if it meant me taking it home to complete it.

**NAZMA**   Oh, right.

**JOE**     No concessions for me. It was just sheer hard work.

**NAZMA**   Well that's good, I suppose, yes, because you didn't let things get you down.

**JOE**     No and I got the grade three and four that I wanted.

*Lights dim on the lounge and come up on the grooming room.*

**AYSHA**   Things like that I don't remember learning, just absorbing as a kid.

**DESIREE**  Trying to get through the last year of college without Braille was a joke.

**AYSHA**   Didn't college do anything?

**DESIREE**     Gave me a discretionary result.

**AYSHA**       Looks better for them than a failure.

**DESIREE**     But that's what I am.

**AYSHA**       If your parents had got you learning Braille, instead of waiting for operations to...

**DESIREE**     I know... but they didn't, and I clung on by my finger tips at college for what? I can't go on to do my solicitor's finals.

**AYSHA**       You can. Use this time now to get yourself together.

**DESIREE**     And pull my finger out?

**AYSHA**       Yeah, point it in the right direction!

**DESIREE**     Towards those damn dots. Well that is my intention you know.

**AYSHA**       But, sore fingers?

**DESIREE**     Oh, very sore. Red, raw and throbbing sometimes.

**AYSHA**       Take it easy. You know, my boarding school sent me out to be the good girl. Don't make waves but what happened when I moved to a new town, started to use a dog, rave all night and then handing in A plus work by the morning? The bright blind thing, just gets stressed right out.

**DESIREE**     But all my friends in the house, you don't understand, they're all nearly qualified now, and what have I got to show? Day after day, spent alone in my room deciphering page after page, and dying amongst the dots.

*Lights dim and come up on the student lounge.*

**NAZMA**       In a way... despite the odds stacked against you, you've been incredibly resourceful in getting around your problems.

**JOE**         Well, if the situation calls for it.

**NAZMA**       And do you call on your family for a lot of support?

**JOE**         Not my parents, no.

**NAZMA**       Brothers and sisters?

**JOE**         Sister.

**NAZMA**       Does she –?

**JOE**         Don't see much of her... we were never that close.

**NAZMA**       Shame.

**JOE**         Well, she went to the local grammar school and I was packed off to Blind School, hundreds of miles away, so what do you expect? I only came home in the holidays and she was never around... out with her friends – who turned out to be a boyfriend. He whipped her away from home at sixteen and that was the end of 'Catherine the Great!'

*Lights dim and come up on grooming room.*

**DESIREE**     How old is, er, your child?

**AYSHA**     Louis? He's three.

**DESIREE**     I'd love to meet him.

**AYSHA**     Well, we all can when Maurice brings him up on visitor's day.

**DESIREE**     Maurice? Is that your boyfriend?

**AYSHA**     Palease! Boy might be right, but the man's no friend of mine.

**DESIREE**     Don't get on then?

**AYSHA** *(pause)* Between me and you, yeah, we're at each other's throats at the moment, over custody of Louis.

**DESIREE** *(sighs)* Seems like we both need to get pissed tonight.

**AYSHA**     Not tonight. I've got to do some serious thinking about changes I want to make in my Affidavit, and get it off to my solicitor by the morning

**DESIREE**     Need any help?

**AYSHA**     Thanks, but it's just a question of selling myself more as I am, instead of always trying to match up to Maurice and his new driving instructor girl friend.

**DESIREE**     Tall order.

**AYSHA**     No. I can think of things that I can offer Louis, that they can't. Like Louis does more with me, because things with us have to be more organised. With Maurice, because everything can be done, nothing gets done. So you see, when I'm in the right frame of mind, I can think of things. *(She sighs)* You know, there was something to be said for those college days. Come in, go out when I wanted, and getting down to all that, *(sings badly)* 'I don't wanna be a freak, but I can't help myself!'

**DESIREE** *(laughs)* God, what a voice!

**AYSHA** *(laughs)* Gotta get it tuned one of these days, and those days, there was no one to trouble my mind but, me, myself, and I. Bye Bye to that life now. *(She sighs)* It's all–

**DESIREE/AYSHA**  Gone.

*Blackout on the grooming room. Lights come up on the lounge.*

**NAZMA**        Would you say you were a good example, generally
   Joe?
**JOE**         Well, I like to think so.
**NAZMA**        Well the bank think so. I know, from my chats with
   Mr Bailey. And tell me, is it your ambition, one day to have his
   job?
**JOE**         Of course!
**NAZMA**        I'm sure you will. Now there's just one other thing I'd
   like to know. I'd like to ask you, and you don't have to answer,
   but do you ever wish you could see?
**JOE**         Well, it's a funny question really. It's like me asking
   you if you ever wish you could fly. You can't, though you might
   occasionally wonder what it's like and you know that some things
   in life would be made easier if you could, but you don't spend
   your whole life thinking about it.
**NAZMA** *(thoughtful)*  No.
**JOE**         Instead, I spend my time thinking about how I can
   adapt to get whatever pleasures I can out of life.
**NAZMA**        And do you adapt by tuning up other senses, like
   your hearing and touch, for instance?
**JOE**         Yeah, and memory training.
**NAZMA**        Now that is something I really would want. My
   memory is dreadful. If I don't write everything down, that's it. I
   also wish I was more musical. You are, aren't you? You like Jazz.
   Do you play an instrument?
**JOE**         Mm, saxophone.
**NAZMA**        And I bet you play it well. Come on, don't be
   modest.
**JOE**         Well, you know, so I've been told.
**NAZMA**        Thought so. Tenor, or alto?
**JOE**         Tenor.
**NAZMA**        I love sax music.

*The lights fade down on their conversation as the sound of the ghost*
*fades in, overlaid by the torturous strains of a saxophone.*

**SCENE 10**

*The music lingers. The phone begins to ring in the corridor. Lights come up. Vince enters the corridor to answer the phone. The music fades away.*

**VINCE**        S.E.D.A., The Mansion House? Oh, hold on a minute. I'll see if she's available.

*Knock on the double doors and Aysha enters the corridor, feeling along the wall.*

**VINCE**        Oh Aysha, phone for you.
**AYSHA**        Thanks. *(She takes the phone)*
**VINCE**        Keep it short, eh. We've got a lecture starting any minute now.
**AYSHA** *(sighs)* Hello? Oh, Stephanie... Hi. No, no, go on, it's alright.

*Vince walks through the corridor, passing Desirée, entering it.*

**VINCE**        Hi, Des, it's Vince here. *(He squeezes her shoulder and she stops)* Alright?
**DESIREE** *(smiles)* Yeah, fine.
**VINCE**        See you in the lounge soon.

*He exits. Desirée sprints along the corridor to the double doors.*

**VINCE** *(bellowing offstage)* Desirée, for God's sake, slow down in the corridor will you?

*Desirée stops abruptly at the doors and stares back up the corridor. After a moment she knocks on the double doors and kicks them open. Exits.*

**AYSHA**        So that means finding a sound one who will do the court report? Well, I know a few social workers, but I don't know if they do welfare probation. I'll have to find out. But how does it work Stephanie? Will all three of us have to be interviewed together, with Louis, or separately? Right, so it's the one who makes the first impression that counts, you think? And when should I expect my appointment to be made for then? Christ, so soon Stephanie? Well no, I don't want any delays. No, of course I don't want to be seen causing them either. *(She sighs)* I've got another two, two and a half weeks here. Well, remember, I did try my utmost to have it different, but look, if you find yourself having to make a date, then do it. Maybe the timing will work out right. I don't know. Yeah, you said it would do my head in. You're right, but I was getting nowhere fast, trying to settle outside Court, so now the ball's rolling...

*Nazma has entered the corridor.*

**AYSHA**        Oh, I'm getting on alright here. Her name's Keller, she's a cute little thing. Louis will love her. Well, I'll do some ringing around, and I'll get back to you. Thanks, Bye.

*She hangs up and goes to exit through the double doors.*

**NAZMA** *(coming forward)* Oh Aysha, could I have a word, a moment?
**AYSHA**        Well yeah, if I know who it's with.
**NAZMA**        Sorry, I'm Nazma...Nazma Zabic. I'm an Assistant Producer for TV West.
**AYSHA**        Oh right, what can I do for you?
**NAZMA**        Well, I don't know if you've heard, but we're planning to film here, in the Centre, for the S.O.S. Today programme. I don't know if you've ever, well, heard of it?
**AYSHA**        Yes, in passing.
**NAZMA**        Well we're filming the training that the S.E.D.A. does here and basically the helpful service it provides for the blind.
**AYSHA** *(half laughing)*  Oh yeah?
**NAZMA**        We'll be starting the filming quite soon, and we are going to follow the progress of one particular person in your class – Joe.
**AYSHA**        Uh huh.
**NAZMA**        And because it's going to be very difficult to film him on his own, as you're all trained together, what I wanted to find

out from you was whether you minded being included in the film as well?

*Knock on the double door and Vince enters the corridor.*

**VINCE** *(to Nazma)* Hi. *(Breezily)* Alright Aysha?
**AYSHA**    Fine thanks.

*Vince nods questioningly at Nazma, who shrugs.*

**VINCE**    Okay. *(exits left)*
**NAZMA**    Well?
**AYSHA**    Just one thing?
**NAZMA**    Yes?
**AYSHA**    Will Joe be talking, em, interviewed?
**NAZMA**    Yes. Vince will be doing an actual commentary on his training, but I think the part that will be really interesting, not that the training isn't, will be the personal profiling of one of the students who's done so extremely well in his career.
**AYSHA**    Right, so it's just Joe and Vince?
**NAZMA**    Well yes, we're limited on time, because there's just so much interesting information to get in.
**AYSHA**    Well I don't, really...
**NAZMA**    I've had permission from all the other students and you will get your name in the credits.
**AYSHA**    Yeah, well I'm sorry but I don't think I want to be involved. *(turns to go)*
**NAZMA**    Hold on, can I ask you why?
**AYSHA**    Well, I just don't feel comfortable about appearing in a film with another person speaking on my behalf.
**NAZMA** *(after a moment's reflection)* Right, yes, I understand.
**AYSHA**    Yeah?
**NAZMA**    Of course I do, he's–
**AYSHA**    You know what I mean?
**NAZMA**    Yeah. *(laughs conspiratorially)*
**AYSHA**    So, you see, I–
**NAZMA**    But don't worry.
**AYSHA**    What?
**NAZMA**    I'll make sure there's another angle in here.

**AYSHA**          You will?

**NAZMA**          Yes, I want to show that black people contribute to charities as well.

**AYSHA** *(suddenly understanding)* Oh! That's not -

**NAZMA**          People like our parents from other cultures really appreciate the work that charities do for the handi-capped because where they originate from, people with handicaps are just left, basically, and get absolutely nothing. No education, no services – they're just beggars, aren't they?

**AYSHA**          And here it's different, yeah?

**NAZMA**          It's so completely different. I mean, take this place.

**AYSHA**          Please. So, Nazma, is it? You'll be showing how much better off we are here?

**NAZMA**          For sure. I mean, there will be a lot of time given over to him – granted... you know, he's really a courageous guy. I admire him.

**AYSHA**          Oh, he's done something brave then? I hadn't heard.

**NAZMA**          Well he's coped with a curse of nature he could have done without – no doubt and achieved so much.

**AYSHA** *(shaking her head)* Tragic.

**NAZMA**          Well no, because he hasn't let his blindness paralyse his ambition.

**AYSHA** *(half laughing)* You put things very clearly.

**NAZMA**          Well, actually that was one my producer coined. He's really keen on all that kind of stuff, but that doesn't stop me from getting our points across.

**AYSHA**          The point is, I don't think you're doing that with me.

**NAZMA**          Believe me, I will. I've been there. Let me tell you something. Before I got this job, I worked mainly on Asian docu-mentaries, yeah? But, the Head of the Multi-Cultural Department at our company was white, okay? He just wanted to commission documentaries on Bhangra music and curry cuisine. Well, me and some other reporters made such a racket about it, and okay, one or two of us found ourselves jobless but we kept on, even used the discrimination act and finally we got an Asian guy in that job. Do you think, after that, I'd let that kind of thing go on outside of Asian programming? Like on this one, for instance? I'll work just as hard to get our voice heard. Don't you see?

**AYSHA**          Yes I do, but we're not talking about the same thing.

NAZMA *(exasperated)* What do you mean, we're not talking about the same thing?

VINCE *(entering corridor right)* Nazma, there's a call for you in my office.

*Nazma sighing, exits with Vince. Aysha knocks on the double doors, ready to exit. A knock sounds from the other side.*

DESIREE *(coming through)* Hello?

AYSHA      It's me – Aysha. Hi. Look, I'll meet you in the lounge in a minute. I've just got to go to my room and sort out some numbers.

DESIREE      Yeah. God, Aysha, you'll never believe what that bloody Vince just said to me. He told me how to walk. He says I do it too fast.

AYSHA      I suppose it's about safety.

DESIREE      What does he want me to do – crawl? I've walked like this, all my life. I don't intend to start clawing along the walls now.

AYSHA      Well you don't exactly have to do that either.

*Lights dim on the two women and brighten on Nazma and Vince who appear at the other end of the corridor.*

VINCE      What exactly is her problem?

NAZMA      God knows. I thought I was getting through but I don't know... she misunderstood me or something.

VINCE      She's a bit aloof. I know she wanted to be trained at home but she didn't request it early enough.

NAZMA      Has that got something to do with it?

VINCE      Well if it has, she shouldn't take it out on us, just because we don't jump, immediately she snaps her fingers.

NAZMA      Hmm, problem.

VINCE      Is it?

NAZMA      I want her in it and anyway it will show the S.E.D.A. benefiting different communities.

VINCE      True.

NAZMA      I mean... let's face it, the Association has to have a few pluses to balance out its minuses.

**VINCE**        Minuses?

**NAZMA**        Well, take the number of women employed here above Kennel girl level.

**VINCE**        Maybe it's because we don't get women like you applying to us.

**NAZMA** *(looks at him and then away)* I can't believe that.

**VINCE**        Let's go into town for a drink, and I'll elaborate.

**NAZMA** *(hesitant)* My time Vince, you know, it's a bit...

**VINCE**        Come on, just one.

**NAZMA** *(suddenly)* Okay! We can use the time to get our heads around the Aysha problem. *(She exits.)*

**VINCE**        Oh right. *(brightens)* In that case, should be over a few.

*He exits, after her. Lights up on the two women. Joe enters, feeling along the wall.*

**DESIREE**        And it was the way he said it. He practically screamed at me.

**AYSHA**        Well you've got a point there, I agree. That's not on.

**JOE**        Hello there.

**AYSHA/DESIREE** Hi.

**JOE**        How are you?

**AYSHA**        Fine.

**DESIREE**        Fine. How are you Joe?

**JOE**        Oh very well thanks. Me and Wonder boy have just been down to the free run. He's superb on re-call.

**DESIREE**        Oh good for you. *(To Aysha)* I'm going to the lounge, I'll see you.

**JOE**        Oh Desirée, yeah, I just wanted to ask you if you've been asked to take part in the TV programme?

**DESIREE**        Yes, Vince has said.

**JOE**        And are you?

**DESIREE**        Couldn't really say no.

**JOE**        Don't know about that. I've just overheard a phone conversation that's all about somebody who's refused.

**DESIREE**        Who?

*Silence.*

**AYSHA**        Didn't your mother ever tell you that eavesdropping led to no good, Joe?

**JOE**            No, but she taught me some things about gratitude, and I'm glad to hear that some of us have got a sense of it, eh Desirée?

**AYSHA**        Well I'd be grateful if you'd excuse me.

**JOE**            Hold on! Don't you think that people like Vince work bloody hard in this place? You've seen them here until ten o'clock at night, here all through the weekends, out in all weathers, and without that kind of dedication, people like us would be left with far less than we have now. With the donations, they give us choice. Isn't that a good thing?

**AYSHA**        Sure, so I've chosen to have nothing to do with it. Now if you don't mind–

**DESIREE**      Aysha, have you really?

**JOE**            You may not realise, but they risk a lot in giving us that choice. There's no guarantee that we're going to pass and if we don't, then they lose quite a bit of money. Now that's the public's money and they don't have to give it and where would we be then? I can't see a better way of paying a little something back for what we get, can you Desirée? I mean, surely it's the least we can do?

**AYSHA**        Look, this is the least I can do, right!

**JOE**            It certainly is, and you're causing a great deal of trouble. For God's sake, you act like you're being hindered here, instead of helped and for that, we're not being asked to prostrate ourselves or anything. Have they asked you to do that Desirée?

**DESIREE**      No, I don't know.

**JOE**            No, it's just being shown in a film, that's all. Being helped by a dog which people watching the film helped to buy. What is the problem? Or is that it? Do I smell the sour odour of grapes here, because it's me who's having the interview? *(sighs)* Well, all I can say is that I'm glad envy hasn't spoilt your sense of conscience, Desirée.

*She exits, bursting through the door and letting out a frustrated cry on the other side.*

**JOE**            Desirée?!

**AYSHA** *(half to herself)* She didn't quite make it to her room.

*She exits.*
*Blackout.*


## ACT TWO
*Lights fade up on the lounge area.*

**VOICEOVER** Okay, you thought that the first week was tough, but
let me tell you, in this, the second week, do not think you are
going to have an easier time of it. You may start to think you
know the ropes because you have been out on a few walks, sat in
on a few lectures and got the dog to respond to you a little more
but take heed, the dogs are now starting to know you are important and that you mean business. They are not going to respect you
for that. In fact, you may find they do the opposite and start to
play up, see how far they can go, and begin to take advantage.


## SCENE 1
*Lights come up on stage right. The military drill music plays. The
three enter wearing dog heads. Nazma hovers on the sidelines.*

**ALL THREE**   Second down kerb, left!

*Vince enters, carrying two headlights, a horn and a bell.*

**VINCE**          First down kerb, right..
**ALL THREE**   First down kerb, right!
**VINCE** *(switching on the lights)* Nazma... Traffic reinforcement,
cars and bikes. Be ready for when they appear! This is not for real
but it could be. I wanna see you keep your heads. *(He smiles at
Nazma)* Okay Joe?
**JOE**              Fine Vince.
**VINCE**          Good. Right, go!
**ALL THREE**   Forward. *(They march)* Straight on.
**VINCE** *(moving around the outside of the stage)* Wonder's got his
nose on the ground. D'you wanna flick his handle Joe? *(He smiles
at Nazma)*

**ALL THREE**   Up to the kerb, sit. *(They look from left to right)*
    Forward.

*Vince runs at Desirée, beeping the horn, and stopping just in front of her.*

**DESIREE**     Good boy, good boy.
**VINCE**     Correct him, don't praise him! He took no notice of
    the car and walked you straight off the kerb.
**DESIREE**     Sorry, no... naughty.
**VINCE**     It's too late now. He doesn't know what he's done.
    Just carry on, carry on!
**DESIREE** *(turning right)*  Right!
**VINCE**     No, second down kerb right. Keep your head.
**DESIREE**     Straight on.
**VINCE;**     Good Aysha, pace has improved. It's looking really
    comfortable..
**ALL THREE**   Up to the kerb, sit. *(They look left and right)*
    Forward. *(Vince, with one headlight, ringing a bell, runs at Aysha*
    *and Joe, stopping in front of them.)*
**AYSHA**     No, stay.
**JOE**     Good boy Wonder, good boy.
**VINCE** *(looking at Nazma and smiling)*  Now that's what I'm
    looking for! *(To Joe)* Good Joe, and Aysha. Excellent correction,
    excellent. Keller made a move, but you let her know that's wrong.
    Superb, you're doing famously. Right, on the up kerb, S.I.T.
**ALL THREE** *(getting in line)* Sit.
**DESIREE**     Sit!
**VINCE**     How many times does he have to be told? Desirée,
    don't loose it.
**JOE**     Sit!
**VINCE** *(laughing and looking at Nazma)* It's a passer-by, stroking
    Wonder. Joe, could you get his attention back?
**JOE**     Wonder, sit!
**VINCE** *(looking at Nazma and patting Joe's shoulder)* Good. That's
    it for now, but more this afternoon.

*The three begin to exit with Nazma following.*

## SCENE 2

*Lights remain up on stage right. As the three exit from the previous scene, Vince puts his hand on Desirée's shoulder.*

**VINCE**        Desirée.
**DESIREE**      Please, just don't say anything.
**VINCE**        Well done.
**DESIREE**      Well done?
**VINCE**        You're looking good.
**DESIREE**      But I don't.....
**VINCE**        This is the first time on the whole course I've felt that I could say that.
**DESIREE**      But didn't you think I did dreadfully?
**VINCE**        You're not perfect by any standards, but now, I can see you're getting there.
**DESIREE** *(relieved)* Can you?
**VINCE**        Oh yeah, easily, but you musn't stop giving it your all. You understand?
**DESIREE**      Yes.

*Nazma enters and watches the two.*

**VINCE**        Good.
**DESIREE**      Thanks Vince and... is your offer of a drink still on in the bar?
**VINCE**        If you're a good girl and get to qualify, we'll crack open a bottle of champagne together.
**DESIREE**      Is that a promise?
**VINCE**        You bet.
**NAZMA** *(smiling)* Er, Mr Stevens?
**VINCE** *(starting)* Oh hi.
**NAZMA**        Could you spare a minute, please?

*She exits and he hurries after her.*

**DESIREE** *(after he has gone)* Well done, you're looking good. You could easily be perfect. *(Pause and then she lets out a whoop of delight. She wraps her arms around the dog's head and clutches it to her stomach)* Forward... and Milton's moving. He's knee high and jiggles, wriggles at the end of the handle. His head goes just before me, and trotting along, he's a fur covered case of keenness.*(Her speech starts to grow more rapid.)* Straight on, and I'm moving now. Sharp heels stab, sounding quick over the concrete, and behind us we leave the pace of normal feet. Hup up, good boy, and we're really going now. Blurred shadows loom and flit as we bear to the right, skirt to the left. *(looking behind her)* Avoiding what? *(laughing)* Who cares! They're gone, and we go on. Wind in your fur. Sun on my face and one of my arms at least swings free. *(Pause)* Up to the kerb and sit. *(Her speech adjusts to a normal rate)* Good boy Milton, good boy. We are going to get through, and then we can leave them all behind. We won't need them and then, no need to smile.

*Blackout.*

**SCENE 3**
*Lights come up on the bar where Nazma and Vince stand.*

**NAZMA**     No, you were great! That's just what we wanted.
**VINCE**     Oh good, because I wasn't sure, you know, if I should have been doing that or not..
**NAZMA**     It was fine, I assure you... it won't matter. The way we're linking the narration in, it's going to work so well having some shots like that of you with Joe. You'll see.
**VINCE**     Right, well as long as you're happy.
**NAZMA**     Joe looked very good out there. He's doing well isn't he?
**VINCE**     Extremely confident.
**NAZMA**     That came across and that's what we were looking for to round off the training sequences.
**VINCE**     That's not the end though?
**NAZMA**     Of this section of filming, yes. We have to start editing, and we don't really need to see him qualify in his last week. Later in the month, we can spend half a day or something, filming him in his home, travelling to work etc.
**VINCE**     But you seemed so keen on getting the whole class on film?

**NAZMA**      I did get them. Remember, I told you. By my third drink, and your fifth, that's what I planned to do.

**VINCE**      Yes, but she has to agree, surely, before you take the film back?

**NAZMA**      Ideally, but we've got to get on. We're still going to be in and out until the beginning of next week, so, there's time.

**VINCE**      Any ideas?

**NAZMA**      Well, we're including some great clips of a Calipso-thon, that a Birmingham community centre held and raised lots of money for charity. If I brought that in to show her, it might drive it home that I want to show black people doing things for each other and not having things done for them. You have got a video here?

**VINCE**      For staff use only, as they're the only ones who'd want to.

**NAZMA**      Oh God, I'm so stupid! Well alright, Mr charming power of persuasion, how are you doing?

**VINCE**      Well I have been piling on the praise. I mean, she is doing alright, but there's no harm in letting her know and getting her feeling good about herself and us.

**NAZMA**      Not quite good enough though?

**VINCE**      Not yet.

**NAZMA**      We might have to be more direct again. Leave it to me.

**VINCE**      I'm sure it's just a question of getting her in the right mood. She's not the easiest person in the world to approach. A bit cut off, pre-occupied.

**NAZMA**      Not too difficult approaching Desirée, so I notice?

**VINCE**      Desirée? Getting her permission was nothing.

**NAZMA**      Camera likes her.

**VINCE**      Oh yeah?

**NAZMA**      Good-looking girl.

**VINCE**      If you like.

**NAZMA**      Do you....?

**VINCE**      What?

**NAZMA**      Do you like the way she's getting on?

**VINCE**      Fine.

**NAZMA**      Hmm. (*Pause*) You talked about a blindfold once.

**VINCE**      That's right, the one we use.

NAZMA        Might give it a try.
VINCE        Oh yeah?
NAZMA        To get a better idea of the staff's response to
   students.
VINCE        Why not?
NAZMA        When you've got a free moment then?
VINCE        Fine.
NAZMA *(pause)* In the meantime though, what we plan to do with
   the remainder of our time here... It'll be sad to go. I've grown
   quite used to it here.
VINCE        Likewise, we've grown very attached to you.
NAZMA *(exiting with Vince)* Right. Well we were going to do
   puppy walkers tomorrow, but they've forecast rain all day, so
   we've rearranged with the Major to do him, in his office, by the
   fire, instead. The next sunny day, hopefully Friday, we're getting
   aerial shots and long shots of the centre.
VINCE *(nodding)* Sounds good.
NAZMA        We also want to film the appeals officer, strolling
   round the grounds, talking to camera, you know...

*They exit.*

**SCENE 4**
*Vince meets Joe in the corridor by the telephone.*

VINCE        Alright Joe?
JOE          Oh, fine thanks Vince. *(sighs)* Just been talking to
   Denise.
VINCE        How's she feeling about the big day then?
JOE          There's another three months to go yet, Vince.
VINCE        Three months of freedom. Enjoy it while you can.
JOE          Yeah, before the yolk goes on. *(They laugh)*
VINCE        Well Joe, You let them think that they've got it on
   you, and that you're eating out of the palm of their hand, but you
   keep a few surprises up your sleeve for them. Keeps them
   interested, and you'll need that once you're married. Things get
   boring you know.
JOE          So speaks a man of experience?
VINCE        Well it was an experience, unfortunately.

**JOE**          Oh right, yeah.

**VINCE**          It's the job.

**JOE** *(nodding)* Oh.

**VINCE**          Big pressures here.

**JOE**          Of course.

**VINCE**          Blame that.

**JOE**          Commitment, right?

**VINCE**          Watch out for that.

**JOE**          Point taken, Vince.

**VINCE**          Priorities Joe. Getting them right. It's a tough one.

**JOE** *(sighs)*          True. But right this minute, mine's the mortgage.

**VINCE**          Well, that seems in order. You've got to have a threshold to carry the blushing bride over.

**JOE**          Well the way things are turning, we'll be lucky to make an offer in time.

**VINCE**          Can be a tricky business.

**JOE**          And what Denise has just told me doesn't help matters. *(Vince looks at his watch and Joe hesitates for a moment)* She's not going to be bringing the same money in from now on.

**VINCE**          Oh? Oh, congratulations Joe! Let's hope the wedding dress still fits her in three months, eh?

**JOE**          What? Oh, no, no, no, I don't mean that Vince. It's the bank.

**VINCE**          The bank?

**JOE**          Yes, they've decided to down rade her pay, she says.

**VINCE**          Oh.

**JOE**          They've made a decision to bring it down, in line with sighted telephonists pay.

**VINCE**          Why did she get more in the first place then?

**JOE**          Our bank was following the example of other firms, who instigated the idea that sighted telephonists could have the opportunity to  move to other departments and up to higher grades.

**VINCE**          And for obvious reasons, someone like her, can't?

**JOE**          Yes, something like that. *(Pause)*

**VINCE**          I see. *(Pause)* It's er...

**JOE**          Yeah, yeah.

**VINCE**          Just one of those things.

| | |
|---|---|
| **JOE** | Yeah. |
| **VINCE** | And I'm sure the bank will make it up in other ways. |
| **JOE** | Sure they will Vince. |
| **VINCE** | They've done well by you, so far. |
| **JOE** | Can't complain. |
| **VINCE** | There you go. |
| **JOE** | Yeah. |
| **VINCE** | Well, got to sort out something with the Major now. |
| **JOE** | And got to feed Wonder. |
| **VINCE** | Then you can have a relaxing half hour with him doing some obedience. |
| **JOE** | Okay Vince, will do. |
| **VINCE** | He's a good dog, Joe. Responds well to your commands. |

*Blackout.*
*Lights come up on the corridor and student lounge. Knock on the double doors. Aysha enters into the corridor, holding a letter. She walks up towards the lounge. Vince, appearing in the doorway sees her, and moments later, follows her. Aysha knocks on the student lounge door and enters. A table against the stage left wall, holds a box for letters. As she is about to post this, Vince appears in the student lounge doorway.*

| | |
|---|---|
| **VINCE** | That won't go until tomorrow now. |
| **AYSHA** *(jumps)* God! |
| **VINCE** *(closing the door)* All the post today has been collected. |
| **AYSHA** | Bloody hell. Yesterday that box was still full at one o'clock. It's only eleven now. The collections should be more organised. What am I going to do about getting this acceptance off now? I'd better phone Stephanie and... *(goes to leave then stops)* |
| **VINCE** | Sorry about that. |
| **AYSHA** | Oh, I'd like to have a word with you, Vince. |
| **VINCE** | Oh yeah? |
| **AYSHA** | It's about what's going on here in the next few days, and my part in it. |
| **VINCE** | Oh right, great! |
| **AYSHA** | Can we sit down? |

**VINCE**          Yes yes, certainly. *(They sit).*

**AYSHA** *(taking a deep breath)* Right... something has come up at home and I'd like to discuss with you, having some time off.

**VINCE** *(catching his breath)* Excuse me!

**AYSHA**          Look, there's something that I have got to be at home for – that's very important.

**VINCE**          When?

**AYSHA**          I need this weekend and Monday.

**VINCE**          Monday? No, it's out of the question, Aysha. I really can't let you go.

**AYSHA**          You don't understand. This is not because I've forgotten to feed the cats or something.

**VINCE**          You just forgot to mention it to us.

**AYSHA**          I just didn't know until now what I was going to do, and I've had so many things to arrange first.

**VINCE**          Things, what things? What's this all to do with?

**AYSHA** *(resentful)* An appointment that I've got to keep. *(Pause)* It's personal. To do with the family.

**VINCE**          I'm sorry Aysha, it's so unexpected. We just can't make those kind of provisions.

**AYSHA**          It's just Saturday and Monday morning that I'm asking for. Nearly all of Sunday here is spent with the visitors, so what will I be really missing?

**VINCE**          Oh just little things, like training with your dog.

**AYSHA** *(thinks)* But, last week, when Marjory was ill for two days with that virus, you arranged things around her so she could catch up. What's different in my case, when I'm only asking for one and a half days?

**VINCE** *(hesitates)* Well, one and a half days, or even two wouldn't be so much of a problem, if I could be confident with the level of work that that student was giving...

**AYSHA** *(confused)* But I've had the impression from you that I've been doing really...

**VINCE**          You're competent, up to a point, but that point stops far short of satisfactory. Aysha, we're basically going to need all the time we can get with you, here at the centre, to get what we want from you. That counts out two days off, I'm afraid. *(Pause. Aysha stands and walks across the room to the door, then stops)* And if I just left?

**VINCE** *(sighs)* Of course there's nothing to stop you.

**AYSHA**     But of course, bang goes the dog.

**VINCE**     Leaving the Centre without approval, means an un-
official termination of your training, so technically you would
have failed the course... and to get your dog.

**AYSHA**     Then I'd have to apply again and wait God knows
how long? I've been dished out this story before, I think. Yes,
when I applied to be trained at home this time. There's me
dreaming that this jolly instructor is going to turn up on the
doorstep one morning, carrying my brand new dog wrapped in
ribbons, that I'm going to be trained on the streets where I live...

**VINCE** *(wearily)* Someone misunderstood.

**AYSHA**     Yes, you did, didn't you? Or rather just ignored my
request, that I made well in advance to avoid problems, and
summoned me here for a month instead.

**VINCE**     The Major received your complaint and we were
going to sort out what you wanted.

**AYSHA**     And I would have waited how long for it? Even the
big boss couldn't give me a date. I had no choice but to come
here. If I had just got what I wanted in the first place, I would be
at home now and I could keep my appointment.

**VINCE** *(standing up)* Yeah I know, but these things happen in an
organisation this size. Look, you don't want to jeopardise your
work with Keller do you? It's far more important that you succeed
with her, than anything else, isn't it? Do that and then you can
deal with other things...you'll see, it'll all turn out for the best.

*He exits. Aysha waits for him to go and then finds the post box. She
is just about to post the letter and hesitates. Then in anger, she rips it
up, and throws the pieces on the floor, before exiting.*
*Blackout.*

**SCENE 6**
*Lights come back up on the lounge and corridor.*

**VOICEOVER** Visitors are very welcome to the centre, but
remember that visits can be a disturbing time for the dogs. Make
sure visitors and dogs meet on neutral territory, not in student
bedrooms. This may lead to a sense of confinement and result in

signs of aggression. If they behave like this, correct the dogs and silence them. We do not want any examples of unruliness while the visitors are here.

*The sound of a murmur of voices.*

**DESIREE** *(knocking on door and entering)* I told you that I didn't want anyone visiting me here. Why did you come? Don't be silly. Stay now you're here. *(sits)*

**JOE** *(entering on a knock)* Come and sit here Denise and I'll make you a drink. What do you want love? Tea or coffee?

*Knock on the double door and enter Aysha into the corridor.*

**AYSHA** *(spinning around)* Oh Michelle! Hi! Why are you so late? *(She bends down)* Come on Louis. *(She stands up)* Why?! Where is he?

**DESIREE** So where's Mum then? She always managed to turn up when I was in hospital? But that was great fun for her, wasn't it, conspiring with the doctors?

**JOE** Yes, there's three Labradors, one Retriever, a German Shepherd and a Lab cross.

**AYSHA** Maurice told me that he was going to bring him around to your place at twelve. You waited till one, yeah. Maybe he turned up after you left. Punctuality isn't one of Maurice's hot points. Did you phone him at his Mum's?

**DESIREE** Auntie Sophie used to live here? Where, in the town? That's right, before she moved to Plymouth. Yes, yes I do remember visiting her. I was about ten wasn't I? It's very pretty around here isn't it? You know I remember walking along with you and Mummy then, holding on both of your hands and closing my eyes, pretending I was blind. It's almost funny isn't it? I'm probably walking those same streets now.

**JOE** Wonder is the tallest dog. He's got the longest fur and he's even got the biggest paws.

**AYSHA** So, she says he did come up from Bristol for the weekend with Louis, but he never mentioned anything about coming here, and now, he's gone back to Bristol! Bastard!

**DESIREE**     That's Joe over there. There's a TV company here doing a documentary on him, but they are filming the rest of us as well. It's awful. We don't know what days the cameras are there, or where they are, or anything. Dad, what does he look like? And don't just say alright, or get embarrassed and stay silent. Is he fat with spots and black lank hair?

**JOE**     And it's not like last time, Denise. Then, they weren't so old and there were more men, and there weren't any bad apples in the barrel. Like that one over there. She seemed like such a nice quiet girl and then she suddenly turns around and gives me such a mouthful the other day. You wouldn't have believed it.

**AYSHA** *(Entering the student lounge after a knock)* Are there any spare seats Michelle?

**JOE**     And here comes another one. The angry type. You know, hasn't come to terms with things.

**DESIREE**     Aysha, hi.

**AYSHA**     Alright Des.

**DESIREE**     Has your friend brought your little boy yet?

**AYSHA**     No, he's still with his Dad. Michelle, this is Desirée.

**DESIREE**     Hi. Aysha, this is my Dad.

**AYSHA**     Hello.

**JOE**     Of course, I'm not avoiding the subject Denise. I just thought you might want to know something about this place, that's all.

*Lights dim on lounge and remain up on the corridor where Vince and Nazma appear. Vince perambulates Nazma along by her shoulders, as she is wearing a blindfold.*

**VINCE**     Right, I'm going to let you go now.

**NAZMA** *(laughing)* No, no. Not yet, not yet!

**VINCE**     Well we could stay like this all day if you like.

**NAZMA**     Okay, I'll do it now.

*Vince steps back and Nazma clings to the wall. Moving slowly along she makes sounds of enjoyable fear.*

**VINCE**     Feel totally helpless? What's it like?

**NAZMA**     Terrifying *(She laughs)*

**VINCE**      Don't worry, I'm here.

**NAZMA**      Oh my god, what's this?!

**VINCE**      Just a door, go on.

**NAZMA**      It's like walking through a tomb.

**VINCE**      Bet you're glad it's not sealed.

**NAZMA**      It's true what they say. You really experience the textures of surfaces in a different... *(She collides with the phone)* Ow!

**VINCE**      The telephone. What did I say about keeping your hands up high? *(Taking her hand and rubbing it)*

**NAZMA** *(removing the blindfold with the other hand)* That was a lot of fun until then.

**VINCE**      Does it hurt?

**NAZMA**      I didn't know first aid was part of the service. Do you provide it for all your students?

**VINCE**      Only the ones I feel particularly sorry for.

**NAZMA**      I see.

*Lights go down on the corridor and come up on the lounge.*

**AYSHA**      You could've been helping me to clean the house out this weekend, Michelle, if I had sent the Welfare Officer's form back, accepting the appointment. Stephanie is trying to arrange another one in about two weeks, when I'll be out of here... Yes, Maurice will be seen first now. God, why didn't I explain it all to Vince? He might have–

**DESIREE**      She's the first human being I've met here. Hers is called Keller... No, it's a Labrador... no, it's her second dog... I don't know what her first dog was called. Look, there's a bit more to her than her bloody dog Dad. Why don't you go and find out!

**JOE**      Calm down Denise, it's not the end of the world. There'll be other houses... Yeah well, maybe not big enough for the dog to have it's own room... Yeah, and not in such a nice area but we can still afford a little place somewhere else... Don't get angry. I know it's not what we wanted, but we will have to compromise a bit at first... Denise, you've got to be joking?

**AYSHA** *(pause)* God this is really freaking me out Michelle... No way! There's no way he forgot. What is he bloody playing at man?

**DESIREE**    Yes, there is a smell here... It's called dog. Even I smell of it. It's all rather odious isn't it?

**JOE**    Oh please Denise, be reasonable... How can I? It's going to cause unnecessary trouble... The interview's done. I can't say anything now, right?... Look, I'm going to take Wonder boy to the run, and leave you to cool down a bit. I'll be back in a minute. *(He exits)*

**DESIREE**    Oh Dad, you haven't got a clue! You don't know what you're talking about... Of course it's going to work. You'll see... I won't need you, or my friends, or anyone then. Keep your doubts to yourself. I really don't need them. *(She jumps up and leaves the room).*

**AYSHA**    Hello. I'm Aysha, and you are?... Denise, oh right... Joe talks a lot about you. This is my friend Michelle... Oh, she's called Keller... No, not at all, sit down. *(Pause)* Is there something wrong?... Do you want to talk about it? Come on.

*The lights fade down on Aysha and the lounge.*

## SCENE 7

*Lights come up on stage right. Desirée's room. Enter Desirée with Aysha following. They both carry dog's heads and Aysha holds a bottle of wine.*

**AYSHA**    They said you'd been asking for me?

**DESIREE**    You've been out?

**AYSHA**    Yeah, I escaped. Michelle rolled me up in the lounge carpet and smuggled me out, but we only got as far as the Off License in town and I got institute sick. I realised then, it didn't matter how far I got, I could never get away from Vince's dear voice in my head, shouting, 'What the hell do you think you're doing Aysha! Call that a correction? I wouldn't blink at that!' So, I came back by cab, but never mind, I brought a bottle of decent wine with me. We've got to get well and truly rat-arsed, it's overdue.

**DESIREE**    Oh, what would I have done if you hadn't been here? Gone mad.

**AYSHA**    Well I know I wouldn't have laughed so much, if not for you. *(They laugh self-consciously).*

**DESIREE**    Let's drink to the S.E.D.A. We might never have met.

**AYSHA**    Woo! *(She pops a cork)* This'll cheer you up, you didn't sound too happy in the lounge?

**DESIREE**    My Dad just turned up unexpectedly. I didn't want him here. I know he felt like he was amongst a bunch of aliens.

**AYSHA**    On the dark forbidding world of Planet Blind.

**DESIREE**    Yeah, and he won't be boarding the space shuttle out here again. Hey, what happened to Louis? I was looking forward to meeting him.

**AYSHA** *(sighs)* Maurice rang me from Bristol about four o'clock, bullshitting me with all this crap that he'd mixed up the dates. He says he'll bring him down next week if he can. Likely story.

**DESIREE**    Why?

**AYSHA**    Oh I don't know, maybe I'm just getting paranoid, but I'm starting to think that Maurice is trying to play happy families. He can do that better with his new woman, if Louis doesn't see me.

**DESIREE**    I wish I was doing my finals. I'd know more about civil law. I might be able to suggest something.

**AYSHA** *(pouring the wine)* The only suggestion I need right now is in this bottle.

**DESIREE**    I gather Joe's fiancée, delectable Denise with the knock knees was here today?

**AYSHA**    How do you know about her knees?

**DESIREE**    My Dad told me.

**AYSHA**    So what? We should be accepted as we are, with our differences. That's what makes us interesting, not wrong!

**DESIREE** *(unconvinced)* Yeah right.

**AYSHA**    Anyway, knock knees or not, she's alright, and God knows what she wants to get herself mixed up with an arsehole like him for.

**DESIREE**    Power. He's management don't you know?

**AYSHA**    Maybe it's the way he manages the power in bed.

**DESIREE** *(laughs)* I think I should let her know that he tried it on with me sort of, on the first day.

**AYSHA**    Doesn't surprise me. Probably feels he owes it to himself.

**DESIREE**    How about you?

**AYSHA**      Me? I don't think I'm his type darling.

**DESIREE**    No, do *you* fancy anyone here?

**AYSHA**      Jesus wept! Are you sure?

**DESIREE**    Not that you could do anything here.

**AYSHA**      You'd be surprised. Last time I trained, I was seeing two guys. One came in Saturday night and I smuggled him out on Sunday morning. I'd just got myself together and the other one turned up on Sunday afternoon.

**DESIREE**    Good God!

**AYSHA**      Didn't last long though. A kennel girl saw me bundling one of them out of the window. The bitch grassed me to the training manager.

**DESIREE**    That's what I mean, you couldn't get away with it, especially if it was an in-house affair.

**AYSHA**      Why? Who've you got in mind?

**DESIREE**    I can't say. It's too embarrassing.

**AYSHA**      Come on, you can tell auntie. Is there some gorgeous Titan here that I've somehow missed? Or are we talking about Amazons?

**DESIREE**    No, no, it's definitely a man.

**AYSHA**      Who, for God sake?

**DESIREE** *(after some hesitation)* His voice belongs to that alter ego, shouting in your head.

**AYSHA**      What, Vince?

**DESIREE**    Chrissie, the deputy kennel manageress, says he's very attractive.

**AYSHA** *(laughing)* Jesus wept.

**DESIREE**    I knew I shouldn't have said anything.

**AYSHA** *(just holding her laughter in)* No, no darling. When Mother Nature creates these stirrings, we've got no defence. *(Aghast)* But why *him,* man!

**DESIREE**    I don't know. He's part of all this I know but...

**AYSHA**      Classic teacher crush.

**DESIREE**    Maybe. *(Pause)* I wonder what he's doing now?

**AYSHA**      Probably at home with his wife, telling her to right, left, back, down, forward, down, stay, good girl.

**DESIREE** *(laughing)* He's not married, well not any more.

**AYSHA**      How do you know?

**DESIREE**    He told me.

**AYSHA**        Oh, so it's got to the, 'she left me, she didn't understand me', stage has it?

**DESIREE**      Oh, it's not at any stage. How could it be? *(Pause)*
Aysha?

**AYSHA**        Don't ask me anything about him. Up till now, I
thought they just got him out of the cupboard marked instructors,
wound him up every morning and off he went.

**DESIREE**      No, don't you wish this wine was enchanted? *(She
holds the glass up in front of her face and the chanting voices
fade in gradually)* ...that it contained some rare, essential, mineral
and as we're drinking it, all its particles are diffusing into our
blood, and as this happens, there's this amazing reaction inspired
amongst the chemicals there, and this new, sparkling, magical
make up of blood pumps its way up, flushing through our eyes,
purifying the filth there, curing that which is diseased, enlivening
that which is dead? *(The chanting, overlaid with clapping hands
and stamping feet grows louder)*.

**AYSHA**        There were about ten of them... all women, including
my mother. I sat in the middle of them, holding a candle. The
folds in the heavy robes they wore didn't touch me but agitated
the air all around, as their hands clapped and swayed above my
head and their voices came at me from every direction. Loud
convicted voices, commanding a miracle to release me, the
convict. My eyes were shut tight and the anticipation was like a
drug rush because I knew, I really knew... *(Music and voices cut
out and she shouts)* Yes! Yes! I do believe!

*Silence.*

**DESIREE** *(after a moment)* But if it had... imagine.

**AYSHA**        What? Maybe Louis playing far away, that's all. They
can have it. I'm not interested. It's all over-rated.

**DESIREE**      Not to me.

**AYSHA**        I know.

**DESIREE**      If I could, just for a day, not even that... an
afternoon... I'd spend my time, well, first of all I'd pour petrol
over that consultant who told me things would be stable and told
my parents otherwise. I'd torch him and then I'd run away... run,
both hands free, into the road. Dodge the traffic, jump on a bus,

no steal a car, a Cheetah convertible, and I'd speed to the nearest lot of shops. Into a newsagents, look at magazines, art, music, fashion... Yeah, an orgy of ogling! I'd run into a TV shop next and flick through the channels until the sets blew up, and then I'd run out, slalom through the crowds, peering into faces, staring right into them...

**AYSHA** You'd end up peering from the dock.

**DESIREE** Absorbing every feature of people's faces, yeah faces. *(Pause)* I wonder what Chrissie meant by attractive? God, it's all so second-hand and futile. What do you do, Aysha? Haven't you found that men run away when they find out? Or if they stay, all you get is their sympathy or the story of their amazing Uncle who was. Isn't it just the biggest turn off?

**AYSHA** Well some blokes think if they jump into bed with you, they'll end up blind in the morning and no amount of convincing them that a condom will do the trick, can get them anywhere near you. But not all.

**DESIREE** But to most, your sexuality is as alive as your sight.

*The sound of the ghost fades up.*

**AYSHA** Unless you find ways of proving the opposite.

**DESIREE** I do it by going out with my friends.

**AYSHA** I loved the feel of fabrics and furniture, so I became their first ever design student. How was that for integration?

**DESIREE** At a pub or a party, if I'm sitting... no one knows.

**AYSHA** While I was there, I was the freak, so why hide the fact? I acted as a mega one.

**DESIREE** When interest is shown, I discretely ask my friends, 'What's he like?'

**AYSHA** And I would drink, smoke, sniff anything and then have it in me to touch up anything that showed any signs of interest. I suppose that's how I proved it.

**DESIREE** While we talk and he doesn't know, I feel something resurrect inside me. That's how I prove it.

**AYSHA** But all that time I gave it out, I thought it was me they wanted. How could they? I didn't even want me then.

**DESIREE**     But of course, it can't last. That fragile, desirable persona gets shattered by the ignored, offered cigarette. Or the glass I reach for, not there. Or, the eyes meeting his, but not quite.

**AYSHA**     And then there came Maurice, who loved the black woman but wanted to hide the clown with crosses for eyes.

**DESIREE**     And it gets shattered by your ugly head rising up, that he sees! *(She smashes her glass)*

**AYSHA** *(imitating)* That wasn't Donna, that was Carol you were congratulating about her new baby. It was so embarrassing – she had a miscarriage two months ago. Why don't you just keep quiet, Aysha? *(Pause)* He can see.

**DESIREE**     If only he would just see me.

**AYSHA**     I can't help worrying when you take Louis out in the pushchair, Aysha... Hang around for half an hour and I'll take you in the car. *(Pause)* He can see.

**DESIREE**     He could drive me in his car and tell me all he was seeing.

**AYSHA** *(imitates)* Stop calling him back all the time Aysha, he's only over there. Go and play Louis, take no notice of Mummy. *(Pause)* He can see.

**DESIREE**     He can see and tell me all about me is lovely.

**AYSHA**     He can see, and boy does he let me know it. *(She smashes her glass).*

**DESIREE**     But I can't have that, because *you* make me ugly. You rocking, head-hanging, excuse for a life!

**AYSHA**     No more excusing me! He can have his sight, and I want to get right out of it.

**DESIREE**     You grovelling, eyeless monster. You're always in the way!

**AYSHA**     Get right away from all that grief.

**DESIREE** *(moaning)* Hideous presence, giving me grief.

**AYSHA**     Freedom. This is me!

**DESIREE**     You're ghastly, shuffling –

**AYSHA**     No more bit brains and fit bodies.

**DESIREE**     Free from your cautious clumsiness.

**AYSHA**     Free from sight! God, does that mean Louis as well then?

**DESIREE**     You fumbling groping...

**AYSHA**     That's what I've been fumbling for?

**DESIREE**     Begging, bent, blind wretch!

**AYSHA**     I've been bent on that?

**DESIREE**     We're all bent double with it.

**AYSHA**     With it? What?

**DESIREE** *(huddled up on the floor)* It's the old, big, ugly blind bogie, that follows us everywhere. Surely you must have met?

**AYSHA**     Blind bogie? Oh right, yeah, yeah, I've met him. Is that who you've been going on at?

**DESIREE**     Well it would be rude to ignore him, as he has so kindly come to see us again. *(Drinks from bottle)*.

**AYSHA** *(pause)* Christ you do need a cure.

**DESIREE** *(slightly hysterical)* Yes dear Lord, drop these scales from my eyes!

**AYSHA**     Not that kind.

**DESIREE**     Then there is no cure.

**AYSHA**     From their phantoms yes, and then we might start feeling a whole heap better.

**DESIREE** *(calling to the ghost)* Did you hear that? Your theirs, not ours, so you can just melt away now and vanish. Go on, fuck off.

**AYSHA**     It takes time Desirée.

**DESIREE**     It must do, because Cyclops is still here.

**AYSHA**     Even in time, when you've thought you've cut it right down to size... to a sleeping little fiend in the corner who doesn't bother you any more, then, people like Louis' father, his teachers, his friends' parents, I'm going to be forced to be involved with the lot of them, I know they'll shake it awake again, and it'll be there to bug me. Well, I am going to have to handle it, I just am, because I want him. Maurice is not going to win. I want my boy! *(Pause)*

**DESIREE**     And I want my dog.

**AYSHA**     If there's anything that makes you feel the phantom well and proper sometimes, it's the dog.

**DESIREE**     No, no, no, that's where you're wrong! You see, because of old Milton here, I'm going to be able to stick two fingers up to the lot of them.

**AYSHA**     Jesus wept! You think the dog is going to cure you of needing them? You will still be blind! You will still need contact with them for all sorts of assistance. It's true. Neither of us can really run away from that.

**DESIREE**     Did you hear that Cyclops? She's changed her mind.
**AYSHA**      We'll have to face the music and get what we want,
without that crap attached to us!
**DESIREE**     Detach ourselves and we don't get it.
**AYSHA**      We try.
**DESIREE**     Cyclops – you and me baby, we're umbilically
bound.
**AYSHA**      Oh God. *(She exits)*
**DESIREE** *(acting out a blind caricature)* I can't see you, I need you.
Don't leave me, please. Help me. Let me touch you. Please help
me. I want help. Please! Help me! Please, help, please, help.
Help!

*Blackout. The ghost sounds grow louder, echoing away into silence.*

**SCENE 8**
*Lights come back up on stage right. The military drill music plays.*

**VINCE** *(enters)* Off the minibus. Complete the route.

*The three enter wearing dogs' heads.*

**VINCE**         Paxton Lane!
**ALL THREE** Paxton Lane!
**VINCE**         High street!
**ALL THREE** High street!
**VINCE**         The station!
**ALL THREE** The station!
**VINCE**         And stay!
**JOE**            And stay!
**DESIREE/AYSHA** Forward!

*The three execute a series of forward marching, right and left turns,
with all the added commands and hand movements. Everything is
synchronised and performed perfectly. They finish.*

**VINCE**         Good, lovely! Lot's of praise. Lot's of praise.
**ALL THREE** Good boy/girl! Good boy/girl!

**VINCE** *(standing at the head of their line)* What do you do when your dog anticipates?
**ALL THREE** Keep to the straight line principle!
**VINCE** When your dog comes up to road works?
**ALL THREE** Do the off kerb obstacle!
**VINCE** Right.
**ALL THREE** Right.
**VINCE** Go!
**ALL THREE** Forward!

*They turn right and march along behind Vince.*

**VINCE** I wanna keep up my good training...
**JOE** I wanna keep up my good training...
**VINCE** With my dog, when I get home.
**AYSHA** With my dog, but alone at home?
**VINCE** I wanna carry a white baton.
**JOE** I wanna carry a white baton
**VINCE** To make sure there are no mistakes.
**DESIREE** These are the lengths that I must take.
**VINCE** I wanna wear my yellow Sam Brown...
**JOE** I wanna wear my yellow Sam Brown...
**VINCE** So I show up in the dark.
**JOE** So I show up in the dark.
**DESIREE** So I show myself up in the dark.
**AYSHA** So I show up what's in the dark.

*They exit behind Vince. Blackout.*

**SCENE 9**
*Lights come up on the corridor.*

**VOICEOVER** Congratulations! This is the third week. By now you must be feeling rather drained, but everyone is surviving and still here, so give yourselves and the dogs a well-deserved pat on the head for that at least. In a few days time, when the training is satisfactorily completed, contracts can be signed and the qualific-ations will be made official. Now, let's just relax a little, and enjoy observing our dogs and their body language.

*In the corridor Aysha is on the phone.*

**AYSHA**        But I thought the next thing was that this welfare guy had to visit me. What's he doing phoning you again? ... What details? ... Oh right. Did he say anything else? ... How often am I away from home receiving help of this kind? ... Maurice told him what?! ... That's not true! ... But did you tell him that I wouldn't have even been here if I could have had my training at home?

*Nazma enters the corridor.*

**NAZMA** *(tapping Aysha on the shoulder)* Aysha, it's Nazma here. Could I have a word with you please? I'll be in the lounge. *(Exits to lounge).*

**AYSHA**        Did he give anything else away about the visit to Maurice?... Yeah, well it sounds like it, I imagine they got on like a house on fire. *(sighs)* Jesus, Steph, what have I done? ... Yeah, the training, I know, and I did try and get the time off, that's right... Of course I couldn't help it... *(Pause)* I'm sure it all hasn't been for the worst... Something good will come out of it... Yeah, we'll get there in the end... Bye Steph. *(putting the receiver down, she rests her head on it.)*

*Lights go down on the corridor and come up on the student lounge, where Desirée is sitting with her dog's head.*

**VOICEOVER**  Show some interest in your dog. You can have some fun for a while, and they will think all the more of you if you pay them some friendly attention.

*Nazma knocks on the lounge door and enters.*

**NAZMA**       Oh hello, Desirée isn't it? I'm Nazma. I'm here working with the–
**DESIREE** *(trying to fasten something around her neck)* Yes, I know.
**NAZMA**        I've seen you around a lot, while I've been here, but we've never had a chance to chat.
**DESIREE**        Oh shit! *(She drops the necklace.)*

**NAZMA** Having trouble with that? *(She picks it up)* Here it is. *(looks)* Very nice.

**DESIREE** *(holding her hand out)* Thank you. *(Nazma drops it into Desirée's hand.)*

*A knock on the door and it opens. Vince enters.*

**VINCE** Oh hi girls!

**NAZMA/DESIREE** Vince!

**VINCE** Well, who first?

**NAZMA** Desirée, I insist.

**DESIREE** Vince, could you look at the catch on this for me?

**VINCE** Sure Des. *(going over to Desirée and looking at Nazma)* Anything wrong Nazma?

*Knock on the lounge door and Aysha enters the room.*

**NAZMA** Nothing that I can't put right, let's hope. *(She indicates Aysha)*

**VINCE** *(nodding)* Right.

**AYSHA** Nazma, did you say you wanted something, or did I imagine it?

**NAZMA** Hi Aysha, no, no you didn't. Come on, let's go over here. *(She leads her to the other side of the lounge)* How are you feeling? You look tired.

**AYSHA** I am.

**NAZMA** You'll be glad to get home?

**AYSHA** *(vague)* Yeah, yeah.

**NAZMA** I heard you wanted to be trained there, is that right?

**AYSHA** *(stiffening)* You heard that where?

**NAZMA** Oh just around. Tell me, what are the advantages of being trained at home, Aysha?

**AYSHA** What is this?

**NAZMA** Well I was just wondering...

**AYSHA** Is this what you wanted to see me about?

**NAZMA** In a way... well no. *(sighs)* Look, I just thought that might have something to do with you not wanting to be filmed.

**AYSHA** Palease, not all this again

**NAZMA**        Aysha, please listen. For the past week, I've been wracking my brains. How am I going to get her to change her mind, and not just me... Vince has tried as well. I wanted to talk to you once more.

**AYSHA**        Vince? I don't remember.

**NAZMA**        Well that just proves my point! People in this place don't really care if there aren't any black faces seen being helped by their money, that we also raise. Most people at my company don't really care either. It's just down to those few like me to change the little we can, and then hopefully attitudes, yeah?

**AYSHA** *(getting up)* Yeah, sure.

*Aysha goes over to make some coffee. Sudden laughter from Desirée which catches Nazma's attention and she wanders over to Desirée and Vince.*

**VINCE** *(trying to fasten the necklace around Desirée's neck)* Keep still!

**NAZMA**        What's going on here then?

**VINCE** *(removing it)* It's no good.

**NAZMA**        More First Aid?

**VINCE**        No luck? *(He nods at Aysha)*

**NAZMA**        No... Desirée, you're far too taxing for him.

**DESIREE**        Oh, I hadn't noticed any signs of strain, Vince?

**VINCE**        Some pressures are pleasurable, and this job, unlike some, knows few of those.

**DESIREE**        A little bit of stress is a good thing.

**VINCE**        You already sound typical of your profession.

**NAZMA**        What's that then?

**VINCE**        Desirée is going to take her solicitor's finals and she can, now she's got Milton.

**NAZMA**        How exciting. So, you're looking forward to going home then?

**DESIREE**        Mmm.

**NAZMA**        Nothing here you're going to miss?

**DESIREE**        Miss?

**NAZMA**        Your instructor? How many out of ten would you give him?

**VINCE** *(laughing slightly)* Time to get some pliers for this, I think. Excuse me.

*Knock on the door and Joe enters, as Vince exits.*

**NAZMA**     Joe, hi! Haven't seen you for a few days. How are you?

**JOE**     Oh hello, Nazma. I'm glad I had a chance to say good bye before you go. Isn't this your last day with us?

**NAZMA**     'Fraid so but you have been told that we'll be arranging a day when we can come over and film you at home soon, with Wonder?

**JOE**     If it cheers things up at home, I look forward to it, and it was certainly an enjoyable experience here.

**NAZMA**     Glad to hear that.

*Aysha, who has been listening to their conversation, moves over to them.*

**AYSHA**     Em?

**NAZMA**     Yes Aysha?

**AYSHA**     Did I just hear you say that this is your last day here?

**JOE**     Who was it who warned about eavesdropping? Want a coffee Nazma? *(He moves away)*

**NAZMA**     Yes please Joe.

**AYSHA**     Well?

**NAZMA**     Yes, that's right, it is.

**AYSHA**     So the filming is over?

**NAZMA**     Well, yes, here it is.

**AYSHA**     Well why are you still asking me for my permission, to be in the film?

**NAZMA** *(hesitant)* Well, because...

**AYSHA**     Uh huh.

**NAZMA**     If you said yes, we could still fix something up.

**AYSHA**     You'd bring all the cameras back, just for me?

**NAZMA**     Sure!

**AYSHA**     But it would have been far simpler to have got me last week, wouldn't it?

**NAZMA**     But we didn't have your consent.

**AYSHA**        No.

**NAZMA** *(pause)* It's a shame that we lost that chance though. Last week I heard you were something of a star student.

**AYSHA**        Star student! You've got to be joking. That wasn't according to Vince.

**NAZMA**        Really?

**AYSHA**        He seemed to change his mind overnight, and he used my bad work as the reason why he wouldn't let me have a couple of days out of this... Jesus wept!

**NAZMA**        What?

**AYSHA**        You said Vince had tried, didn't you? I don't believe it. He kept me here, in case I changed my mind, didn't he?

**NAZMA**        Sorry?

**AYSHA**        Everything's got messed up for me because of your film!

**NAZMA**        I don't understand. What's our film got to do with anything?

**AYSHA** *(pause)* Oh nothing. It's got nothing to do with you really.

**JOE**          Here's your coffee Nazma.

**NAZMA** *(moving over to Joe)* Lovely.

**AYSHA**        It was me.

**JOE**          We were talking about the film. What are you doing next?

**NAZMA**        Technical stuff, working with the editor. Trying to get some continuity between coins dropping in tins – you – and Wonder's appealing eyes. *(She laughs)*

**AYSHA**        How often is she away receiving help of this kind?

**JOE**          Tell me Nazma, with editing, you can take things out but you can't put anything in, no?

**NAZMA**        Well it depends, on how important something was.

**AYSHA**        He would have still had the same impression, even if Maurice hadn't got at him first.

**NAZMA**        I mean if it was saying something new.

**JOE**          You can bring the cameras back yeah, but could that be for... say an interview?

**NAZMA**        We have enough of those, explaining, appealing, thanking...

**AYSHA**        Because of 'Thank you.' Thank you for your help! Your kind generous help

| | |
|---|---|
| NAZMA | Are you talking to me Aysha? |
| AYSHA | Yes, and your whole film that stinks of gratitude! |
| JOE | She's got a slight problem with gratitude. |
| AYSHA | Because I've got an idea of what thank you does. |
| NAZMA | Well aren't you glad you've got your dog? |

AYSHA     Oh wise up woman! You think I'm glad that you're showing us as people who just *take* all the time, *take* any bit of help that might be chucked our way. No wonder I get looked down on.

NAZMA     Hold on a minute! I think you'd better get that chip off of your shoulder. What do you think we've got a whole feature on Joe for? He doesn't come across as any of those things for your information.

AYSHA     Oh no.

NAZMA     You know nothing about it. Through his interview he shows that the handicapped *do* achieve and that they *do* contribute. He is a positive image.

AYSHA     About as positive as Mother Theresa's pregnancy test.

NAZMA     How can she say that about you?

JOE     Free country.

AYSHA     Not for the other disabled people in your bank though.

JOE     What disabled people?

AYSHA     Denise.

JOE     What's Denise got to do with it?

AYSHA     Oh come on, Joe.

JOE     I really don't know what you're talking about, Aysha.

AYSHA     You don't know about your own employer's acts of discrimination against people like you, that your own fiancee told me about?

NAZMA     What's this?

AYSHA     Ask your positive image.

NAZMA     Joe?

JOE     I have never said that things are totally fair at the bank.

NAZMA     Well yes, you told me about that 'inconsistency of appearance' job.

AYSHA          Oh, so there's other things and you're going to keep
your mouth shut about it all.

JOE          You don't understand. Nazma said it's hard to edit
things in.

AYSHA          But if they are important enough?

NAZMA *(pause)* I don't know. I'd have to think about its relevance.

*A knock on the door and Vince enters, coming over to Joe and
Aysha, as Nazma wanders over to Desirée.*

VINCE          I thought an unscheduled lecture had started by the
sounds of things in here. Keep your voices down, yeah? We don't
want people to think we're a pack of wild animals. *(goes over to
Nazma and Desirée)*

VOICEOVER Dogs are a pack animal and within the pack, posit-
ions are constantly being established and re-established. You
must be alert and ready to check if any signs of this show.

*The sound of barking dogs, which runs through this entire scene
begins to distort gradually into snarls and howls.*

VINCE          Did I miss something?

NAZMA          Aysha's problem.

VINCE          Oh yeah?

NAZMA          Something and nothing, I don't know. Desirée, what
did you think about taking part in our film?

VINCE          There were no problems with Desirée.

NAZMA          Yeah? What did you think of the film then?

DESIREE *(shrugging)* Not much.

VINCE          And most people here took it like that, with a pinch
of salt.

NAZMA          Yes, that's what I felt..

VINCE          And that's what you got. It's in the can as they say.

NAZMA          But the transmission isn't quite.

VINCE          Hasn't a date been set yet?

NAZMA          Soon... and it will go out then unless we discover
huge errors in content or there are power failures.

**VINCE**      Well, we made sure all our facts were straight and our figures like Desirée, were looking good. *(He rubs her shoulder)*

**DESIREE**      Have you done my necklace, Vince?

**NAZMA**      So, you're admitting it now? You seemed reluctant to agree before, when I pointed out that Desirée was rather camera-genic.

**VINCE**      No, I haven't quite finished with your necklace yet Desirée.

**AYSHA**      What's wrong with her? There's nothing to think about. She's giving you the chance to say something, you do something!

**JOE**      Give me the benefit of choosing where I speak, and understand that I don't intend to do it there.

**AYSHA**      Where would you choose to do it then?

**JOE**      Through my job, where they see me working to the best of my ability. That means I'm valued for my competence and my blindness does not get in the way of me earning my respect.

**AYSHA**      But it does though, for those like Denise or, doesn't she work hard enough? Isn't she as competent?

**JOE**      Of course she is, but she's, she's...

**AYSHA**      She's not the marvellous exception to the rule, like you, with your head buried, going on proving that there's no differences with us, that we don't need any recognition for who we are?

**JOE**      Jesus Christ! I'm just an ordinary guy, adapting to this situation called life. If I start whining on the television about how unfair things are... why are they going to take any notice of me? We all do it – cope the best way we can and if that means without concessions, or recognition, or whatever you call it, then–

**AYSHA**      Then we all have to bust our arses being amazing, when we should have...

**JOE**      Of course we should have, and they could do more... We all know that but the brick wall just gives you a bumpy forehead. Haven't you noticed, and you stay at the bottom for your pains.

**AYSHA**      I think it's pretty painful being the silent survivor.

**JOE** *(pause)* Anyway, I thought you were against receiving help?

AYSHA          As a smiley face, used to ease  a quid out of a
pocket, and a quid of guilt off a mind – yes. But financial
compensation from an employer who won't bring down the wall
to let us through, that's something else, isn't it? Isn't it?

JOE            Denise had no bloody business talking to you!

VINCE *(to Nazma)* Stay there, I'll sort this out. *(coming over to
Aysha and Joe)* Aye, aye, what did I tell you?

AYSHA          Come here, go there, keep it short, hurry up, do this,
do that. Stop telling me what to do!

VINCE          Are you alright mate?

JOE *(walking around angrily)*  Yeah, yeah.

VINCE          What's it all about Joe?

JOE            She's just exercising her mouth Vince.

VINCE          What's the routine then, Aysha?

AYSHA          You want to know? Okay. You have not got a clue,
and you don't give a shit about anything, apart from keeping your
job safe, keeping everything the way you want it, and keeping the
blasted money rolling in.

VINCE *(low and in her ear)* What utter blind ignorance. Are you
getting wound up over that, Joe? Don't let her get to you! *(To
Aysha)* So that's the rubbish that stopped you from doing the film
then?

AYSHA          No, it was the rubbish already in the film that
stopped me, and having no chance to say it was rubbish.

VINCE          Well, thank God. The malicious voice from the
wilderness is just a fart in the breeze, eh Joe?

AYSHA          But loud enough to hear, eh Joe?

*Joe stays silent.*

NAZMA          Are you pleased with Milton?

DESIREE        What?

NAZMA          Oh, you're listening. What's happening in the minor
dispute. You can probably hear better than me.

DESIREE        For something so minor, it's going on a bit.

NAZMA          Don't worry, he'll mend your necklace soon.

DESIREE        What?

NAZMA          Who is it that usually helps you with your odd jobs?
Your boyfriend?

**DESIREE**     I haven't got a boyfriend.

**NAZMA**     Really? That must be hard.

**DESIREE**     I can always find someone who gets a buzz out of helping.

**NAZMA** *(looking at Vince)* Well I bet when you get to college, all the boys will be queuing up for you there.

**VINCE**     D'you know what this programme means to us, Joe?

**AYSHA**     D'you know what this programme means to us, Joe?

**VINCE**     Yes, it means finishing off our rebuilding work here and opening three other centres like this around the country, for you!

**JOE**     How else do we get trained, Aysha?

**AYSHA**     We could – without places like this and people like him... why don't they take a bit of notice of us in the running of this place?

**VINCE**     You' re so pompous, you've gone cross-eyed with confusion and lost sight of what you're talking about! It so happens that Joe has been invited onto the S.E.D.A. Board of Management, next month. *(He puts the dog's head on Joe.)*

**AYSHA**     Well if your record at the bank is anything to go by Joe, I won't hold my breath.

**VINCE**     Oh, I wish you would.

**AYSHA**     Joe's the one who's perfected that technique quite well, aren't you?

**JOE**     What's the bank got to do with what's going on here?

**VINCE**     She's lost it, Joe.

**AYSHA**     Changes Joe! The way we're treated at your bank and the way we're treated here. Don't ignore the changes needed to make this place slightly more humane.

**VINCE**     How is this place inhumane? For god's sake, what we do here is to give you people the opportunity to get your mobility, get out there and live like human beings.

**AYSHA** *(putting on her dog's head)* But before that you have to turn us into something with just a few less rights, with just a little less dignity, something that's just a little less than human.

**VINCE** *(moving away)* God, come on, that's taking it just a little bit too far!

*The faint sound of the ghost fades in and grows steadily louder.*

| | |
|---|---|
| **NAZMA** | And did you find it easy to learn Braille? |
| **DESIREE** | What? |
| **NAZMA** | I suppose it's like anything – practise makes perfect. |
| **VINCE** | You have to learn a lot of new things after losing your sight. |
| **DESIREE** | Yes. |
| **NAZMA** | Did it go very quickly? |
| **DESIREE** | Over a few months. |
| **NAZMA** | You could see perfectly before? |
| **DESIREE** | Perfectly, then partially. |
| **NAZMA** | God... and then nothing at all? |
| **VINCE** | Not nothing, she's got some left. |
| **NAZMA** | Really? Well that's something, at least but it's such a shame because she's so pretty, isn't she? |
| **VINCE** | The film will testify to that. |
| **DESIREE** | Will it? |
| **NAZMA** | Can you see the television? |
| **DESIREE** | Not your programme. |
| **VINCE** | What? |

**AYSHA** *(addressing the room)* And if they don't show us like this, how will they get their money, Joe?

**JOE**          I don't know.

*Nazma and Vince stand up.*

**VINCE** *(storming over)* Look – get your facts right! People give us money because of the dogs, right?

**JOE**          The way they talk to us sometimes, you wonder if they know there's a difference.

**AYSHA**          Anyway, who is it who has to say thank you?

**VINCE**          What's wrong with a bit of fucking gratitude?

*Aysha and Joe are silent.*

**VOICEOVER** *(losing its benign quality)* Your head position can be under threat at any time and it is up to you to maintain that role as Alpha dog. There are many ways in which you can keep your status. Never take your eyes off the dog. Always remain

physically on a higher level and keep your voice low and steady
to cover any traces of fear.

**DESIREE**     Vince...

**VINCE**        Yes, Desirée? You were saying something about the
film?

**NAZMA** *(beginning to move around Desirée)* How much can you
see then?

**DESIREE**     Some things, if I force myself.

**VINCE**        Aren't you going to force yourself to see the film?

**DESIREE**     I don't want to.

**NAZMA**        Can you see me?

**DESIREE**     Yes.

**VINCE**        You won't see how good you look.

**DESIREE**     Can I have my necklace?

**NAZMA**        What do you see me as?

**DESIREE**     For God's sake – you're a blob. Have you got my
necklace?

**NAZMA** *(laughing uncertainly)* Well that's the first time I've been
described like that.

**VINCE**        Well Desirée, I can tell you... anything like a blob,
Nazma definitely is not.

**NAZMA** *(a smile of triumph)* Thank you Vince.

**DESIREE**     But I will be, on her film, and I don't want to be.

**VINCE**        Don't talk rubbish Desirée.

**NAZMA**        We've already told you now, you'll look lovely.
*(She places the dog's head on Desirée.)*

**DESIREE**     I've never wanted to do it Vince.

**NAZMA**        If you were unhappy, why didn't you say something
earlier?

**DESIREE**     I'm sorry.

**VINCE**        I don't like this Desirée.

**DESIREE**     Can I have my necklace, please? *(holding her hand
out.)*

**VINCE** *(passing it over her palm)* Won't you think again?

**NAZMA**        It would save us a lot of headaches.

**DESIREE**     I have thought, please.

**NAZMA**        Well if that's how you feel, then we ought to –

**VINCE** *(making her grab for the necklace)* Change your mind
Desirée.

**DESIREE**       Please, let me have it!
**NAZMA**        Yes, give it to her Vince.
**VINCE** *(throwing it down)* She can get it herself.
**DESIREE** *(on the floor)* Where is it?
**NAZMA** *(going to retrieve it)* Here it –
**VINCE** *(kicking it away)* No you don't.
**NAZMA**        Vince! *(expecting him to follow)* Come on, let's go
for a drink and think about all this, yeah?
**VINCE**         Think about it, Desirée.
**NAZMA** *(shocked he is not following, she runs and holds his arm)*
Look Vince – you and me. I thought you've been wanting to get
together again after the last time? Let's go.
**DESIREE**       I can't find it!
**VINCE**         You said, yes, Desirée. Say it again!
**NAZMA**        Stop it! She's blind.
**DESIREE**       Where is it, please?
**NAZMA**        Please! *(she stands helpless, then backs off, watching
the scene. Not knowing where to turn, she runs to Aysha and Joe,
frightened)* I don't know... what can I do?
**JOE**           What the hell is going on?
**AYSHA**        Help.
**DESIREE**       I want it!
**VINCE**         Say yes, first!
**NAZMA**        Vince!
**AYSHA** *(calm)* Help her, help her.
**NAZMA**        What? How?
**JOE**           Do something.
**NAZMA**        I want to... help me!
**AYSHA**        You help us, remember your film?
**DESIREE**       Give it to me! Give it to me!
**VINCE**         I said, say yes!
**NAZMA**        Oh God! Please stop! *(running around)*
**AYSHA** *(following her voice)* Feeling good, yeah?
**NAZMA**        Joe!
**JOE**           What's happening, what's happening?
**NAZMA**        Help, someone, please! Help! Help!
**AYSHA**        Your cameras – bring them back! Bring them back
now!
**VINCE**         Say yes, say yes!

**NAZMA** *(holding onto the door and half way out, but looking back)*
  Stop this! Stop this Vince!!
**DESIREE** *(banging her fist on the floor)* It's mine, it's mine, it's
  mine!
**VINCE**          Say yes, fuck you!
**DESIREE** *(pulling her dog's head off and crying out)* No!

*The sound of the ghost, which is very distorted, the screaming sax
and the howling hounds, cut to silence.*

*Lights fade.*
*The End.*

## Maria Oshodi

Her first play, *The S Bend*, was produced as part of the Royal Court Theatre's Young Writers' Festival in 1984. She went on to write four more plays that were produced, published and toured nationally, including *Blood, Sweat and Fears, From Choices to Chocolate*, and *Here Comes a Candle.*

While studying for her degree, she wrote *Hound*, and the screenplay *Mug,* which was produced as a short film for Channel 4 in 1990. In 1992 she graduated from Middlesex University with a 1st class BA Honors in Drama and English. Since then she has worked in arts development, acted, and currently runs her own arts company *Extant,* as well as working for BBC Drama production as a Diversity Project Co-ordinator.

# Soft Vengeance

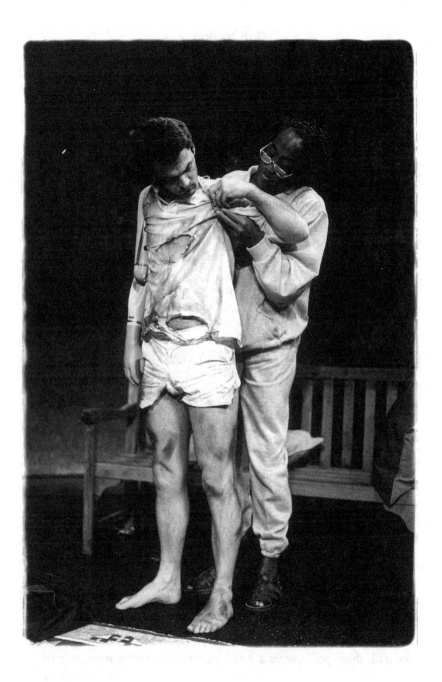

## Soft Vengeance

Grae*ae* approached me and asked me if I would consider adapting Albie Sach's autobiographical novel *'Soft Vengeance of a Freedom Fighter'* for the stage. They had four actors in mind with specific disabilities. It seemed to make sense to try workshopping the material with actors first, to see how the adaptation might work.

Ray Harrison Graham, Sarah Scott, Deborah Williams and Ewan Marshall improvised with the material for a week. What attracted the actor/director, Ewan Marshall to the material was its obvious relevance to a company like Grae*ae* – a contemporary political story set in Mozambique detailing resistance to the Apartheid regime, as well as a graphic and moving account of Albie's coming to terms with a newly acquired disability and the effect of this on his politics. It was extraordinary material but it did prove difficult to dramatise because, unsurprisingly for a man confined to a hospital bed and recovering from a bomb blast, the novel was full of Albie's internal monologues on the state of his mental and physical well-being.

The best way to dramatise this was to create two Albies which reflected two of the aspects of Albie's character which emerged from the novel – as I named them Daytime Albie and Albie Nightime; the politically correct Albie, and the more childish, but perhaps freer to express the unsayable, Albie. The conflict of these two personas became the spine of the play.

The director and I decided that I should write these parts for Ray Harrison Graham, a black, deaf actor, and Ewan Marshall, a white actor/director with one arm. The qualities/disabilities these performers had, seemed to lend themselves well to the telling of Albie's story.

After the piece was written, I attended rehearsals and was happy to rewrite as we went along. Ray and Sarah, who are both deaf actors asked me if they could rewrite a scene, in which Albie had his first date, as an amputee and a man blind in one eye, in sign language. It became, to my mind, one of the most compelling scenes of the play. I want to say, to finish, that the play was written with the performers strongly in mind and the performers were extraordinarily good. So good, that as I write this I am reminded what a great pity it is that such disabled performers are still excluded from the mainstream!

**April De Angelis**

# Soft Vengeance

## April De Angelis
Adapted from *Soft Vengeance of a Freedom Fighter*
by Albie Sachs

This play was first performed on 14th September, 1993 at Lilian Baylis Theatre, Sadlers Wells, London with the following cast:

| CHARACTERS | CAST |
| --- | --- |
| Albie | Ray Harrison Graham |
| Albie 2 | Ewan Marshall |
| Ivo Garrido, Mother | Sarah Scott |
| Margit, Woman in Bath, Limb Fitter | Deborah A. Williams |
| Woman Ironing | Sarah Scott |
| Dr Olga, Nurse, Policeman. | Deborah A. Williams |
| Father John, Melba, Zuma, Lecturer | Deborah A. Williams |

| | |
| --- | --- |
| Director | Ewan Marshall |
| Designer | Annabel Temple |
| Lighting Designer | Jenny Cane |

## ACT ONE
### SCENE I
*Four actors on stage. The first throws a beer can to the second, etc, until Albie catches it. He then packs it in his bag along with his swimming trunks and a towel. He zips up the zipper. He stands up, satisfied, holding his bag.*

CAST        Maputo... a summer's day... small breeze... someone drives by... they wave hello... a blue car...you can smell the sea... a hot day... etc.

*As he does this, the other actors who have been describing the day and the location go completely and instantly quiet. They move away leaving Albie alone.*

**ALBIE**          Oh shit. *(Pause)*
Everything has gone dark.
I am feeling strange and cannot see anything.
The beach. I am going to the beach. I packed a frosty beer for
after my run. *(Pause)*
Oh shit. I must have banged my head like I used to climbing
Table Mountain and dreaming of the struggle. It will go away. I
must just be calm and wait. *(He waits)*
Shit. How can I be so careless?
Banging my head like that. *(Short pause)*
The darkness is not clearing.
This is something serious. A terrible thing is happening to me, I
am swirling! I cannot steady myself.

*Albie 2 gives a cry.*

**ALBIE 2**        Ah!
**ALBIE**          A punch against the back of my neck.
And another! I am being dominated, overwhelmed. I have to
fight! I can feel arms coming from behind me, pulling at me
under my shoulders.
**ALBIE 2**        D'Larme!
**ALBIE**          I am being kidnapped!
**ALBIE 2**        Leave me!
**ALBIE**          They have come from Pretoria to drag me over the
border and lock me up.
**ALBIE 2**        Leave me! Leave me!
**ALBIE**          I jerk my shoulders and thrash my arms as violently
as I can.
**ALBIE 2**        Leave me alone! D'Larme!

*Repeats the cry in Portuguese.*

**ALBIE**          I am shouting in both English and Portuguese. I am
screaming for my life but with some politeness. After all, I am a
middle-aged lawyer in a public place.
**ALBIE 2**        I would rather die here. Leave me. I'd rather die
here.

**ALBIE**          I feel a surge of elation and strength as I struggle. I may be an intellectual but at this critical moment I am fighting bravely and with all the courage of the youth of Soweto!

*Voices give a snatch of an ANC song or chant*

**ALBIE**          Dark still. Voices.
**VOICES**          Lift him. Lift him up. Put him there.
**ALBIE 2**          I am not a him, I am me.
**ALBIE**          We are travelling fast.
**VOICES**          Lift him, careful, careful. Move him this way, this way. Mind out. Quick, quick. Move him this way, that way.
**ALBIE**          I am wrapped in darkness and tranquillity, drifting... If I am dead I am not aware of it. If I am alive I am not aware of it. I have no awareness, nothing...

*Short pause.*

**VOICE**          Albie...
**ALBIE**          *Albie*... through the darkness a voice, speaking to me, using my name.
**VOICE**          Albie, this is Ivo Garrido speaking to you.
**ALBIE**          Ivo? I know Ivo.
**VOICE**          You are in Maputo Central Hospital and your arm is in a lamentable condition.
**ALBIE**          Lamentable. How tactful the Mozambican culture is compared to the English.
**VOICE**          We are going to operate and you must face the future with courage.
**ALBIE**          I feel a glow of joy. I am in the arms of Frelimo. I am safe. What happened? A voice answers, close to my ears, I think it is a woman's.
**VOICE**          A car bomb.
**ALBIE**          She says. *(Pause)* So it has happened.

**SCENE 2**
*Albie moves so as to break the reality of the preceding scene.*
*However he still faces the audience in order to explore his injuries.*

**ALBIE**      Here is an old Jewish joke.
Himie Cohen falls off a bus. As he gets up, he makes what
appears to be a large sign of the cross over his body.
Himie's friend is watching in astonishment.
'Himie' he says, 'I didn't know you were a Catholic.'
'What do you mean, Catholic?' Himie answers.
'I was just checking; spectacles, testicles, wallet and watch.'
*(Pause)* I'm going to alter the order a little. I'm sure Himie would
not mind in the circumstances. Testicles...
*(Albie lifts his arm and sends it over his body. First on his
crotch.)* My balls, one and two. All present and correct.
Perhaps I should call them testes since I am in hospital.
My penis is there. My good old cock.
I'm alone, I can say the word. No doubt it will lead me into as
much happiness and as much despair, in the future, as it has in the
past. Good. I am moving my hand up to my chest.
Wallet... ribs seem intact, my heart is there. My blood will pump,
I will live and live robustly! Spectacles...
*(He feels his face with his fingers.)*
I cannot feel any craters or jagged bits and I am thinking clearly.
Watch... *(Albie feels for his right arm. A pause.)*
My hand creeps over my shoulder and slides down my upper arm
and suddenly there is nothing there.
*(Pause)* So I have lost an arm.
*(Pause)* They did not say they were going to cut it off.
*(Pause)* It's the right arm that's missing, because it's my left that's
doing all the feeling.
*(Pause)* So I have lost an arm. That's all. I've lost an arm.
They tried to kill me but I have only lost an am. An arm.
*(Pause)* Spectacles, testicles, wallet and watch.
I joke, therefore I am.

**SCENE 3**
*A bed is wheeled forward. Albie gets onto the bed. The nurses speak
in whispers or sign to each other silently so as not to disturb Albie.
They walk very softly. They check his pulse and temperature, perhaps
they blindfold him. A doctor speaks to Albie. Albie is in discomfort.*

**DOCTOR**      Professor Sachs...

**ALBIE**    Please, call me Albie.

**DOCTOR**    I am Dr. Olga.

**ALBIE**    How am I doing?

**DOCTOR**    Apart from the loss of an arm, you have sustained four broken ribs, a fractured heel on the right leg and a severed nerve in the left. There are considerable surface wounds as a result of the shrapnel. Both eardrums are ruptured. We are all grateful that you escaped alive, Professor. I am going to test your eyes.

**ALBIE**    My eyes?

**DOCTOR**    First the right side... *(She mimes unbandaging. Albie looks at her)* It's you. We met before. When I went to get my eyes tested at the hospital, remember? *(Pause)* I was the queue barger. You sent me back.

**DOCTOR**    Three times I believe.

**ALBIE**    I was in a hurry.

**DOCTOR**    Now the left side.*(begins to unbandage his left side)*

**ALBIE**    I had an important meeting concerning our democracy.

**DOCTOR**    It would have been undemocratic of me to favour famous professors over office workers no matter how much of a hurry they were in.

**ALBIE**    I was terribly late. Still, I would like to take this fortuitous opportunity to apologise.

**DOCTOR**    You can't see anything from this side? *(Pause)*

**ALBIE**    No.... So, I have lost the sight of my left eye. *(Pause)* Doctor Olga?

**DOCTOR**    Yes, Albie?

**ALBIE**    Something is puzzling me. I have been through a terrible experience. I'm lying here a mass of fractures and wounds. So tell me, why am I feeling so wonderful?

*The doctor does not answer, perhaps she shakes her head in puzzlement.*

**SCENE 4**
*Night time. The airport. Albie is wheeled in onto the tarmac. As he is wheeled he speaks.*

**ALBIE**          I nearly died. I nearly died but I did not.
*(He is left alone.)*
On the tarmac. Warm night air.
The sky is dark. Just the bright lights of the airport building.
They've left me a moment. *(Pause)*
I want someone. Someone to hold me.
All the women I've ever held in my arms to hold me. Rescue me.
Remind me that once my body was lovable and loved.

*A woman steps out. She wears an unfashionable hat and holds a battered bag. She is Albie's mother.*

**MOTHER**          Albie? *(Albie looks at her)* Hello, Albie.
**ALBIE**          What are you doing here?
**MOTHER**          I brought you these. *(holds out a paper bag)*
**ALBIE**          You gave me a start. Stepping out of the dark like
that.
**MOTHER**          I'm glad I caught you. A nice man let me through.
**ALBIE**          I was just having a quiet moment. There's a lot of
people to see when you've been blown up.

*She proffers the bag again*

**MOTHER**          I've brought you some tomatoes.
**ALBIE**          You came here to give me some tomatoes?
**MOTHER**          I grow them now, in my garden.
**ALBIE**          I'm afraid I can't eat them.
**MOTHER**          Oh.
**ALBIE**          I'm intravenous at the moment. Most of the time you
can't recognise me for the tubes. *(Pause)* They're putting me on a
plane. I'm going to London. For treatment.
**MOTHER**          From age six you wouldn't hold my hand. Not even
crossing the road.
**ALBIE**          Mum.
**MOTHER**          And now look. My son the lawyer going to hospital.
**ALBIE**          Better than your son the lawyer going to prison like
last time.
**MOTHER**          I was proud. *(Pause)*
I was remembering when Josie Mpama and me were sent to

organise the mineworkers because it was easier for women to get through. It was freezing cold and we only had one pair of gloves between us. So we wore one each and swapped left for right every so often.

**ALBIE**     I know it must be hard for you.

**MOTHER**     All the way here I kept thinking... one glove.

*She makes a step towards Albie, he retreats*

**ALBIE**     They're coming now. *(Pause)* I just want to get this over. To come back and start my life again. Like before. *(Pause)* When I've learned to write again, I'll write.

**MOTHER**     You don't want these? *(holds up bag of tomatoes)* They're good for your skin.

**ALBIE**     My skin isn't the problem.

**MOTHER**     I've always liked them. I'll say goodbye then, Albie.

*She leaves. Pause.*

**ALBIE**     I will be back. I will have my run on the beach and my frosty beer. I will complete my run. And this time nothing will stop me! *(Pause)* Khanimambo, Maputo, until we meet again.

*He is wheeled off.*

## SCENE 5

*London, hospital. Albie tries to get on a pot. As he does so, he sings a revolutionary ANC song. He manages with difficulty to get onto it. He sits.*

**ALBIE**     'The success of the revolution depends on the tiny daily acts of each one of us...'
What is really heroic is the act of pulling myself across the bed and toppling on to this pot. Commode. That's technically inaccurate. There's nothing commodious about them.
*(He strains. Fails.)*
It is my duty to myself, to those who love me, to the comrades to get better, to make myself as physically whole as possible, to

emerge radiantly and forcefully from the blast.

*(He strains again without success. He picks up a book. Reads.)*
*'Murder by the Book.'* One of Rex Stout's best and usually an
excellent laxative, but today, even after three murders, nothing's
happening. *(Pause)* What I need right now is a plan for recovery
with a decent time scale that I can stick to. Then, in say three
months time I can be walking, okay, I'll concede a stick, but
walking onto a plane home with two arms.
A prosthetic arm. I've heard they can do things.
Driving. Tidying up. Good. I've never liked tidying up. Back in
Maputo, back in Johannesburg people will say
'Albie is his old self again, he's restored.'
Their spirits will rise and they'll take heart in their struggle. I'll
have lost three months of my life. Three months. That's all my
assassins will get from me. Tactics. I just need the right tactics.
*(Pause)* I can feel something! A stirring! My muscles beginning
to move on their own and a tiny bit of substance entering the
passage. Eureka! The movement continues. It is coming, it is
coming. A tiny plop! Joy! A revolutionary movement! *(Pause)*
Now for the toilet paper. It is not merely for the sake of lavatory
humour that I call this – the frontier of struggle.

*(He leans over with great difficulty and manages to put the roll
between his knees. He unwinds a short length and pulls. The
paper does not break.)*
Christ. *(He tries again)* One... two... three...
*(This time it works)* Victory! I shit, therefore I am.

## SCENE 6
*The whole cast sing softly as Albie climbs painfully into his bed.*

**CAST**          It's me, it's me O Lord
                  It's me, it's me O Lord
**ALBIE**         What time is it? Not light, not dark.
    Don't talk to yourself, Albie, that's a bad habit.

*Albie 2 appears.*

**ALBIE 2**       I can't help it. I like talking to myself. I get lonely.

**ALBIE**          Well, I would like to get some sleep. I need my rest.
I have a lot of recovering to do. *(pulls the covers over his head)*

**ALBIE 2** *(sings mournfully)* It's me, it's me O Lord
                   It's me, it's me, it's...

**ALBIE**          Are you deliberately trying to provoke me?

**ALBIE 2**        It's not my fault. The words keep rattling around my
skull. Ow!

**ALBIE**          What now?

**ALBIE 2**        I feel sore all over.

**ALBIE**          If you tried getting some sleep it wouldn't bother you
so much.

**ALBIE 2**        Daytime Albie. The perfect patient. I can't sleep.
My scalp feels like it's clamping down on my skull. My whole
right side aches like a raw wound.

**ALBIE**          Everything will get better. It's a matter of patience.

**ALBIE 2**        Not everything will get better.

**ALBIE**          There was no need to bring that up.

**ALBIE 2**        We never used to think about it and now it's gone. I
can't get used to the extra space. I miss it. Do you miss it?

**ALBIE**          Goodnight.

**ALBIE 2**        It's morning.

**ALBIE**          Shhhh. *(Pause)*

**ALBIE 2**        Technically it is morning. Legally it is.

**ALBIE**          Shut up. *(Pause)*

**ALBIE 2**        Aaagh!

**ALBIE**          What is it now?

**ALBIE 2**        I felt it. A ghostly tingling...like my fingers were
clenched into a fist.

**ALBIE**          It's all in your imagination. Phantom limb they call
it.

**ALBIE 2**        Phantom!

**ALBIE**          It's gone. Along with my watch, my signature and
the callus on my finger where I held my pen.

**ALBIE 2**        That crusty thing.

**ALBIE**          I happened to be very proud of that. That was my
answer to the calluses of the workers.

**ALBIE 2**        I always wanted to scrub at that with a pumice.

**ALBIE**          Listen and take heed. I'm going to sleep now. Sleep.
That's my priority. I don't want to lie here listening to any more of

your questionable opinions. Wake me on pain of death.

*Silence. Albie closes his eyes*

**ALBIE 2**      Albie?
**ALBIE**        I don't believe it.
**ALBIE 2**      What to you think they did with it?
**ALBIE**        Did with it?
**ALBIE 2**      The doctors. Did they burn it?
**ALBIE**        That is a disturbed and unproductive way to think. It
was the assassins that *did it* not the doctors.
**ALBIE 2**      I'm not disturbed.
**ALBIE**        No, you're just a symptom.
**ALBIE 2**      A symptom!
**ALBIE**        You'll probably evaporate in a few days time.
**ALBIE 2**      I certainly will not evaporate!
**ALBIE**        You're a psychological splinter. *(Pause)*
**ALBIE 2**      It was in tatters, Albie. Our arm. Bloody bone and
tatters.
**ALBIE**        Like I said, I need my rest.
**ALBIE 2**      You miss it too. You can't lie to me. I'm the expert
witness.
**ALBIE**        Expert! You've got nothing, no strategy, no goal.
You just creep about at night. Whining. It's quite pathetic. I'll be
glad to see the back of you, Albie night-time.
**ALBIE 2**      It's easy for you to say. You have a nice bright room
and nurses buzzing about. I only have the darkness and a sore
neck. I don't get post or visitors. I don't have friends. Nobody
wants to know me. Only you. Albie daytime.
**ALBIE**        No wonder. Look at you. Full of sickening self pity.
**ALBIE 2** *(sings again mournfully)* It's me, it's me O Lord...
**ALBIE**        If you're going to sing, do it with some vim!
*(Albie joins in. They sing together)*
                 It's me O Lord standing in the need of prayer
                 Not my brother not my sister but me O Lord
                 Standing in the need of prayer. *(Pause)*
If you want to get through this you'll have to follow my example.
That'll pull you through.

*Albie puts his head down. Albie 2 watches him.*

**ALBIE 2** *(whispers)* It's me... it's me...

**SCENE 7**
*Albie puts on or is revealed to be wearing a brightly coloured
patterned T-shirt and shorts. It has a tropical fruit motif or
something similarly garish and upbeat. He displays this to his visitor,
Margit. Margit bursts into tears.*

**ALBIE**      It's not that bad, is it?

*Margit tries to stop crying*

**MARGIT**      Sorry.
**ALBIE**      I wanted a new image. Something lively. *(Pause)*
Margit? *(He hugs her)* Calm down. That's it. It's alright. It's al-
right.
**MARGIT**      It's not the outfit, Albie.
**ALBIE**      I know.
**MARGIT**      I'm sorry. I shouldn't be crying. Seeing you...
**ALBIE**      See this?

*He hands something the size of a button to Margit. She takes it.*

**MARGIT**      What is it?
**ALBIE**      Yesterday when the nurses changed my bandages,
she was swabbing my chest and she hit a tender place. I tell her
'that was sore' and she says 'there's something there, I can feel it'
She gets a pair of tweezers and inserts them into the wound. A
little tug and she has pulled it out. She holds it towards me, a
jagged piece of metal. "That's another piece of rubbish out', she
says. I look closely. 'That's not rubbish' I say, 'That's my car!'
You see. That piece of shrapnel worked its own way out.
I must really be on the mend.
**MARGIT**      Here. *(hands it back)*
**ALBIE**      Now it's all I have left of my lovely Honda.
**MARGIT** *(laughs)* I'm okay now.
**ALBIE**      Sure?

**MARGIT**     Yes.

**ALBIE**      Good. Then you can tell me how it happened.

**MARGIT**     What?

**ALBIE**      How it happened. I know I can trust you to be accurate. I haven't read the newspapers you see. And my visitors are too tactful to raise the subject.

**MARGIT**     I can't tell you, Albie.

**ALBIE**      I'm fine. Remember the piece of Honda. *(Pause)* Margit. I don't know what happened that day. I need facts, for my recovery. *(Pause)*

**MARGIT**     What I am going to tell you is based on newspaper stories, letters and telephone calls. *(Pause)* It was about nine am. You were planning to go to the beach. The date was seventh of April, 1988. You went to your car which was parked just in front of your building, put something in the trunk, walked to the side in front where you placed a small bag...

**ALBIE**      That was the frosty beer.

**MARGIT**     And then you went to open the door next to the driver's seat.

**ALBIE**      I don't remember that.

**MARGIT**     At that moment Sam Barnes, your American friend drove past on the other side of the road with her baby in the back of her car and you looked up to wave at her ...and according to one version that probably saved your life.

**ALBIE**      And then?

**MARGIT**     And then the explosion took place. Your car was thrown to one side and you were thrown to the other. I don't know if you saw pictures of your car? *(Albie shakes his head)* It was crumpled up like a ball and you were lying some distance away. Some people came to pull you away in case there was another explosion. You were speaking to them. Giving them instructions how to carry you.

**ALBIE**      Speaking! I thought I was shouting, fighting for my life.

**MARGIT**     A team were setting up to make a film about woman's day nearby and they pulled up in their van and took you to hospital. It was just a hundred yards away.

**ALBIE**      I thought I was being kidnapped. Dragged for miles over the border. That is a joke! *(He laughs)* Life is crazy! *(laughs again)* Thanks for telling me, Margit.

**MARGIT**      You're sure you'll be okay?

**ALBIE**      Of course. I'm making the fastest recovery in history.

**MARGIT**      Well, if you're sure.

**ALBIE**      I'm sure. *(He squeezes her hand)*

**MARGIT**      You're going to have to get some replacements for those, Albie. *(She indicates his clothes)*

**ALBIE**      Aren't they affirmative and witty?

**MARGIT**      Shortie pyjamas?

**ALBIE**      You could be my producer. Get me something stylish. Produce me.

**MARGIT**      Are you serious?

**ALBIE**      I'm serious. These are all I have in the world. My suitcase never arrived from Maputo, so I not only lost my arm and my car and my job and my home and my country... I lost my clothing as well. I'm like a newborn baby. I start with nothing. Produce me.

**MARGIT**      I think that's a wonderful idea. I know just the shop – it's expensive.

**ALBIE**      Good. I don't want to sneak back into Maputo. I want to do it in style.

**MARGIT**      We miss you back home, Albie. It feels like there's a great hole in our department. We need you.

**ALBIE**      I'll be back before you know it.

**MARGIT**      I know. *(stands to leave)* Someone was telling me about this guy they know. He's a professional skier. Professional. And Albie, he has one leg.

**ALBIE**      Really. One leg.

**MARGIT**      Really. *(kisses him goodbye)* See you in Maputo.

*She leaves. Pause. He picks up a little bell. He rings it frantically. A nurse appears.*

**ALBIE**      Nurse... Nurse... Please, tonight or tomorrow, as soon as possible, I want to see a psychiatrist. A psychiatrist, you hear!

**SCENE 8**
*A policeman stands by Albie's bed.*

**POLICEMAN** I'll just stand if that's alright.

**ALBIE**          Please do.

**POLICEMAN** Liaise is French in origin. I expect you know that, seeing as you're a professor. It's one of those mysteries. Why didn't we have our own word? Why did we have to take one of theirs? *(Pause)* Let's get it over with, shall we? *(takes out a note book. He takes a breath and recites)* Have you seen anything out of the ordinary, peculiar, noticed any suspicious behaviour as to say, out of character, or had a sighting? Someone just hanging about, don't be deceived by uniforms, perhaps you have had a garbled message or a parcel?

**ALBIE**          Nothing of that sort.

**POLICEMAN** I must repeat no matter how small or insignificant the thing may be, it may only exist at the level of recurrent unease at a minor detail please do not hesitate to report it to me now that's my job. We're  here to protect and survey.

**ALBIE**          I can't say there's anything...

**POLICEMAN** Well that's that then. *(He puts away his notebook)* I've missed the tea have I?

**ALBIE**          By five minutes. I can't imagine they'd try again.

**POLICEMAN** Vigilance is confidence. You never can tell with these political types. They don't think like the rest of us. Now this ANC – I don't mean to worry you, but better safe than sorry. I'm sure you're happier knowing we've got our tabs on you.

**ALBIE**          I've been a member of the ANC for most of my life. *(Pause)*

**POLICEMAN** Turned against you, did they?

**ALBIE**          They're not responsible for this.

**POLICEMAN** No?

**ALBIE**          No. White extremists. *(Pause)*

**POLICEMAN** I've never got myself involved in politics, Mr Sachs. I don't understand it. I'm just happy being myself. Well now, I'll take another look down the corridor and then I'll be off. Same time next Tuesday?

**ALBIE**          You know, it's quite funny. For the first time in my
life I'm on the same side as the police. *(He laughs, the policeman
doesn't)*
**POLICEMAN** Till next week then.

*He exits. Albie picks up a shoe and begins to practice tying a lace
with one hand. Albie two appears. He also has a shoe, untied. Albie
continues with his task.*

**ALBIE 2**       There's a policeman in the corridor.
**ALBIE**          He's hunting down assassins. He comes on
Tuesdays. Vigilance is confidence.
**ALBIE 2**       What if the assassins come on a Wednesday?
**ALBIE**          That would be bad luck.
**ALBIE 2**       It's not funny. They could be plotting against us right
this minute. And we're fiddling about with a shoe. One of your
guys was assassinated in a hospital bed.
**ALBIE**          This is London not South Africa. They're not going
to try here.
**ALBIE 2** *(whispers)* Don't say that. You might provoke them.
**ALBIE**          Don't be paranoid.
**ALBIE 2**       Have you checked the room? Bugs!
**ALBIE**          Try to get a grip on things, okay, Albie Nighttime?
**ALBIE 2**       Christ, they have devices now that are small enough
to hide in earwax. They can do anything. They can bore a hole in
your ceiling, drop down And slice your throat. Then they're out
before anyone's the wiser.
**ALBIE**          I would be the wiser. Now please. I want to achieve
this. *(indicates shoe)*
**ALBIE 2**       Never let it be said that I hindered your recovery.
*(Albie two begins to search under the bed, feel around its edges,
etc. Albie watches him. Albie two looks at his shoe)* This is bloody
fiddly. Can't we just tell the occupational therapist from now on
we'll wear sandals?
**ALBIE**          There. I've done it.
**ALBIE 2**       You've done it?
**ALBIE**          And now I've undone it.
**ALBIE 2**       Why did you do that?
**ALBIE**          So I can try again. *(He begins again)*

**ALBIE 2**          You're making it into a drill. This isn't the army.

**ALBIE**          Victory does not come – it has to be organised.

**ALBIE 2**          I'm sick of all those stupid principles.

**ALBIE**          Where would we be without them?

**ALBIE 2**          We'd still have an arm. *(Pause)*

**ALBIE**          It'll have been worth losing an arm if we win our struggle.

**ALBIE 2**          Struggle, struggle. Everything's a struggle for you. Even a shoelace. We were just going for a run and now look at us. Stuck in here. Have you looked in a mirror lately? You weren't exactly a beaut' before... but now...! Tragic! Shaved head and scars, scars, scars.

**ALBIE**          I think of it like dad would. Battle scars. Remember the postcard?

**ALBIE 2**          When we were six?

**ALBIE**          Grow up and be a soldier in the fight for freedom, that's what he wrote us.

**ALBIE 2**          But I don't want to be a soldier. I have bad knees. I just want an ordinary life. I want to be an artist. Or a filmmaker. I want to collect rare and exquisite pieces of Mozambican sculpture. And I want to go swimming. It's time you left. Time we lived a little. You're not getting any younger. You almost made sure we never got any older. Haven't we given enough? *(Pause)*

**ALBIE**          I'm not leaving the ANC. Never.

**ALBIE 2**          You never think about me. What I want. *(Pause)*

**ALBIE**          Look. I've got something for you. *(Pause)* A poster.

**ALBIE 2**          What is it? Revolutionary art? The youth in struggle? *(Albie brings out a poster)*

**ALBIE**          It's a Matisse.

**ALBIE 2** *(looks at it)* A Matisse?

**ALBIE**          That's right. Blue and orange. *(Pause)*

**ALBIE 2** *(grudgingly)* It's quite nice.

**ALBIE**          Perhaps now I can get on with this in peace. *(indicates shoe)*

**ALBIE 2**          You got this for me?

**ALBIE**          That's right.

**ALBIE 2**          You made a concession? Despite the fact that there is so much suffering in the world, that beauty is contaminated for you and often intolerable?

| | |
|---|---|
| **ALBIE** | Don't quote me, it's annoying. |
| **ALBIE 2** | Well, thank you very much. |
| **ALBIE** | My pleasure. *(Pause)* |
| **ALBIE 2** | He put you up to it. Didn't he? |
| **ALBIE** | *He?* |
| **ALBIE 2** | The psychiatrist. The one you asked to see. He |

thinks you can buy me a few colourful pictures and I'll go. Well, I won't. We could have been killed.

| | |
|---|---|
| **ALBIE** | I – I, not we. |
| **ALBIE 2** | Maybe you want to die, but I don't. |
| **ALBIE** | It's nothing to do with wanting to die. I am part of an |

historic struggle. I will go on being part of it. Right now I'm struggling to get whole and active again. To triumph over the bomb despite you and your childish negativity.

*(There is a knock)*

You better go. I don't want you hanging round with comrade Zuma visiting.

| | |
|---|---|
| **ALBIE 2** | Don't worry. I don't care if I never lay eyes on |

another comrade again.

*Albie two exits. Zuma enters*

| | |
|---|---|
| **ALBIE** | Zuma. |

*(They go to shake hands. Albie twists his hand to make it possible)* Well, what has my post person brought today? *(Zuma hands him his letters)*

| | |
|---|---|
| **ZUMA** | Here... And how is Comrade Albie this morning? |
| **ALBIE** | Great. Apparently my liver is mending nicely. |
| **ZUMA** | Your liver? |
| **ALBIE** | It was sewn together very neatly in Maputo only no- |

one mentioned it to me.

| | |
|---|---|
| **ZUMA** | It just quietly got on with its own business? That is a |

well brought up liver. *(Albie laughs. A pause)*

You're not opening your post?

| | |
|---|---|
| **ALBIE** | Did you know about the others? |
| **ZUMA** | What others? |
| **ALBIE** | The others who were hit when the car exploded. |

*(Pause)* Yesterday, I read it in a letter. *(He quotes)* "I hope you are satisfied with the arrangement whereby the bulk of the money

collected goes to the family of Mr Mussagy who is still in a coma in Central Hospital." It appears from the letter that Mr Mussagy and his son had been walking along when they were hit by shrapnel from my car.

**ZUMA**     Yes... It's unfortunate.

**ALBIE**     Unfortunate! A piece of my car is lodged in the head of a Mozambican who was taking his son for a walk.

**ZUMA**     You can't blame yourself for that.

**ALBIE**     If I didn't live in that particular street, park my car in that particular place, Mr Mussagy wouldn't be lying in hospital now.

**ZUMA**     That's a lawyer talking. We always say, in such circumstances, try to consider things as part of a wider political situation.

**ALBIE**     He has three other children.

**ZUMA**     Albie, this line of thinking is not productive.

**ALBIE**     It's too hard for me to depersonalise it.

**ZUMA**     I have been a soldier. And trust me, a good recovery is dependent on healthy thoughts. You are a lawyer, and we need lawyers.

**ALBIE**     Yes, yes. I know.

**ZUMA**     You rest, Albie. That is the best thing you can do.

**ALBIE**     You're right. *(Pause)* How is Mr Mussagy? Has there been any more news?

**ZUMA**     Mr Mussagy died at three am this morning. He never came out of his coma.

**ALBIE**     I'm angry.

**ZUMA**     Yes.

**ALBIE**     Because I'm not the only one, not the only victim. I've lost my monopoly status – my right to determine levels of rage. That's me... D'you see?

**ZUMA**     Rest, Albie.

*Zuma leaves.*

**ALBIE**     Rest...

*Albie's physiotherapist enters. She wears a white coat, checks her notes.*

| | |
|---|---|
| **PHYSIO** | Now, stand. |
| **ALBIE** | What? |
| **PHYSIO** | Stand up. |
| **ALBIE** | Are you crazy? I've got a broken heel. Shattered to bits. |
| **PHYSIO** | That's alright, you can stand on it. |
| **ALBIE** | I want to see the orthopod. |
| **PHYSIO** | I am afraid that is not possible. |
| **ALBIE** | I demand to see the orthopod. |
| **PHYSIO** | He's in New Zealand. |
| **ALBIE** | New Zealand! Didn't he leave any written instructions? |
| **PHYSIO** | Yes. Here. Have a look. *(offers him a look)* |
| **ALBIE** *(reads)* | ...should not bear pressure for six weeks. |
| **PHYSIO** | Six weeks are up. Manoeuvre yourself to the side of the bed. *(He does so)* |
| **ALBIE** | Look. My legs are far too feeble. The muscles have almost gone. It will hurt like anything and it'll be me feeling it, not you. |
| **PHYSIO** | Just let your feet touch the ground. |
| **ALBIE** | I might do permanent damage to my heel! The bones will break and it will be misshapen for life. |
| **PHYSIO** | Sit forward as much as you can, tuck your bottom in and slowly stand. |
| **ALBIE** | I've forgotten how to do it. Before... I just used to stand. Can I use my hand to steady myself? |
| **PHYSIO** | If you want. Go up slowly. *(He does so)* Lean forward a little. |
| **ALBIE** | I want you to know I'm doing this for the ANC. |
| **PHYSIO** | Slowly. |
| **ALBIE** | I can't do it. There must be another way. |
| **PHYSIO** | You're doing fine. |
| **ALBIE** | I'm shaking. *(He stands slowly)* |
| **PHYSIO** | Brilliant. *(Albie stands upright for a moment)* Now sit down. Move your backside slowly. Bend your knees... *(Albie sits on the edge of the bed)* Wonderful. |
| **ALBIE** | Of one thing I am now sure, when Jesus appealed to his followers to rise up and walk, he had a physiotherapist with him. How much longer till I can run? |

**PHYSIO**        Run! Four months until you can walk.

*She exits briskly.*

## SCENE 9
*Albie hobbles over to the bath. He uses a stick. A nurse stands with a towel. He stops*

**ALBIE**        A bath! *(Cue for strains of classical music)* Nurse, I can't tell you how excited I am. My first bath. I've always loved bathing. That delicious moment as you plunge into the water and feel its heat on your skin. The pleasure of total immersion as the water swallows and caresses you and finally the long dream-filled soak when your imagination takes over and all sorts of problems solve themselves. The world is divided into shower people and bath people and I'm definitely a bath person. *(He looks about him)* There is something wrong with this bathroom. It has a bath, taps, a bathmat... but there are no half-used tubes of toothpaste, no damp facecloths, no powders, no pills. This isn't a bathroom, it's a space with bathing facilities. Never mind. The taps are running and soon I will be plunging into lovely warm water. *(He manoeuvres off his track suit top. The nurse beckons him over. He begins the exceedingly difficult task of getting into the bath. The nurse may give a few single word instructions. Albie may reply. In the bath, he begins to sink.)* I'm slipping.

*The music which is still in the background may now represent a storm at sea. (Perhaps Kachachurian) Albie 2 approaches, he is not registered by the nurse. Albie 2 has a long rough-looking brush.*

**ALBIE 2**      I found this. Under your pillow.
**ALBIE**        Put it back.
**ALBIE 2**      What is it?
**ALBIE**        It's a back scrubber
**ALBIE 2**      A back scrubber!
**ALBIE**        Put it away.
**ALBIE 2**      I expect they went to a lot of trouble at the OT department making you this. What's wrong with it?

*He flourishes it at Albie.*

**ALBIE**          I just don't like it.
**ALBIE 2**          It does the job, doesn't it? Doesn't it?
**ALBIE**          It's ugly.
**ALBIE 2**          What's that, soldier? Ugly? What's wrong with ugly?
**ALBIE**          I don't want ugly things around me. It's for my
recovery. I need beautiful things. I'm not going to explain to you,
you wouldn't understand.
**ALBIE 2**          Oh, I understand. You're slipping, Albie.

*Albie slips once more. He steadies himself. Albie 2 puts the back
scrubber on the bath. Stands back. As the nurse helps Albie out,
Albie addresses the audience.*

**ALBIE**          I hate the bath. I hate the water. I hate my optimism.
The truth is that I have been severely mutilated and my body has
lost its equilibrium. I want to cry. To weep. I want the nurse to
hold my hand and tell me it will be alright.
*(He looks at the nurse. Decides against it)*
I have been betrayed by the water.
I was a fool to imagine happiness.

**SCENE 10**
*Albie in front of a mirror attempting a tie a necktie. He has attached
one end by means of a peg to his shirt. Around him black plastic bin-
liners. A few small parcels (presents). Albie 2 enters.*

**ALBIE 2**          So, we're all ready then? *(Albie does not answer)*
Moving lock, stock and bin-liner to brother Johnny's. Excited?
**ALBIE**          Ecstatic. Apparently sexual intercourse is a long way
off and will be very tiring.
**ALBIE 2**          Bad luck. *(Pause)* Why have you got a peg attached
to your collar?
**ALBIE**          It's a strategy. For tying a necktie.
**ALBIE 2**          Another bloody strategy. *(Pause)* Three months eh?
Since the bomb. *(Pause. Picks up parcel, reads:)* To Carol, All
my thanks. Love, Albie. Three kisses. *(puts it down)*
**ALBIE**          You're not coming to Johnny's.

**ALBIE 2**          It's annoying, I know, my lack of evaporation. *(picks up another parcel)* To Audrey. Gratitude isn't enough. I'll never forget you. Albie. Also three kisses.

**ALBIE**          Look. These people have been very good to me. I want to thank them.

**ALBIE 2** *(picks up another present)* Julie. Thank you. Thank you. Thank you for the endless swabs. Fondest regards, Albie. One kiss only. But it's a big one.

**ALBIE**          It's very common for patients to have strong feelings for those who care for them.

**ALBIE 2** *(reads)* Eddie. Thanks mate. A. Sachs. Eddie doesn't get anything. How come you never had strong feelings for Eddie?

**ALBIE**          Just leave things alone.

**ALBIE 2**          Sor-ry.

**ALBIE**          I've said my goodbyes so that I can move on cleanly to the next stage in my recovery. *(fails with his necktie)* Shit!

*A knock at he door*

**ALBIE 2**          A visitor.

*A Limbfitter enters.*

**LIMBFITTER** Mr Sachs?

**ALBIE**          That's right.

**LIMBFITTER** I've just come to measure you up. Before you leave the premises.

**ALBIE**          Measure me up?

**LIMBFITTER** Your stump.

**ALBIE**          I take it you're referring to my arm?

**LIMBFITTER** Stump is the correct scientific terminology.

**ALBIE 2**          He's right, you know.

**ALBIE** *(To Albie 2)* It's my arm and I'll call it what I like!

**LIMBFITTER** When you're home you can do what you want. Only down at the unit we call them stumps. *(gets out a tape and begins to measure Albie's arm.)* It's a bit too long.

**ALBIE**          Too long?

**LIMBFITTER** For an elbow. I'd recommend having a bit more off.

**ALBIE**          A bit more off?

**ALBIE 2**          Tell him we've had enough off, thank you.

**LIMBFITTER** That would facilitate the use of an elbow joint. It all depends what you want the arm for.

**ALBIE**          What does anyone want an arm for?

**LIMBFITTER** Balance, minimal grip or cosmetic purposes.

**ALBIE 2**          Tell him it's for political purposes.

**ALBIE**          Shut up!

**LIMBFITTER** I beg your pardon?

**ALBIE**          Sorry.

**LIMBFITTER** People do get emotional.

**ALBIE**          I'm not getting emotional.

**ALBIE 2**          You are.

**LIMBFITTER** We like to stress that all our limbs are both functional and elegant. Our arms come with a selection of detachable appliances.

*Zuma enters.*

**ALBIE 2**          Comrade Zuma.

**ALBIE**          Join the party.

**LIMBFITTER** Tanned or plain?

**ALBIE**          What?

**LIMBFITTER** The prosthesis?

**ALBIE 2**          Plain.

**ALBIE**          Tanned.

**ZUMA**          How are you feeling today?

**ALBIE**          You want to know how I'm feeling?

**ZUMA**          Yes, that's why I'm here.

**ALBIE**          I feel like shit. That's how I feel. How would you be feeling if you'd been blown up and had your arm cut off and lost the sight of an eye? How do you expect me to feel? I feel like shit! Shit! *(Silence)* Don't just stand there with a stupid grin on your face, shout back at me. Go on. Go on! *(Silence)* Shout at me and then I can shout at you some more.

**ZUMA**          I'll see you another day, Comrade Albie.

**LIMBFITTER** We'll be in touch Mr Sachs.

*Both exit.*

**ALBIE**          Please shout!
**ALBIE 2**          Poor Comrade Zuma. What has he ever done to you?
*(Pause)* You've changed. The bomb has shaken you up. Shaken
you to bits. *(Albie stands with his necktie and shoelaces loose)*
**ALBIE**          I have to get better as quickly as possible. That is my
duty.
**ALBIE 2**          My advice to you is to follow my example. If you're
lucky that may pull you through.
**ALBIE**          Go away, leave me alone.
**ALBIE 2**          You're shaken to bits. Shattered...

*Albie 2 exits. Albie stands bereft.*
*Lights down.*


**ACT TWO**
**SCENE 1**
*Johnny's apartment. No bed. Albie sits. A stick near him. He reads*
*the newspaper, with some difficulty. The phone rings. Albie searches*
*for the phone. He is obviously in pain. Finally he finds the phone.*

**ALBIE**          Hello.*(phone goes dead with a prrrr sound)* Damn!
*(He sits down exhausted. The sound of a doorbell.)* Oh no.
*(shouts)* Who is it?
**MELBA**          It's me. Melba.
**ALBIE**          Melba. Wonderful. Come up... I'm in love with
Melba. Melba, attractive, vivacious, sophisticated and mine for
fixed periods every week, Monday to Friday, five pounds an hour.

*Melba enters.*

**MELBA**          Is too much.
**ALBIE**          No, no.
**MELBA**          Too much. I take less.
**ALBIE**          That's ridiculous.
**MELBA**          No ridiculous. Five pounds too much for you.
**ALBIE**          It's five pounds or nothing. I couldn't possibly pay
you less.
**MELBA**          Less. Yes, yes.

ALBIE          Absolutely not! *(addresses audience)*
Don't be alarmed if we are speaking in an excited way with a lot
of volume and vivacity. It's a cultural thing.

MELBA          Are you good today?

ALBIE          How are you feeling today?

MELBA          You feeling how today?

ALBIE          How are you feeling today?

MELBA          How are you feeling today?

ALBIE          Terrible, thank you.

MELBA          You must not feel that.

ALBIE          But I do. I want to lie down and cry.

MELBA          Men not cry.

ALBIE          Men cry.

MELBA          Not in Columbia. What problem?

ALBIE          I've got a boil on my ankle and my arm came today.

MELBA          It come?

ALBIE          In the bag. *(He indicates. Melba goes to look)* No.
Don't look. *(Melba stops)*

MELBA          I have something for you. Is big surprise.

ALBIE          Really? *(She gives him a box)*

MELBA          Cakes. Turkish cakes.

ALBIE          Melba, how kind of you.

MELBA          Not me. From my boyfriend, Mehmet.

ALBIE          From Mehmet. Well, that's wonderful, marvellous.

*Albie gets into his bath.*

MELBA          The water is good?

ALBIE          Perfect.

MELBA          Ready?

ALBIE          Ready.

*Melba begins to wash Albie. She gives instructions.*

MELBA          Left leg. *(lifts his leg)*

ALBIE          Left leg.

MELBA          I am going round the sore.

ALBIE          Yes.

MELBA          Carefully. Carefully round. Now right leg.

**ALBIE**          Right leg.

*Albie gives a sigh of pleasure.*

**ALBIE**          One day I might react. I don't know which is better,
     to concentrate on not having a physical reaction or to think about
     something altogether different like Eugene Terrablanc.
**MELBA**          Good?
**ALBIE**          Yes.

*Melba uses shower spray to spray Albie's back. Albie finds this*
*pleasurable. Melba finishes.*

**ALBIE**          Thank you.
**MELBA**          It was nothing. Nada.

*She drops the shower nozzle into the bath.*

**ALBIE**          Aaagh! The spray. It's rubbing against my sore.

*She quickly lifts it out.*

**MELBA**          You are angry with me.
**ALBIE**          No, no. It was an accident.
**MELBA**          I hurt you. You are angry.
**ALBIE**          No, no.
**MELBA**          Hit me.
**ALBIE**          I don't want to hit you, I want...
**MELBA**          Hit me!
**ALBIE**          Melba... pass me the towel.

*She does so. She helps him out of his bath and helps him to dress.*

**MELBA**          Are you still angry?
**ALBIE**          I was never angry. Melba... I have to say something.
**MELBA**          Yes?
**ALBIE**          Since the bomb, things have changed for me. It's as
     if a touch, just a touch has the power to transform all the negative
     energy, the terrible hatred of the bomb into something...

| | |
|---|---|
| **MELBA** | You are very brave man. I've never met a man like you. |
| **ALBIE** | Really? Not just anybody's touch, a woman's touch. |
| **MELBA** | Yes. I'm glad to help you. |
| **ALBIE** | You are helping me, Melba. |
| **MELBA** | Of course. Three days a week. |
| **ALBIE** | No, I meant helping me to recover. Helping me with your... |
| **MELBA** | Cooking? |
| **ALBIE** | Yes, yes... and Melba... |
| **MELBA** | Yes. |
| **ALBIE** | There's something else I wanted to say. About women. |
| **MELBA** | Women? |
| **ALBIE** | The love and comfort of women. Their warmth, stroking. It does more than the doctors. And then with you it's– |
| **MELBA** | Next I do the hoovering. First I put on your shoe. |
| **ALBIE** | No, no. I can do that. |
| **MELBA** | It is simple for me. For you it is hard. Very hard. |
| **ALBIE** | Oh. Yes. Hard. *(She puts on his shoe)* My darling, I want to say, I wish to put my arm around you and hug you and say that you are wonderful and I love having you near and that you are helping me with your love and affection even more than with the laundry and the food, and that it is a case of good coming out of bad, that I would never have got to know you if it wasn't for the bomb... |
| **MELBA** | I have to tell you something. *(Pause)* The cakes. |
| **ALBIE** | The cakes? |
| **MELBA** | They are not for nothing. |
| **ALBIE** | You want me to pay you for the cakes? |
| **MELBA** | No, no. They are for goodbye. |
| **ALBIE** | Good-bye? |
| **MELBA** | After today, I don't come. *(Pause)* For the past few weeks, it has been terrible for me, coming here. I get nervous every time I touch you. So I cannot come anymore. Next week my friend from Columbia come. She is very good and will look after you better than me. |
| **ALBIE** | Melba... |
| **MELBA** | I have to wash the dishes and then the hoovering... |

**ALBIE**        Melba...
**MELBA**      You carry on full of good spirits. You still have your
   beliefs in spite of everything. My life is nothing. I am not
   important at all.
**ALBIE**        Melba...
**MELBA**      This is my address and phone number if you ever
   come to Bogota.

*She exits.*

**ALBIE**        Adios, Melba.

*Albie sits alone. Very still. Albie 2 enters.*

**ALBIE 2**      Aren't you going to put it on? *(Pause)* Every day for
   two weeks. Come rain or shine you'd try it out. That's what you
   said. *(picks up arm, examines it)* One arm. Complete with biceps,
   hook and additional hand. While not in active use the hand can
   double as a burglar deterrent. Just leave it lying casually about
   your flat...
**ALBIE**       Go away.
**ALBIE 2**      If you don't like it you can always switch bags with
   one of your visitors. Imagine their surprise... Dear Albie... I left a
   bag identical to this one in your flat containing my swimming
   trunks, towel and a Jackie Collins novel. Here is your arm.
   *(Pause)*
**ALBIE 2**      We could bury it somewhere. See the back of it.
**ALBIE**       I have to think of others. Friends, comrades.
**ALBIE 2**      Oh them.

*Zuma enters.*

**ZUMA**      Beer!

*Albie picks up the bag with his prosthesis in it, looks for somewhere
to put it, tucks it to one side.*

**ZUMA**        I brought some beer to celebrate Albie in the outside
   world.

**ALBIE**        Thanks.
**ZUMA**         I haven't come at a bad time?
**ALBIE**        No, no. *(Pause)* I'm sorry. At the hospital. I was tense, you know.
**ZUMA**         Of course.
**ALBIE**        Sit down Zuma, sit down.

*Zuma sits, he uses the bag as a cushion.*

**ZUMA**         The word is out in the movement.
**ALBIE**        The word?
**ZUMA**         The first thing Comrade Albie did in hospital was feel for his balls.
**ALBIE**        That is... unfortunately true. *(They laugh)* You know, there's something on my mind. *(Pause)* If I wasn't sick already, I'd say it would have driven me sick with worry.
**ZUMA**         Go on.
**ALBIE**        I've been reading the newspapers. There was one report that some of our leading comrades connected with military action had said the time had come to hit white civilian targets so as to show the white population that their government couldn't protect them. Bombs have been going off in rubbish trays outside the Ellis Park Sports stadium. The Ellis Park tendency they call it. They say the talk in the ANC is all bombs, bombs and more bombs. That's what I read. *(Pause)* Is it true?
**ZUMA**         There have been explosions.
**ALBIE**        I thought we wanted our ideas to break through to the white population? Bombing them won't help.
**ZUMA**         Some people are tired of waiting for our ideas to 'break through' to whites. *(Pause)* The young are impatient, Albie. It's hard to blame them. They don't like waiting for change. They want to use every resource available.
**ALBIE**        And the international community? Are we prepared to alienate them?
**ZUMA**         With all respect, the international community doesn't have to live in Soweto. *(Pause)*
**ALBIE**        I sit around here on my own. I don't get a chance to discuss things. To put my point.

**ZUMA**          You can tell me. I'll pass it on. That's what I'm here
    for.
**ALBIE**          I think we should be patient. We are closer than
    ever. We have historic justice on our side.
**ZUMA**          For the sake of argument, Albie – one could say that
    black people are dying while waiting for historic justice to arrive.
    Perhaps historic justice would come a little faster if whites
    suffered too?
**ALBIE**          I'm worried about us. What it will do to us. Our
    spirit. Our morale. If we use the tactics of the right how are we
    any different from them? We'll be indistinguishable. Won't that
    erode us?
**ZUMA**          Erode? What does that mean to a young comrade?
    She may have seen her friends die, her family split up, suffering...
**ALBIE**          Do you think I'm reacting as a white? *(Pause)* An
    eye for an eye? An arm for an arm? Is that what we're fighting
    for?
**ZUMA**          It's under debate, Albie.
**ALBIE**          What about you?
**ZUMA**          My son was blown up by a bomb. That was ten years
    ago. He was nineteen. Waiting is dangerous if you are black. I
    have one more son. For his sake, I hope the waiting will not be
    for much longer.
**ALBIE**          I don't know what to think.

*Zuma shifts, moves the bag.*

**ZUMA**          This is bloody uncomfortable.
**ALBIE**          It's my arm.
**ZUMA**          Sorry, man. *(jumps up)*
**ALBIE**          Today is my first day for trying it.
**ZUMA**          Yes? *(crumples up his can)* Wear it for the ANC,
    eh? Show them.
**ALBIE**          Will you hear soon? The decision?
**ZUMA**          When I do, I'll pass it on.

*Zuma exits. Albie gets up slowly and fetches the bag with the arm in
it. He does so carefully. Surreptitiously. He puts the bag down on the
bed, looks at it. Unzips bag. However he cannot summon up the*

*enthusiasm to take the arm out. He lies back down, curls himself up protectively. Albie 2 enters. He looks in the bag.*

**ALBIE 2**     It'll be a kind of magic for them, like I've grown a new arm. That's what they want to see. Albie whole again. Not like this.

**ALBIE**     What are you doing?

**ALBIE 2**     Trying it on, having a go. Slip into the shoulder holster. Straighten the lower portion. Adjust the harness behind my back. Pull the strap at the end under my left shoulder, thread it through clasp, one, two, three holes, that's it, just the right tension. *(displays effect)* Magic. What do you think?

*It is as if Albie is wearing the prosthesis too.*

**ALBIE**     Is it comfortable?

**ALBIE 2**     It's not uncomfortable.

**ALBIE**     What can it do?

*They lift their arms a little.*

**ALBIE 2**     Bit of carrying. Bit of picking.

*They both pick. Albie takes some steps back. Looks at Albie 2, who, in turn looks at Albie.*

**ALBIE**     You wouldn't know. From a distance.

**ALBIE 2**     Well?

**ALBIE**     A real hand feels, it touches. You make love with a hand, greet, negotiate. It's your anger, your instinct and imagination. It doesn't pretend to be a hand, it is one.

**ALBIE 2**     Let's bin it then.

*Albie 2 begins to take off prosthesis.*

**ALBIE**     No.

**ALBIE 2**     Why not?

**ALBIE**     You can't just get rid of it like that. These things have to be decided upon correctly.

**ALBIE 2**      Agonised over.

**ALBIE**        Considered.

**ALBIE 2**      Never let it be said I hindered your considering. I'm calling the first witness.

**ALBIE**        Who?

**ALBIE 2**      Father John. His hand was blown off opening a parcel. Remember?

**ALBIE**        He brought us some cherries. He carried them in his teeth.

*He questions Father John.*

**ALBIE 2**      Father John?

**FATHER JOHN**  Yes, Albie?

**ALBIE 2**      I'm conducting a survey. Can I ask you about your prosthesis?

**FATHER JOHN**  Of course..

**ALBIE 2**      Where is it?

**FATHER JOHN**  I'm not sure.

**ALBIE**        Not sure?

**FATHER JOHN**  It's in a cupboard, I think.

**ALBIE**        You never used it?

**FATHER JOHN**  Not after the first day. I had no need for it.

**ALBIE 2**      How do you manage?

**FATHER JOHN**  I use my good hand.

**ALBIE**        For everything?

**FATHER JOHN**  I get my friends to cut my meat.

**ALBIE**        Thank you.

**ALBIE 2**      See. So far nil in favour.

*Woman enters. Begins ironing.*

**WOMAN**        Marvellous weather.

**ALBIE**        Yes. *(Pause)*

**WOMAN**        Marvellous.

**ALBIE**        Yes.

**ALBIE 2**      Can I ask you about your prosthesis?

**WOMAN**        I've never regretted it.

**ALBIE**        You?

**WOMAN**        My right arm is artificial.
**ALBIE**        Is it? I couldn't tell.
**WOMAN**        That's what I've been told. That it's almost
impossible to tell.
**ALBIE**        It is almost impossible.
**WOMAN**        Yes.
**ALBIE**        Mmmm.
**WOMAN**        Of course being here's a bit of a give-away. The
upper limb unit. *(Both laugh)* I wouldn't be without it now.
**ALBIE**        Really? You're happy with it? In yourself.
**WOMAN**        Absolutely. Ironing for example is no problem. Ride
the hiccups. It's well worth it in the end.
**ALBIE**        Thank you. Thank you for the encouragement.
**WOMAN**        Don't mention it. My only fear is that one day a
friend will drop by. You know... catch me, when I'm not wearing
it. That would be terrible. My biggest nightmare. Just terrible.

*The woman continues to iron.*

**ALBIE 2**        Two-nil.
**ALBIE**        Don't cheat. That was a recommendation. It's one-
all.

*The woman leaves.*

**ALBIE 2**        Next there was the man who needed his for driving
and golf and holding paper down... a sort of prosthetic paper-
weight.
**ALBIE**        Which brings it to two-one.
**ALBIE 2**        Witness number four...
**ALBIE**        Tommy's mother. *(Pause)* Tommy was a little kid I
saw at the training centre. His arms were tiny little protuberances
which we used to skilfully manipulate the plasticine he played
with. He chatted to me on a toy phone. "Mister, your head's on
fire" you know, the usual thing. And then his mother walked in.
Strode gracefully to the middle of the room and took her little
boy. I became aware that she was lovely and that one arm was
missing, or rather that she had a very short arm. I looked at the
way she bore herself. Proudly, gracefully. With sparkle and

conviction. It never stopped the men. She told me.

**ALBIE 2**      Two all. It's a draw. So you decide. *(Pause)*

**ALBIE**        Take it off.

*Albie takes off arm. Albie 2 puts it in the bag.*

**ALBIE**        I won't wear it again. She decided it for me. I want to be like her. *(He zips up bag)*

**ALBIE 2**      That's that then.

**ALBIE**        Maybe I've let myself down. Let the ANC down.

**ALBIE 2**      Too bad, Albie – the decision's legal.

*Albie puts bag away, out of sight.*

## SCENE 2

*A park bench. Albie seems anxious. Albie 2 enters ostentatiously attired to enjoy the sun. Sits next to Albie.*

**ALBIE 2**      Lovely.

**ALBIE**        What are you doing here? Outside?

**ALBIE 2**      Basking. I can smell the roses. Beautiful. And the sun is shining! This was a good choice for our first outing.

**ALBIE**        For a start I'm not talking to you in public.

**ALBIE 2**      Why not?

**ALBIE**        Because it looks bloody odd. That's why.

**ALBIE 2**      That doesn't matter. There are a lot of odd people about. This is London. You know, the sun is quite warm.

*Albie smiles at a passer-by. Albie 2 begins to take off his shirt.*

**ALBIE**        What are you doing?

**ALBIE 2**      I'm taking off my shirt.

**ALBIE**        Stop that.

**ALBIE 2**      But I'm getting uncomfortable. Hot. I'm beginning to sweat, Albie.

**ALBIE**        If I can put up with it, so can you.

**ALBIE 2**      So, you're hot too?

**ALBIE**        What if I am?

**ALBIE 2** *(feels him)* Your shirt is damp. Take it off. Feel the
sunlight on your skin.

**ALBIE**          There's a moral issue involved which you, as usual,
have overlooked.

**ALBIE 2**        A moral issue! You're only taking off your top.

**ALBIE**          The point here is that people have come here to look
at beautiful things not at mutilated limbs.

**ALBIE 2**        This is as bad as the shrivelled orange.

**ALBIE**          The shrivelled orange is irrelevant to this discussion.

**ALBIE 2**        We held up the whole of a canteen queue while you
decided whether it was your revolutionary duty to choose the
rotten orange.

**ALBIE**          I took it.

**ALBIE 2**        It was dry inside. Like eating tobacco.

**ALBIE**          Stop complaining.

**ALBIE 2**        Is that what the struggle is about? You eating crappy
fruit. Eating what a sane person would throw in the bin? Is that
going to be the brave new world? *(takes off his top)*

**ALBIE**          You did it!

**ALBIE 2**        I felt like it.

*He lays back & enjoys the sun. Albie looks. A pause. He then takes
off his own top using his teeth to help. He sits awkwardly at first then
relaxes. He smiles at a passer-by. Relaxes more. Pause.*

**ALBIE**          You know...

**ALBIE 2**        What?

**ALBIE**          I have taken the most critical single decision of my
life surrounded by roses.

### SCENE 3
*Scene changes: Albie and a woman are sitting by the bath. Classical
music.*

**WOMAN**          Well, that's my definition of post-modernism.

**ALBIE**          Thank you. That's almost comprehensible. Can I
have the cushion?

*Woman passes him the cushion*

**WOMAN**      Your turn. Tell me the story about the occupational
    therapist.
**ALBIE**      Again?
**WOMAN**      I like it.
**ALBIE**      I'll tell you in a bit. I'm thinking.
**WOMAN**      What? *(Pause)* Is it about sex?
**ALBIE**      You win. Here's the story. I go to the OT... She says
    "Why have you come? What do you want from Occupational
    Therapy? We are very democratic here and like to take our
    initiatives from the patient." I am a bit in love with my
    Occupational Therapist and want to impress her and show her
    how liberated I am, so I say, "Cooking... I really want to be able
    to cook again." "Fine," she says, "What sort of cooker have you
    got at home? Gas or electric?" "I don't know," I say. "I never
    looked"

*Woman laughs.*

**WOMAN**      So what did you think about the sex?
**ALBIE**      It's different without an elbow to lean on.
**WOMAN**      Please, don't spare my feelings.
**ALBIE**      You are my first post-bomb encounter.
**WOMAN**      You put things so nicely.
**ALBIE**      But it's interesting. I was much more dependent on
    the positioning of my partner. A passage of De Beauvoir came
    into my head!
**WOMAN**      While we were making love?
**ALBIE**      Yes. About men being all arms and legs, snatching
    and catching and pushing the woman's body, leaving her without
    an inch of physical autonomy. Overwhelming her.
**WOMAN**      That's too right-on for words.
**ALBIE**      I found myself in a state of physical uncertainty.
    *(Pause)* I liked it. *(Pause)* I began to discover something lovely
    was happening. That it's not a choice of women reaching for men,
    or men reaching for women, each struggling to arouse the other or
    get the timing right but that each partner could move the part of
    the body that he or she wished to be engaged and place it against
    the other's hand or mouth, taking away the waiting and sense of

passivity on the one hand and the feeling of encroaching on the other.

**WOMAN**    I thought I'd vetoed speeches, Albie.

**ALBIE**    Perhaps all men should have an arm chopped off?

**WOMAN**    As long as it's the right arm.

**ALBIE**    Why's that?

**WOMAN**    The right arm is the aggressive one. Especially in men. We keep the world away with our right arms. We try to dominate everything with them. The left arm expresses the gentle and receiving side of our nature. The feminine, if you like.

**ALBIE**    That was a speech.

**WOMAN**    I'm allowed.

**ALBIE**    Of course. *(She gets something out of a bag)* What's that?

**WOMAN**    Massage oil.

**ALBIE**    What's it do?

**WOMAN**    It renders you reactionary.

**ALBIE**    I'm getting out.

**WOMAN**    It relaxes you, Albie. It's a therapy.

**ALBIE**    Do you believe in all that?

**WOMAN**    We are muscle and bone and skin. That's as much a part of us as any mental construct. Give me your foot.

**ALBIE**    Only temporarily. *(She begins to massage it)*

**WOMAN**    The nerve endings in your feet reach into all parts of your body. And the relationship between your feet and the rest of you indicates what kind of person you are.

**ALBIE**    Are you trying to tell me my personality is in my foot?

**WOMAN**    Just relax.

**ALBIE**    Christ... Maybe it is. *(She continues to massage)*

**WOMAN**    Massage helps to release feelings. Things held in. *(She continues)* How's that?

**ALBIE**    Mmmm? *(She stops)* It hasn't worked.

**WOMAN**    No?

**ALBIE**    No.

**WOMAN**    You seem more relaxed.

**ALBIE** *(relaxed)* Do I? *(Pause)* I don't seem to be letting things out.

**WOMAN**    You haven't tried.

**ALBIE** *(feebly)* You bloody bastards who blew off my arm...

| | |
|---|---|
| **WOMAN** | Albie! You can't use bastards. That's not PC. |
| **ALBIE** | Buggers then. You bloody buggers that blew off my arm. |
| **WOMAN** | Buggers is homophobic. |
| **ALBIE** | Shit. *(He shouts)* You bloody shits! You tried to kill me. Cockroaches! You bloody rats! *(Shouts really loud)* You bloody scum who planted the bomb. *(He is enjoying himself)* Cockroaches, rats, scum, we'll get you one day. Don't think you'll escape! *(ecstatically)* Scum! |

*The scene changes. Albie 2 appears.*

| | |
|---|---|
| **ALBIE 2** | They know who *he* is, Albie. |
| **ALBIE** | Who? |
| **ALBIE** | Him. Him. The man who did it to us. *(Pause)* I've seen his picture. Thirty years old, heavily built, a little moustache. Like a little Hitler moustache. The sort of thing you want to rip off and grind into the ground with your heel. He's a black Angolan recruited into the South African Army Special Forces Unit. He came into Mozambique two years ago with explosives and a mission to kill us. |
| **ALBIE** | Oh. |
| **ALBIE 2** | To kill us. |
| **ALBIE** | Yes. |
| **ALBIE 2** | What are you going to do? |
| **ALBIE** | Do? What can I do? |
| **ALBIE 2** | You must know people. |
| **ALBIE** | What people? |
| **ALBIE 2** | In our organisation. People who will deal with him. |
| **ALBIE** | He'll be tried in a civil court and if the evidence is not strong enough for a conviction, he'll be acquitted. |
| **ALBIE 2** | Acquitted? But he's human lice, Albie. He can't do what he did to us and get away with it. |
| **ALBIE** | The risk of acquittal is fundamental to the creation of a strong system of justice. |
| **ALBIE 2** | Albie... He never gave us the chance of a trial. |
| **ALBIE** | I know. And that's our victory. Our moral victory that he should have the chance. |

**ALBIE 2**      I don't want a moral victory. I want to see the bastard that did this to us suffer. I want to see him strung up and dripping blood.

**ALBIE**      Well, you're not going to see that.

**ALBIE 2**      You're not going to help me?

**ALBIE**      Not in that way.

**ALBIE 2**      I helped you. *(Pause)* I feel rage, Albie... rage.

**ALBIE**      I'm sorry

**ALBIE 2**      I can't believe this. Where's the soldier when you need him?

**ALBIE**      It's not just a question of what you want.

**ALBIE 2**      You think you can splash a bit in your bath, release a little anger and things will be okay? You're wrong. This rage is bigger than me. It's not something you can reason with. It's raging inside me and it'll break out.

**ALBIE**      I won't be bullied. Do what you like. Break out. *(Pause)* The moral victory is ours. Isn't that enough?

**ALBIE 2**      It's nothing.

**ALBIE**      It's not nothing. It's what I've been working for all these years. For ten years in Maputo. Endless meetings. Working into the night. I helped put the laws in place that will assure our assassin gets a fair and honest trial.

**ALBIE 2**      You did that?

**ALBIE**      Yes.

**ALBIE 2**      For ten years.

**ALBIE**      Yes.

**ALBIE 2**      And you're pleased?

**ALBIE**      Yes.

**ALBIE 2**      But look at you now. *(Pause)* Look what justice has done for you. Blown up. Months of pain and now left to live out your half life. The man that did it to you won't suffer like you did. Not for one second. He still has both arms and both eyes. What will he get? A few years in jail and then he'll be out running and swimming and doing as he likes. He'll be free to laugh in your face. Because people like you haven't got the guts to take a gun and blast back. That's the only language murderers understand. Violence is their language. They won't listen to anything else. They're not the sort that are going to read your damn books, Albie. They don't weigh up the niceties like you do. The pros and cons. The morals. They go out and get what they want the only way they know how. That's what the real world's like.

**ALBIE**          I know what the world's like.

**ALBIE 2**        Do you? You've gone soft, Albie. Sitting at a desk too long, head stuffed with theories. But that's weak. That's a dream and it just lets the bastards go free. *(Pause)* I need the soldier, Albie. Will you help me?

**ALBIE**          Why does it have to be, in that way?

**ALBIE 2**        Some of your comrades feel the same. They want retaliation too. They're sick of being the ones to suffer.

**ALBIE**          There's no decision on that yet.

**ALBIE 2**        Soon there will be. Maybe it will go my way. Then what would you do? Leave them? *(Pause)* Your type of justice is okay for your type of person, Albie. But for most of us it's soft. Nothing.

**ALBIE**          Is that what I lost an arm for? A war of vengeance?

**ALBIE 2**        It's not just you, you have to think of now, Albie. It's others. People will go on and on being maimed, if no one will stop the maimers. You were saved. Others might not be. Think of them. Not of yourself. Of them. *(Pause)* They won't get flown to London for treatment.

**ALBIE**          I do. I do think of them...

**ALBIE 2**        Prove it.

*He exits.*

**SCENE 4**
*Albie comes forward to address a meeting. He places down a bag. He has his notes with him. He seems nervous. He is introduced by a lecturer. Albie two watches the proceedings.*

**LECTURER** Ladies and gentlemen, friends. It gives me great pleasure to see you all here at the London School of Economics and Political Science on the occasion of the annual D.N.Pritt Memorial Lecture which tonight will be given by Albie Sachs. Thank you. *(Pause)*

**ALBIE**          Firstly, firstly... *(Pause)* There have been a lot of firsts for me. My first shoelace, my first onion and now this, my first post-bomb talk. *(Pause)* So... *(A long pause)* I have been

living in Mozambique for ten years. *(Pause)* In the beginning
everything seemed wide open. Here was a newly liberated
African country, a democracy, where black and white people
could live together in dignity. I helped in building up a system of
courts from scratch. We were determined to have justice enshrin-
ed in our legal system. *(Pause)* Over the years the same question
kept running round and around in my mind. Do rich and poor
have the same human rights problems? In Mozambique we were
fighting against hunger, to eliminate diseases like measles that
killed thousands of kids every year, for schools, for elementary
knowledge, to be a nation. And then the might of South Africa
was pitted against us – raiding our villages, destroying clinics,
schools, courts. Terrorising our people and destabilising our
nation. *(Pause)* The West's response? They accused us of civil
rights abuses; of detentions without trial, even torture. The
smugness of the West angered me. And so I began to argue for
law in context; due process, the right to a fair trial may sometimes
have to be waived. *(Pause)* And now? *(Long pause)* After I was
blown up I wanted to be myself again. I wanted to be well,
healed, whole as I put it, and I wanted nothing to get in my way. I
was in a race. But against who? Against myself – because another
part of me was saying, 'Wait, look, listen. Who are you now? You
are still Albie but Albie without an arm and an eye, so how are
you going to live and be in the world?' *(Pause)* At first I fought
against this. I just wanted to be me again, exactly as before. I
would wear a prosthetic arm and then what would be the difference? Who could tell the difference? Only me. Me. *(Pause)* I
would be able to tell. And when I listened to myself, I heard a
new voice. It said that I was the important one. And in the very
personal matter of myself I must please myself. I would be Albie
without an arm and an eye and I would move freely in the world
proud and unashamed. And I could say this is who I am. What has
this to do with justice? *(Pause)* So now I can answer my own
question. There are certain values and procedures thatbelong to
all humanity. Simply – a fair trial, justice for all. Even my assassin must come to court and be tried legally and I must bow to that
process. Take a look at me. I survived against the odds. In that
sense I am the message. *(Pause)* I've got something for you. *(He
opens his bag and takes out a plant in a pot)* It's so dull in these

places. Grey. I bought you these. Flowers. *(He places down the pot)* If my voice was half decent I'd sing you a song. We always sing in Maputo. And we always have a plant in a tin pot. We're hearts as well as minds.

*He exits.*

## SCENE 5
*Lights focus on Albie 2, sitting in a 'cell.' Prison bars effect. Albie has been watching with his mother. She reads from her programme.*

**MOTHER** *(reads)* The Jail Diary of Albie Sachs. *(looks about her)* There's a lot of people here, Albie. Come to see your play.
**ALBIE**          It's not strictly my play. David Edgar wrote it.
**MOTHER**      That's picking straws.
**ALBIE**          I don't think David would agree with you.
**MOTHER**      But you wrote the book first.
**ALBIE**          Yes, yes, I wrote the book first.
**MOTHER**      It seems a long time ago. Those prison times.
    *(Pause)* There's a strange man waving at you, Albie.
**ALBIE**          That's Neil Kinnock, mother. *(Pause)* I'm glad you
    could come.
**MOTHER**      I flew over. I wouldn't have missed it. *(Pause)* I'd
    have come to the hospital. But I thought I'll wait till he writes.
**ALBIE**          But I never wrote.
**MOTHER**      Till now.
**ALBIE**          I was thinking... When I qualified as a lawyer, dad
    wanted me to go to England and be a member of parliament. I
    wouldn't go and we had a dreadful row. It's the best way to further
    the struggle he said.
**MOTHER**      But that's not Albie's way. I told him that.
**ALBIE**          Did you?
**MOTHER**      Let him find his own way, I said. That's important.
**ALBIE**          I remember now.
**MOTHER**      There's more than one way to fight. *(Pause)*
**ALBIE**          Soon I make a speech.
**MOTHER**      To all these people? What will you say?

**ALBIE**        I'll thank them for coming tonight. Tell them the proceeds will be of great help to me in my recovery. *(Pause)* Will you come with me?

**MOTHER**      You never used to want me at your prize days. Just your dad, remember?

**ALBIE**        That was before all this.

**MOTHER**      I used to think it was my hats.

**ALBIE**        Your hats?

**MOTHER**      Everybody wore them then.

**ALBIE**        Will you come? *(Pause)*

**MOTHER**      Will it be okay for you now, Albie? I'm old now, remember? I want it to be okay.

*She joins him. Walks deliberately to Albie's left side to enable Albie to put his arm around her.*

**MOTHER**      Yes, Albie. I knew it wasn't my hats.

**SCENE 6**
*Albie runs on the spot in the gym. Albie 2 enters.*

**ALBIE 2**      Always the gym.

**ALBIE**        I'm running.

**ALBIE 2**      You'd better be careful. You could do yourself a nasty injury.

**ALBIE**        I've done three lengths.

**ALBIE 2**      Your whole body is shaking. Is that any way for an invalid to behave?

**ALBIE**        Now I'll do six.

**ZUMA** *(enters)* Olympic training?

**ALBIE**        Even I'll admit I'm a little old for that.

**ZUMA**         Still, you can do it for the ANC, eh?

**ALBIE**        Of course.

**ZUMA**         I've some news for you. There have been discussions. The national executive committee met. There was debate, votes for and against. The final decision reaffirmed ANC policy not to go for civilian targets.

**ALBIE**        I'm glad.

**ZUMA**         I came as soon as I knew. You're going back.

| | |
|---|---|
| **ALBIE** | Soon, soon. |
| **ALBIE 2** | Everything's worked out for you. |
| **ALBIE** | I can do eight lengths if my lungs hold out. |
| **ALBIE 2** | Still a bloody masochist. |
| **ALBIE** | No. It's joy that's driving me. |
| **ALBIE 2** | Joy? You're crying. |
| **ALBIE** | Tears. Good for me. |
| **ALBIE 2** | We had our chance, Albie and we lost it. |
| **ALBIE** | I don't want revenge. I want to run. That's my soft vengeance, running and being alive. Feeling the sun on my skin and the sand tickling the soles of my feet. |
| **ALBIE 2** | What about me? |
| **ALBIE** | You can stand still if you like. Stay here. |
| **ALBIE 2** | Stay here? |
| **ALBIE** | On your own. But the rest of us – we're not standing still. We are in motion. All of us freedom fighters. The detainees, exiles and underground workers. Nothing can stop us. Our generation is indestructible. We're going forward. Twenty lengths. Are you coming? |
| **ALBIE 2** | Running? |
| **ALBIE** | On the beach at Maputo. I can see the sea! |

*Albie runs faster, Albie 2 watches him. It is apparent that Albie is no longer in the gym. That he is running outside, on the beach. That the sun is shining.*

| | |
|---|---|
| **ALBIE 2** | Wait! |
| **ALBIE** | May the day come when the whole world walks around in bathing costumes without a place to put their guns! |

*Albie 2 begins to run as well. They run together. The effect builds to a crescendo.*

| | |
|---|---|
| **ALBIE** | I 'm back, therefore I am. |

*Sudden darkness.*
*The end.*

## April De Angelis

Other plays by April De Angelis include:

*Ironmistress* 1989

*Crux* (Paines Plough / national tour) 1990 (also published by Aurora Metro Press in *'Seven Plays by Women'*)

*The Life and Times of Fanny Hill* (BAC)1990

*Hush* 1992 (Royal Court)

*Playhouse Creatures* (Sphinx/Old Vic)1993

*Positive Hour* (Hampstead / Out Of Joint Theatre Co.) 1996

Libretto: *Flight.* (Glyndebourne) 1997/8

*Warwickshire Testimony* (RSC)1999

She is currently writing a new play for Out of Joint Theatre Co.

# <u>Sympathy for the Devil</u>

# Sympathy for the Devil

The play is based on the raw material of my own personal experience as a Black deaf man when I was travelling in Jamaica and the States.

It tells the story of a group of black performers diverse in character, united by disability, who are invited to America to an International 'Special Arts Festival'. Billed 'A Help in Handicapped' by its patronising hosts, the glitzy event is tarnished when disillusioned performers plan to boycott what they feel is a glorified freak show. Harmony is destroyed when growing tension explodes into fierce confrontation and the smiling face of charity is replaced by the cold stare of oppression.

The play takes a ruthless look at bleeding heart liberals, black attitudes to disability and the whole good causes industry.

**Ray Harrison Graham**

# Sympathy for the Devil

## Ray Harrison Graham

*Winner of the Raspberry Ripple Award for Best Drama.*

The play was first performed on 31st October, 1996 at Oval House Theatre, London and later transferred to the Tricycle Theatre, London with the following cast:

| CHARACTERS | CAST |
|---|---|
| **Fitzroy Chambers** | Ray Harrison Graham |
| **Jackie Phillips/Pearl Chambers** | Deborah A. Williams |
| **Chantelle Williams** | Maria Oshodi |
| **Curtis Frazer** | Raymond Baugh |
| **Jean-Marie Kellerman** | Emma Healey |
| **Bob Fitzgerald/Jud Davies** | Jonathon Keeble |
| **Reverend Al Jeremiah/Peter Dwyer** | Simon Crouch |
| **Chorus of gospel singers** | (played by cast) |

Director Ray Harrison Graham
Designer Miranda Melville
Lighting Designer Simon Gray
Producer Ewan Marshall

**ACT ONE**
**SCENE 1**
*The stage is empty. A rehearsal is in progress.*

**KEITH** *(enters)* Fitz! Are we doing this or what? We got the church group coming in half an hour.
**FITZROY** *(offstage)* Yeah, two minutes, two minutes. OK, let's do the ending once more... this time give it everything you've got!

*A rhythmic African drumming starts.*

**VOICE** *(mysterious)* Everyone in this world is different. God
  made it that way. And like the animals of the jungle, we survive
  in different ways.

*Lights fade up to reveal Chantelle centre stage. She wears a black
leotard and tights with bare feet. She wears classic, mime white face
make-up (as they all do). As the voice speaks, she mimes.*

**CHANTELLE** *(voiceover)* See, the bat – it could be just like me
  As it flies through the air it cannot see
  Go on ... close your eyes ... dark, isn't it?
  Scary? ... you feel alone ... trapped
  You want to run, escape, scream!
**ALL**          AAAAAAHHHH!
**CHANTELLE** *(voiceover)* But God has made my hands my eyes
  They give me the freedom to see what's there
  I can feel your face, your lips, I can even stroke your hair.

*Chantelle steps back and Jackie takes centre stage.*

**JACKIE** *(voiceover)* But what for me? I am not the same as her?

*She raises her arms then mimes to the voiceover.*

**GOD** *(voiceover)* Fear not said He.
  Look at the python, he has *no* hands.
**ALL**          Ssssss.......
**GOD** *(voiceover)* Yet he's feared throughout the jungle for his
  poisonous glands.
  Look, as he slithers along, black and powerful
  Agile and strong.
**JACKIE** *(voiceover)* They say that two is better than one
  But not for me cos' this one's just as fun. *(All cheer)*
  So! I cannot play basketball out there in the sun
  But with these god-given legs, I can surely run!

*Jackie steps back. Curtis moves centre stage mournfully in a wheel-
chair. He mimes to the chant.*

**CURTIS** *(voiceover)* Running has never been much fun for me
   I cannot join in, or ever climb a tree.
**GOD** *(voiceover)* My child, look up to the sky
   See the birds in the heavens – they need no legs to fly
   Like the wings of an eagle, your arms I've made strong
   On the wheels of your chariot you can fly
   Join us! You belong!

*Curtis moves back. The drums become louder. Fitzroy comes
dancing in (over the top). He mimes to the voice.*

**FITZROY** *(voiceover)* As I run through the jungle, I love all I see
   But the roar of lion, the elephant, the song of
   the bird in the tree.
   All these sounds, Lord you've taken from me!
**GOD** *(voiceover)* Look at the fishes beneath the sea, they have
   no fear.
   In their silent world they use their eyes,
   their bodies to hear.
   The clever dolphin, the cunning shark, the
   might of the great whale!
   Learn from these and you cannot fail.
   Look to the octopus with its many arms
   These two I have given, are your voice
   to express and command.
**ALL** *(chant)*
   We may not be able to be like you
   But we hope you can see there are many
   things we can do!
   Some cannot hear
   *(Fitzroy steps forward)*
   Some cannot see
   *(Chantelle steps forward)*
   Some cannot walk
   *(Pause)*
   Some cannot walk

*Pause. Curtis has gone offstage.*

**ALL**              Some cannot walk. *(Pause)*
**FITZROY**     Curtis!
**CURTIS**       Eh?
**JACKIE/CHANTELLE** *(exasperated)* Oh Curtis!
**FITZROY** *(angry)* What you doing? You're supposed to be on.
**CURTIS**       What? I thought –
**FITZROY** *(can't hear him)* What did he say?
**JACKIE**       What? *(The music is too loud)*
**FITZROY** *(shouts)* Curtis!... Oh shit, man... look, just turn off the
   music, put the lights on, it's ruined now.

*Lights come up and music is switched off. Curtis enters. He is eating.*

**FITZROY**     What are you doing man? You missed the ending!
**CURTIS**       What? I thought it had finished.
**FITZROY**     No, man... I told you before. You don't go off 'til
   after the last words...
**CURTIS**       We said the last words.
**FITZROY**     No that's – the old bit.
**CHANTELLE** Don't you remember? We changed it.
**CURTIS**       When?
**JACKIE**       You're so stupid... remember we added a bit.
**CURTIS**       Nah.
**JACKIE**       Oh shit. Look – *(She acts it out slowly to him)*
   You watching, right? He does – 'Some can't hear,' she does –
   'Some can't see,' then *you* do – 'Some can't walk.'
**CURTIS**       Me?
**FITZROY**     Well, who hell else is it gonna be?
**JACKIE**       Yes, *you*! Curtis, *you*! Then I do my bit and we
   bow and that's the end.
**CURTIS**       No one told me that bit.
**JACKIE/CHANTELLE** *(shouting)* We did Curtis, you just don't
   remem –
**FITZROY**     Alright, alright... ease up on the man. There ain't no
   point arguing about it... You know what to do now, don't you?
**CURTIS**       Yeah, I do *now*. Now you've told me.
   *(Jackie kisses her teeth.)*
**FITZROY** *(calming things)* Alright... OK everyone, listen up.
   *(He turns to the lighting box)* Thanks Keith, that was nice. We'll

be two minutes, yeah... Alright, now forgetting about Curtis messing up the ending, that was looking good. You're starting to get into it now and Chantelle, that beginning bit is wicked! Jackie you just gotta loosen up and enjoy it, you're still giving it too much attitude... otherwise you might as well say we're ready, next stop America!

*All cheer, except Jackie.*

| | |
|---|---|
| **JACKIE** | Are you sure they're gonna like this? |
| **FITZROY** | What do you mean? |
| **JACKIE** | Well, it just seems a bit – |
| **FITZROY** | What? A bit what? |
| **JACKIE** | Well, it's crap! |
| **CURTIS** | Ease up, nuh Jackie. |
| **CHANTELLE** | Yeah Jackie. |
| **JACKIE** | I just don't think it's that good. It don't feel right. |
| **CHANTELLE** | It's only a play. |
| **FITZROY** | What's wrong with it? |
| **JACKIE** | I don't know... just some of the things we're saying, all that God bit. |
| **FITZROY** | Look – look, we've gone through this before so why you starting all this up now? What's the matter – you don't believe in God? |
| **JACKIE** | I – I just don't see why we can't do what we did on the talent night. Everyone thought that was good, all of us doing our own thing. It's better like that – you and Chantelle dancing, him – |
| **FITZROY** | Look, this festival is a big thing. There's gonna be people from all over the world doing shows. |
| **JACKIE** | So...? |
| **FITZROY** | So, it's 'special' art. We got to do something about disability, about black culture... we can't just get up there dance a bit, sing a bit and tell jokes. |
| **JACKIE** | I think it was saying more about us than this is. Even if we just – |
| **FITZROY** | I ain't gonna argue about this, right. Cos that's what is on the video we sent them and that's what they want. |
| **JACKIE** | What *they* want? |

**FITZROY**     What I want then.

**JACKIE**       What about –?

**CURTIS**       Ah, give it a rest Jackie. Who's running this thing?

**CHANTELLE**  Yeah, we sorted all this out.

**FITZROY**     See... we're all happy about it. No one else is complaining... So, can we just leave it at that now?

**JACKIE**       Fine.

**FITZROY**     So, is everybody set for tomorrow, yeah? Passports,
tickets –

**CURTIS** *(puts his hand up)* Listen, I wanted to ask how much is it
gonna cost, where we're staying?

*The others sigh.*

**FITZROY**     How many times...? We don't pay *anything*. It's free,
we're guests, they pay for everything. When we reach there, we
just rest up in a nice big posh hotel, eat plenty, do the show and
enjoy ourselves. All we got to worry about is a bit of spending
money.

**CURTIS**       We don't pay for the food?

**FITZROY**     No, man – it's free!

**CURTIS**       Murder she wrote!

**FITZROY**     Alright, look – if no one's got any questions we
better get changed, pack up our things so we can get home and
get ready for the morning. *(They start to leave)* Eh, and listen...
the flight is at ten o'clock. That means we gotta be there at eight.

**ALL**          Yeah...

**FITZROY**     No, I'm serious. I don't want any of this 'BMT' –
black man time rubbish. I mean eight o'clock! Cos anyone ain't
there, I'm on the plane without them.

**ALL**          Yeah.

**JACKIE** *(to Chantelle)* See ya.

**CHANTELLE**  See you tomorrow.

**CURTIS**       Later, yeah.

**FITZROY**     Yeah, cool.

*Jackie and Curtis exit.*

**FITZROY** *(puts his arms around Chantelle)* You all set for it, then?

**CHANTELLE** Yeah, I'm really looking forward to it. I won't be able to sleep tonight.

**FITZROY** Wait up. I can't hear you. *(He goes to face her)*

**CHANTELLE** I said, I won't be able to sleep tonight.

**FITZROY** Maybe I should come round then?

**CHANTELLE** *(laughs)* Ain't you excited?

**FITZROY** Course... in fact, I'm probably more excited than you.

**CHANTELLE** I doubt it.

**FITZROY** *(mysteriously)* No, I think I am.

**CHANTELLE** Why? What you hiding from me?

**FITZROY** Nothing – just I might have a little bit of a surprise for you.

**CHANTELLE** Oh don't... I hate surprises. Tell me now.

**FITZROY** Don't worry about it. I think you'll like it.

**CHANTELLE** Why can't you tell me?

**FITZROY** Because.

**CHANTELLE** *(mock fights with him)* Fitzroy!

**FITZROY** Look, I'll give you a clue. How long we been seeing each other?

**CHANTELLE** Just coming up for two years.

**FITZROY** Well, it's something you've always wanted.

**CHANTELLE** What – ear-rings? *(Fitzroy kisses his teeth)* Well, tell me!

**FITZROY** Come on, we gotta go.

**CHANTELLE** *(takes his arm)* If you tell me, you can come round tonight.

**FITZROY** Bribery –!

*They exit.*

## SCENE 2
*An emotional black soul version of 'The Star Spangled Banner' is sung/played whilst images of disabled people achieving are projected onto a large screen. There is a podium on a platform which is heavily decorated with ISA flags and banners. Above the podium, centre stage, is a large banner which reads 'ISA – taking the Dis out of Ability'. Red, yellow and blue ribbons hang from almost*

*everything. The stage is a mass of colour. Bob Fitzgerald Jnr. sits on the platform, with Jean-Marie Kellerman.*

**ANNOUNCER**  Just some of the wonderful work done by I.S.A. in the last year. Now please welcome co-founder of I.S.A. Miss Jean Marie Kellerman.

*Applause.*

**JMK**  Ladies and gentlemen, it is my honour and very great pleasure to welcome you all to International Special Arts 1996. This is the fourth time we've had this festival and – my! It seems to get bigger and better, each time. For the next seven days, each of you will participate in performance, workshops and exhibits, celebrating the creative spirit, whether you write a poem, perform a dance, sing a song, or express yourself through the visual arts, you reveal what is truly unique about you. By sharing your creative gifts, you communicate through the universal language of the Arts. Before we begin, what promises to be a wonderful and fulfilling week of activities, it is again my honour to introduce you to someone, without whom, none of this could have been poss – *(turns over a page)* – ible. Way back when I.S.A. was a tiny embryo in the huge womb of American conscience and no one was willing to offer us funding, one man searched his heart and dug deep into his pocket and offered us a sum too generous to mention. 'Why – *(turns a page)* – did he do this?' I hear you ask. Well... because he had seen, himself, the injustice of impairment, nursing his lovely wife, Linda for six long years until her death from multiple sclerosis. Ladies and gentlemen – to open I.S.A. 1996 – a man who needs no further introduction, our 'saviour' and President – Mr Robert Glenn Fitzgerald... *Bob!*

*Loud applause. Bob acknowledges it. He moves to the central microphone.*

**BOB**  I wish – I wish I was as nice as she says I am, or at least half as pretty. Well, first off, I want to take this opportunity to praise Miss Kellerman and all of her team who have worked tirelessly not just to make this festival possible, but for the last ten years, to make I.S.A. what it is today. So Jean, on behalf of I.S.A., I say thank you for the joy that you brought – certainly, to me and I'm sure, to all of us here. *(Pause)* OK pride... Pride. *(He spells)* P.R.I.D.E. is not such a long word but it has a big meaning. People are proud of many things. Proud to come first and pick up an Olympic gold... some of you out there, I'm sure, are proud Americans... proud of your homes... fellas are proud to have beautiful women by their side – I know I am. But seriously, I've felt pride many times, not least seeing the spirit with which my dear wife faced out her last days. Miss Kellerman spoke earlier of my generosity, but I say lucky, because nothing has made me as proud as I am to be standing here today as your president. You know, I was sitting having a coffee earlier and I was looking through the programme for this week. I was astounded at the many different skills we have at this festival. I mean, let's have a look – *(He opens the programme)* What have we got here? Wheelchair dancers from Taiwan, a deaf group from Milwaukee who sing with their hands, Luigi Mendoza, an Italian blind magician, Billy Dale – paralysed from the chest down, plays piano with his forehead and many more. You know what I thought, 'I'll be dammed, look what the human spirit can achieve and me I don't want to get out of bed if I've got a headache!' You know what amazes me, us able-bodied people get so angry at life. I believe we could learn something from all of you, because when I look at *you,* I see great unity, a family and despite your misfort-unes, despite the ridicule and prejudice you sometimes face, I'll be damned if you people aren't always smiling. I'm a grown man and I don't mind admitting, that it brings a tear to my eye when I see the courage and joy, with which you approach life. Yeah, that makes me proud and it should make you damn proud! So you keep smiling and together we'll kick the 'Dis out of Ability!' Thank you.

*Loud applause. Lights fade.*

**SCENE 3**

*A function room next to the main party hall. There is lively music in the background. The group take in the atmosphere. Enter Jean-Marie Kellerman and Peter Dwyer.*

**FITZROY**     It's a lot bigger than I thought. I was only expecting one hall.

**JMK**          Hello, hello, welcome to D.C. From the UK, right? Did you have a nice flight? *(checks her clipboard. They nod)*

**FITZROY**     Um...Yeah, we did.

**JMK**          Not too turbulent?

**FITZROY**     Sorry?

**JMK**          Not too much turbulence?

**FITZROY**     Oh, turbulence? No, we just had sandwiches.

**JMK**          OK, let's see... *(she tries to guess the names. She points at Fitzroy)* Curtis. *(points at Jackie)* Chantelle. *(to Curtis she talks loudly and signs badly)* I think we both know who you are – Fitzroy right? And you must be J –

**FITZROY**     Um... I'm Fitzroy.

**JMK** *(surprised)* You're Fitzroy! Oh, I beg your pardon.

**FITZROY**     That's OK.

**JMK**          But you speak so well!

**FITZROY** *(smiles)* Thanks.

**JMK**          Really you do... full marks there, huh! *(To Curtis)* So, you're Jackie, right?

**JACKIE**       Wrong.

**CURTIS**       I ain't a woman.

**JMK**          Oh, I see... *(She laughs too much)* No, you definitely are not ... *(still signing and talking loud)* 'Curtis' pleased to meet you, sir. *(Curtis looks around puzzled)* And you are...?

**JACKIE** *(quickly)* I'm Jackie, she's Chantelle.

**JMK**          Well, you certainly don't need assertiveness training, do you? *(She laughs. Jackie pretends to laugh)* Well, it's great to meet you all. I'm Jean-Marie Kellerman, organiser of this event and co-founder of the I.S.A. A grand title, I know, but I'd like it very much if you'd ignore that. I want you to know I'm not one of those big shots behind closed doors. I like to be very much a part of things. OK. This is Peter Dwyer, Head of Activities.

**PETER**        Hi – and Recreation.

| | |
|---|---|
| **JMK** | What? |
| **PETER** | And Recreation. |
| **JMK** | OK... Well, Alice, your team leader, who I believe you've met, will be looking after you, during the festival. Your dormitories – Peter? |
| **PETER** | They're on the B Wing, Village C. |
| **JMK** | You can collect your keys from Housekeeping. |
| **PETER** | Yep, right across the parking lot. |
| **CHANTELLE** | Dormitories? *(Fitzroy nudges her)* |
| **JMK** | Everything you need, you'll find in your rooms... Peter–? |
| **PETER** | Sure. Timetables, meal times, map of the campus etc. |
| **JMK** | A general information pack. |
| **FITZROY** | Nice. |
| **JMK** | Now, you'll be pleased to know that we've managed to arrange lots of activities for you, so you won't get bored. |
| **PETER** | No way. Can't happen. If anyone gets bored I'll make it my personal duty to do something about it. |
| **JMK** | Now on the final night – the Gala, which is when you'll be performing – it's actually going to be a VIP evening and that is with a capital V. Rehearsal – |
| **CHANTELLE** | Really. Who's coming? |
| **JMK** | Well, I don't want to give too much away, but there will be a few faces you'll recognise from the movies and if I tell you that the guest of honour is none other than the former Vice President of the United States – Dan Quayle – you'll get the picture. *(They try to be impressed)* |
| **PETER** | Oh yes! |
| **CURTIS** | *Who?* |
| **JMK** | Rehearsal space is available in the studio theatre. |
| **PETER** | Make sure you check with me for times. |
| **JMK** | On the subject of the performance, can I just say that I saw the video that you guys sent of your piece... *(pause)* Stunning! Really absolutely right there! I was truly moved. It is *so* powerful. *(All except Jackie are genuinely pleased)* I think it's going to go down really well! And I think, you in particular Fitzroy, are going to have quite a fan club afterwards. *(Fitzroy smiles shyly)* Well, I guess you're all keen to get partying. OK, |

the main party is in the Lincoln Assembly Hall. There's a disco and later a live band till ten thirty.

**PETER**           Plus, we have Mad Cap Larry.

**JMK**              Oh, you'll love him. He's a kind of comic-stroke-clown.

**PETER**           Seriously, hold on to your hats – he's a *blast!*

**JMK**              If you're hungry, there's a buffet in the Ford Suite, G5.

**CURTIS**         Chicken?

**JMK**              Excuse me?

**CURTIS**         Will there be chicken?

**JMK**              Oh, you mean at the buffet? Oh gosh, there'll be all sorts there... fish, steak, salads, potatoes, everything.

**CURTIS** *(seriously)* And chicken?

**CHANTELLE**  Curtis!

**CURTIS**         What? I'm just asking...

**JMK** *(laughs)* Oh plenty. More than you can eat, I'm sure. OK then, it only leaves me to give you these – *(gives them all a badge)* – your 'Special People' pins and to personally welcome you to I.S.A. '96. *(shakes everyone's hand. Jackie deliberately offers her left arm. Jean-Marie Kellerman hesitates, then gives it an extra strong shake.)*

**JMK**              Curtis – last but not least.

**CURTIS**         Nice baby.

**FITZROY**        Thank you... and on behalf of all of us, I'd like to say thank you.

**JMK**              My pleasure... enjoy.

*Peter gives them a thumbs up. They exit.*

**CURTIS**         Stop at ten thirty! What kinda party is that? *(They all burst out laughing)* No way man, that's sad! *(They all speak at once.)*

**CHANTELLE**  Fitzroy – you said we'd be in a hotel.

**CURTIS**         Yeah man, what happened about that?

**FITZROY**        That's what they said.

**JACKIE**         Can I join your fan club?

*The others laugh.*

**SCENE 4**
*Party. The group are in a smaller room adjoining the main hall.*
*Music can be heard.*

**JACKIE**　　　You're not gonna believe this.
**ALL**　　　What?
**JACKIE**　　　No drink. No alcohol.
**CHANTELLE**　You're kidding?
**FITZROY**　　There's a bar over there.
**JACKIE**　　　It's all soft drinks. The only real bar is in the hotel
　where the leaders are staying.
**CHANTELLE**　Are you serious?
**JACKIE**　　　You see me laughing?
**CHANTELLE**　What kind of party is it, without drink?
**CURTIS**　　　Relax yourselves. Fitzroy, reach into my bag.
**FITZROY** *(pulls out a bottle of overproof rum from Curtis' bag)*
　Backside! What the hell is this? Murder she wrote!
**JACKIE**　　　Yes Curtis! Nice one.
**CURTIS**　　　You see – and you all think I'm stupid.

*Jackie exits.*

**CHANTELLE**　What's he got?
**FITZROY**　　White rum.
**CHANTELLE**　How did you get that here?
**CURTIS**　　　I have my means.

*Enter Jackie with cups and coke.*

**FITZROY**　　You're a sly man, Curtis.
**CURTIS**　　　Just pour me a drink. I'm gonna drink then nyam
　out! Chicken time.
**FITZROY**　　Eh, look we can't be getting drunk so we'll just have
　one of these OK, and that's it.

*Lights fade. Music changes to live band 'Old MacDonald' some time*
*later.*

**FITZROY** *(passing the bottle to Jackie)* Not once... not once has that man been on time for anything, even when they buried his granny...

*Enter Curtis.*

**CURTIS** *(angry, kisses his teeth)* Idiots! You'd think in a big place like this, people would know what they're doing, plan ahead... it's ridiculous!

**JACKIE**      Eh?

**FITZROY**      What's matter? What's happened?

**CURTIS**      No chicken.

*They all burst out laughing.*

**FITZROY**      You bitch you!

**CURTIS**      It's not funny. They've run out.

**FITZROY**      Look at him. He's serious, you know. *(goes to him)* Eh, Curtis, you can't get vex over chicken, man *(laughing)* Come have another drink with me.

**CURTIS**      I thought you didn't drink.

**FITZROY**      I don't, but this is a special occasion.

**CURTIS**      Special how?

**FITZROY**      You'll find out in a minute. I got something in my heart and something in my head and now I feel the time is right.

**CURTIS**      Why have you always got to talk in riddles?

**FITZROY**      This ain't no riddle. You make sure they stay here and listen. *(exits)*

**CURTIS**    What?

**JACKIE** *(quite drunk)* I mean I don't really know you... don't get me wrong, but I think you're brilliant.

**CHANTELLE**  Me! Why?

**JACKIE**      Cos you are.

**CHANTELLE**  Where's he gone? He's too drunk.

**JACKIE**      You're alright, you know.

**CHANTELLE**  What's he doing?

**JACKIE**      Do you know what I'm saying? You could do anything.

**CHANTELLE**  How much have you had?

**JACKIE**          No, I'm serious. Like, even though you can't see and
stuff, nothing seems to bother you, you just take it in your stride.

**CHANTELLE**  You're joking.

**JACKIE**          I ain't... and well, do you want to feel my face?

**CHANTELLE**  What?

**JACKIE**          You know feel my face so you know what I look
like? *(Chantelle laughs)* What?

**CHANTELLE**  We don't really do that.

**JACKIE**          No?

**CHANTELLE**  No.

**JACKIE**          Why's that, then?

**CHANTELLE**  I don't know. We just don't.

**JACKIE**          Oh... Audrey Hepburn did it.

**CHANTELLE**  What's he doing, Curtis?

**CURTIS**          Don't know.

**JACKIE**          So you've never done it?

**CHANTELLE**  Never! Oh I tell a lie, I did it once when I was
younger and the bloke – right – teacher, he said I should do it and
I reached and I was feeling his face and he had like crusty bits
round his mouth and snot coming out of his nose.

**JACKIE** *(laughs)* Oh god!

**CHANTELLE**  Never again.

**BANDLEADER** *(offstage)* Before we do our next song we have a
young man from England who's got something important he'd
like to say. It's all yours, son.

**FITZROY**          Um... this is a message for Chantelle... Chani –
we've been seeing each other for a while now and I love you and
I think you feel the same, so I'm asking you if you'd like to be
my fiancé.

*Cheers from the crowd.*

**CHANTELLE**  Oh – my – God!

**BANDLEADER**  OK, Chantelle, it's up to you. He's on his way
back, so you better make up your mind. *(Chantelle laughs.)*

**JACKIE**          What are you gonna do?

**CHANTELLE**  I don't know. I – what do you think?

**JACKIE**          It's up to you. It's your life.

*Enter Fitzroy.*

**CHANTELLE**  Oh god! I don't know.
**FITZROY**      You'd better know.
**CHANTELLE**  I don't believe you just did that!
**FITZROY**      I told him to put our song on. *(goes to her)* C'mon,
   what do you say?
**JACKIE** *(joking)* No, don't do it. *(Pause)*
**FITZROY**      You lot, shut up. This is serious... *(He looks at
   Chantelle)* C'mon the music soon finish.
**CHANTELLE** *(puts her arms around him)* Of course, I will.

*Music swells. ('Hello' by Lionel Richie.) They dance. Lights fade.
Music changes to faster tempo.*

**JMK**          Oh, well... My! – My! – My! Way to go, you guys.
   Way to go! Congratulations.
**FITZROY**      Thanks.

*Enter Peter. He carries flowers and balloons.*

**JMK**          This is just a little something from I.S.A. *(quietly)*
   Flowers.
**CHANTELLE**  Oh – no thank you.
**JMK** *(to Chantelle)* Are you pleased? You must be. He's such a
   catch. I'm so pleased for you both really.
**FITZROY/CHANTELLE**  Thank you very much.
**JMK**          Quite the knight in shining armour, aren't you?
**FITZROY**      Well, I got my style.
**JMK**          Haven't you just? I wish someone would do that for
   me. You better keep a tight rein on him. They'll be after him.
   *(laughs)* Why aren't you celebrating? You should be out there
   dancing, showing us how it's done.
**CURTIS**      Hey! It's the same as that film.
**JMK**          What's that?
**CURTIS**      Your name – Jean Marie Kellerman. J.M.K.
**JACKIE**      That was J.F.K. Fool!
**JMK**          I guess it is a bit the same but sad to say that's where
   the similarities end. I am certainly not a President!

**JACKIE**    No, but you should be shot.
**CHANTELLE** Jackie!

*Enter Jud Davies.*

**JUD**    Congratulations.
**CHANTELLE** Who's that?
**JMK**    Aren't they great? I must go, but thank you, you've really made my day.
**FITZROY/CHANTELLE** Thanks.

*She exits.*

**JUD**    Hi, I'm Jud. I'm with a group from England. Congratulations. Well done.
**FITZROY**    Thanks.
**JUD**    We didn't realise there was another UK group here, so when I heard the announcement, I thought I'd come and introduce myself.
**JACKIE**    Hi, I'm Jackie. This is Curtis and you know these two.
**JUD**    Yeah.
**CURTIS**    Pour me a drink, Jackie.
**JACKIE**    It's over there.
**JUD**    Well, there seems to be more action in here than out there. I've been trying to find some sanity amongst all the orange squash and smiles.
**FITZROY**    Have a drink man. Loosen up your white self.
**JUD**    Cheers! *(He sips)* Jesus Christ! What is this stuff? *(They all laugh)* Got a bit of a kick to it though, hasn't it.?
**FITZROY**    I like this guy. If you're a friend of overproof, you're a friend of mine. *(He crosses to Curtis)*
**JACKIE**    I thought you were Christian.
**FITZROY**    Listen, even Jesus drank wine. *(They laugh)* I want to make a toast to everybody. Come Jackie, I know we've had our fights, but you know I love you. I reckon this week is gonna be kicking and wouldn't want to be anywhere else. You lot – well you're cool.
**CURTIS**    You should ease up. You're gonna drunk yourself.

**FITZROY**      No I'm alright, I can hold my drink... besides I'm
   happy tonight. I don't care about anything. I feel good.
**CURTIS**       Yeah, I'm happy for you.
**FITZROY**      It's what you should be doing... find yourself a
   woman, settle down.
**CURTIS**       Who me? No chance. You think I'm a fool? I ain't
   into that one-woman business. Me right – I'm gonna save up my
   money, then when I get older I'm gonna go to Jamaica, sit on
   beach and get fat... yeah man, that's the life – pattie in one hand,
   pussy in the other.

*Lights fade. Jackie enters with food.*

**JUD**          Just as bad out there, is it?
**JACKIE**       Worse!
**JUD**          What's going on now?
**JACKIE**       Line dancing. Mad Cap Larry's on with the
   Dingbats.
**JUD**          Oh no – my lot will be killing themselves. 'Hold on
   to your hats'...
**JACKIE/JUD**   'He's a *blast!*' *(They laugh)*
**JUD**          It's unbelievable, isn't it, that Kellerman woman?
**CHANTELLE**  She's really nice.
**JUD**          What with that smile – *(He impersonates)* she could
   put that in the Guinness Book of Records under 'Endurance'.
   *(They laugh)* I can't get over this place. So, how are you lot gonna
   spend your fun-filled week? Trips to the zoo? Mask-making?
   'Cos you have to wait till the end of the week for the firework
   display.
**JACKIE**       Well, me and Chantelle are going on a coach trip
   tomorrow.
**JUD** *(in disgust)* You're not going on the 'Funday' excursion?
**JACKIE**       Well, yeah our names are on the list.
**JUD**          So what? Take them off.
**JACKIE**       Well, we really want to see the Monument.
**JUD**          So do I, but you don't have to go with that lot.
**CHANTELLE**  We might as well.
**JUD**          You left school years ago. If you want to see it, do it
   in your own time.

**CHANTELLE**  It's been organised.

**JUD**          Listen, they invited you here, to perform. That doesn't mean they've got control of what you do in your free time. *(They laugh)* Did anyone ask you, if you wanted to go?

**JACKIE**          Well – no.

**JUD**          No. They're telling you to do it, like they're telling you when to eat, when to go to parties when not to drink. *(Chantelle laughs)* It's no joke. They think anyone with a disability has automatically got a mental age of a four year old. If you're in difficulty please seek a special volunteer... etc.

**CHANTELLE**  Well, it is their festival.

**JUD**          Wrong. What does it say on all the banners and publicity? 'Disability Festival' – it's meant to be *our* festival. If it wasn't for us, they couldn't do any of this.

**CHANTELLE**  But they've done it for us.

**JUD**          Sure. With the money they couldn't get *without* us. Don't be feeling grateful to them. You're paying their wages. Putting it simply – they raise this money by showing people how sad and tragic our lives would be, without them.

**CHANTELLE**  I'm not sure I agree with that. Look at all the people who benefit.

**JUD**          What do they benefit?

**JACKIE**          We only want to see the Monument.

**CHANTELLE**  And it's all free.

**JUD**          You pay a high price by losing dignity.

**CHANTELLE**  *(laughs)* You're mad.

**JUD**          You think so? I'm telling you they don't want us here to perform plays and songs about our lives. No chance. They want us to show how much like them we can be. Know what I mean? Look at me – I ain't really got a limp. I can tap dance... it's bullshit. It's a fucking freak show.

*Enter Fitzroy and Curtis.*

**FITZROY**          Chani... Chani... come here baby-love.

**CHANTELLE**  You're drunk.

**FITZROY** *(drunk)* You are gonna love your present.

**CHANTELLE**  Will I?

**FITZROY**          Yeah, you will. I shouldn't really talk about it now.

**JUD**              Are you gonna tell us what it is?
**FITZROY**          No, that's strictly between me and Chani. You know
what it is, innit? Something we both really want. Something you
can't buy. You got it now.
**CURTIS**           Yeah, I think so but I don't understand how?
**FITZROY**          Sssssssh!
**JUD**              Oooooooh, mystery. Are you gonna come and meet
the group then?
**JACKIE**           Yeah alright.
**CHANTELLE**  Are you alright, Fitzroy?
**FITZROY**          Yeah. *(To Jud)* Eh, you trying to steal my woman?
**JUD**              I couldn't, if I tried.
**JACKIE**           Eh Curtis, what's this? *(She holds up a chicken leg)*
**CURTIS**           Yes! Chicken.
**JACKIE**           No – the last piece of chicken. *(She puts the whole
thing in her mouth)*

*Lights fade.*

**SCENE 5**
*Foyer. A tannoy announcement is heard.*

**ANNOUNCER**  Any delegates still requiring excursion passes
please go to the front desk in the main foyer.
**JMK**              Let me see if I've got this right – Peter, you want to
divide people up into groups according to their disability and
have a mini football tournament.
**PETER**            What do you say?
**JMK**              Peter, have you really thought this through? *(Enter
Fitzroy. To Peter)* One moment. *(To Fitzroy)* Hi, well if it isn't
the star of the show. How are you doing?
**FITZROY**          Hi. Yeah, I'm OK thanks. How are you?
**JMK**              Busy, but we're surviving and we're having fun.
**FITZROY** *(looking round for Chantelle)* Well, that's important.
**JMK**              I notice Fitzroy, that you don't use sign language.
**FITZROY**          No I don't.
**JMK**              Is there a reason for that?
**FITZROY**          I don't really need it.

**JMK**          OK... it's just you seem to understand me better
when I use it.

**FITZROY**          That's because the movements are expressive.

**JMK**          You know there's quite a few people here at the
festival in the same boat as you – partially deaf. They've got a
group going... They use sign language. They seem to enjoy it.

**FITZROY**          I think that's more for the deafer people.

**JMK**          Right. Hey, caught a sneak look at your rehearsal.

**FITZROY**          Oh yeah?

**JMK**          Honestly, I'm not kidding. Your dancing is really
sensational.

**FITZROY**          Thanks.

**JMK**          Where did you learn to dance like that?

**FITZROY**          Just picked it up.

**JMK**          The natural rhythm thing, right?...and you keep
yourself in such great shape. How do you manage that? *(He
shrugs)* C'mon, you must have a strict diet, right? Lots of working
out.

**FITZROY**          No, I don't do any of that stuff. Just do my dancing
now and again.

**JMK** *(pinching his arm)* God, I'm so jealous. *(laughs)* And here's
me, all wrinkles and flab.

**FITZROY** *(nods, pause)* Sorry – what did you say?

**JMK**          I said, I'm an out-of-shape has-been.

**FITZROY**          No, you look really good. Look sweet.

**JMK**          Sweet? I've never been called that but I think I can
live with it.

**FITZROY**          Well, it's true.

**JMK** *(laughs)* Well, thank you!

**PETER**          Miss Kellerman *(points to his watch)*.

**JMK**          Thank you Peter. I'll see you around. Hey and why
don't you think about joining that sign language group. I think
you may benefit a lot from it.

*She exits.*

**SCENE 6**
*Lights come up to reveal Fitzroy on a telephone.*

**OPERATOR**   One minute sir, I'll try and connect your call.

**PEARL** *(English accent)* Hello.

**OPERATOR**   Good afternoon, I have a call for a Mrs Chambers. From Washington DC.

*Lights reveal Pearl Chambers in her living room sitting on an easy chair.*

**PEARL**          One moment. *(calls to someone)* Samuel there's a woman on the phone from America... I think Fitzroy... plane crash or he's sick...

**OPERATOR**   Hello... Hello...?

**PEARL**          Hello... Sorry to have kept you.

**OPERATOR**   Connecting you now.

**FITZROY**      Hello... *(struggles to hear)*

**PEARL**          Fitzroy?

**FITZROY**      Hello.

**PEARL**          What happened Fitzroy? You sick!

**FITZROY**      No Mum, I'm fine.

**PEARL**          You in trouble?

**FITZROY**      No... no trouble

**PEARL**          Police arrest you?

**FITZROY**      No Mum... listen, there's no problem, everything is fine.

**PEARL**          So what did you ring for?

**FITZROY**      Just to talk. *(Pause)*

**PEARL**          What you want to talk about?

**FITZROY**      I've – I've got a surprise for you.

**PEARL**          That's nice – have you seen Carol and Tyrone yet?

**FITZROY**      I – what?

**PEARL**          Have you seen Carol and Tyrone?

**FITZROY**      Who are Carol and Tyrone?

**PEARL**          Your cousins! They live in America.

**FITZROY** *(laughs)* No... No, Mum I haven't seen them.

**PEARL**          Why you laughing? Did I say something funny?

**FITZROY**      No...

**PEARL**          Then you must be a damn fool because only mad people laugh at nothing.

**FITZROY**     Look Mum... it's hard to hear you on this phone and I haven't got much money...

**PEARL**        Alright then, Fitzroy... I'll tell your Daddy 'Hello' from you...

**FITZROY**     What?

**PEARL**        And you take care now son, thanks for ring –

**FITZROY**     Mum! Wait!

**PEARL**        Yes?

**FITZROY**     I haven't told you the surprise.

**PEARL**        Oh yes, sorry. What's the surprise then?

**FITZROY**     Well, you know Chantelle, the girl in the group... we're gonna be engaged.

**PEARL** *(Pause)* Which girl is that?

**FITZROY**     You know Chantelle... you liked her... fair skin long hair... pretty.

**PEARL**        I don't remember no girl look like that.

**FITZROY**     She been to the house a couple of times.

**PEARL**        What? You mean the blind girl?

**FITZROY** *(hesitates)* Yeah, that's her. *(Pause)* Mum?

**PEARL**        I thought surprises were supposed to be something nice.

**FITZROY**     I can't hear you Mum.

**PEARL**        I didn't say anything.

**FITZROY**     Mum, it's really hard on this phone... can you speak up a bit?

**PEARL**        What made you get engaged to her?

**FITZROY**     What do you mean?

**PEARL**        I mean... did something happen why you have to get engaged to her?

**FITZROY**     How do you mean...? No, nothing's happened.

**PEARL**        Well, I can't pretend I'm happy.

**FITZROY** *(frustrated)* Why?

**PEARL**        What's the matter with you? Did something lick you in your head on the plane and turn you into a fool so can't remember anything I told you before you left?

**FITZROY**     Of course I ain't forgotten.

**PEARL**        Then what happen – you can't hear!

*Lights change. We are now in Pearl Chambers' living room several months earlier. It is a heated argument.*

PEARL          You can't hear?

FITZROY        Don't keep saying that.

PEARL          Well, you don't seem to understand me.

FITZROY        I understand you... but that's your opinion.

PEARL          Alright, it's my opinion... Just how far are you planning to take this thing?

FITZROY        What?

PEARL          Where do you see yourself going with this girl?

FITZROY        I don't know... I love her... and if it worked out I'd probably want to marry her.

PEARL          Is it? *(kisses her teeth)* Let me ask you something young man, how long have you known this girl?

FITZROY        Long time... I don't know, almost two years.

PEARL          That's a long time? You think you know her well enough to marry her? *(kisses her teeth)* Let me tell you, it's forty years I married to your Daddy and I'm still not sure it's a good idea.

FITZROY *(laughs)* I'm serious you know.

PEARL          So am I... you think you love this girl but it's not so.

FITZROY        I know what I feel... I love her.

PEARL          No son... what you feel for this girl is care, not love.

FITZROY        No Mum.

PEARL          Yes... You talk about marriage – have you thought about it?

FITZROY        What do you mean?

PEARL          I mean the future when you have children... can she have children?

FITZROY        Of course she can have children!

PEARL          What make this girl blind?

FITZROY        Eh?

PEARL          How did this girl came to be blind?

FITZROY        No reason, she was born like it.

PEARL          Exactly, so that means it could be in her blood, hereditary.

FITZROY        So?

**PEARL**          That means your children could be blind! *(Pause)*
See you don't think about those things.

**FITZROY**          It wouldn't matter.

**PEARL**          Boy, don't be so damn stupid! How will you
manage? The poor girl can't move from one place to another
without you helping her. She can't see to dress herself, she can't
clean or cook, so how can she take care of a baby? You'd have to
do everything.

**FITZROY**          You can probably get people to take care of all that.

**PEARL**          Is it? *(Pause)* Well, you can't get people to take care
of how you feel.

**FITZROY** *(irritated)* What are you saying now?

**PEARL**          Have you stopped to think how you're going to feel
when all the children are running round kicking ball with their
fathers and you have to stand at the side? You can't even take
your son and show him a cat or dog. No sir, you can't do none of
that.

**FITZROY**          Look – just stop this, alright!

**PEARL**          Yes, because you can't stand to hear the truth.

**FITZROY**          No it's not that!

**PEARL**          Of course... you just like to dream, you don't like
reality...

**FITZROY**          We don't even know if they wouldn't be able to see.
Maybe they would!

**PEARL**          You can take that risk? Son, you must come to
realise that you are not the Good Samaritan. You can't take on
everyone's problems... I know you feel sorry for this girl, but
you're just a normal young man who wants someone.

**FITZROY**          I've got someone! *(Pause)*

**PEARL**          Fitzroy... I am your mother. *(He nods reluctantly)* I
know how you feel... Alright son, you're not a good-looking man
like your brothers and I know you feel shame because your ears
aren't good, but that doesn't mean you can't find another woman.

**FITZROY**          What are you talking about?

**PEARL**          There is somebody out there I'm sure who would
happily accept you.

**FITZROY**          I don't want –

**PEARL**          A woman that could look after you, take care of *you*. This girl doesn't have any use! She just clings to you, because she knows no man don't want her, she can't cope without you.

**FITZROY**          I'm happy to take care of her!

**PEARL**          And who's going to take care of you?

**FITZROY**          We'll take care of each other.

**PEARL**          Lord, yes! What a house full of mumu that'll be. She can't see nothing, you can't hear nothing. The children will be walking around like duppies licking their heads on the furniture with their pants full of filth.

**FITZROY**          I can't be bothered to talk to you.

**PEARL**          It's no use you getting angry and sulking because it's what you're going to have to get used to, if you choose this life. People will make fun of you.

**FITZROY**          Why would they?

**PEARL**          Because people don't like it.

**FITZROY**          You don't half chat some rubbish! Most places we go, people are all over us... they can't do enough for us.

**PEARL**          That's white people you're talking about. Of course they'll be nice and smile because them lie, damn two-faced.

**FITZROY**          It's black people as well.

**PEARL**          Is it? I don't know which black people you're talking about because I know people don't like it. They don't want it in their families. I even remember back home, when I went to people's house that have 'mumu' children, they hide them, push them under the bed so no one can see them. *(He kisses his teeth)* It's true – because it carries a stigma!

**FITZROY**          That's back then, years ago... people don't think like that no more.

**PEARL**          People are not like 'party frocks' boy. They don't go in and out of fashion. And let me remind you, it's only since you joined this group, that you started to mix with these people. When you were a child and I tried to take you to the handicapped Christmas party, you used to scream and bawl saying you didn't want to go in there... you were scared of them.

**FITZROY**          That was way back before I had sense!

**PEARL**          And now it's those same handicapped children you want to bring into the world.

**FITZROY**          Chantelle ain't handicapped!

**PEARL**          No? What do you think gonna happen when you
take her to people's house to eat? They'll say, 'Oh God, look how
she's nasty, pushing her hand in the plate, feel up the food like a
monkey.'

**FITZROY**          That's it! *(He starts to leave)*

**PEARL** *(quickly)* Son, that's not me talking. I'm just showing you
how people are. I'm just looking out for you... I like the girl.

**FITZROY**          Don't lie!

**PEARL**          Don't call me a liar in my own house.

**FITZROY**          You're just trying to stop me being with her. I don't
know why, but you just don't wanna see me happy... You're
saying it's other people, but really it's you who thinks that way.
You're the one who can't accept her.

**PEARL**          That's not true at all.

**FITZROY**          Of course it is. You're just plain bad minded, cruel!

**PEARL** *(hurt)* No, no son, you know I'm not trying to be cruel. I'm
not a wicked person. You know and God knows I am a Christian
woman. How could I think these things? *(He looks away)* Fitzroy,
look at me, I know you turn away so you can't hear what I'm
saying... I would never do anything to hurt you. I know how it is.
From when I gave birth to you, I've lived through it. Life is hard
enough already for a young black man, never mind the problems
you want to take on, but... if you say you like this girl and you
truly came to love her, of course I would have to accept her.

**FITZROY**          Could you do that?

**PEARL**          How could I face my God if I lied to you? But son, I
know you and I beg you to stop and think...Yes, you care for this
girl... but can you really put your hand on your heart and tell me
you don't feel any of the things I am saying?

**FITZROY**          There's got to be a way Mum. I can't let her go.

*He looks at his mother but cannot say anything.*

**PEARL**          If there is, son, then the Lord will point you to it. If
not, then you have to be fair to this girl and let her go, before you
really hurt her.

*Lights slowly cross fade to Fitzroy on the telephone.*

**FITZROY**     Mum, I remember everything you said. No wait...
you said, you could accept it. I have prayed about it, it's gonna be
alright... that's what I am trying to say! Mum, I'm gonna have to
go... I got no more money... Just don't worry. Trust me, it'll be
alright.

*Lights fade.*

**SCENE 7**
*Outside the conference centre, Jud paces. He shouts through a
megaphone.*

**JUD**          Don't get on the coaches. Don't let them take you
for a ride. This festival, which is supposed to be bettering the
lives of disabled people, is actually doing a great deal of harm. By
putting us forward as needy dependants, it perpetuates the false
perception non-disabled society already has of us, as people who
offer little or nothing. Fifty years ago, Hitler called us 'non-
productive consumers'. Today I.S.A. wants to take the 'Dis' out
of 'Ability' – spot the difference, if you can. The only people this
festival benefits are the organisers, the leaders who get a free
holiday and a piss-up in the States. So don't get on these coaches.
Don't let them take *you* for a ride.

*He exits. Jackie and Chantelle stand waiting for a coach to take them
on a day trip. They wear colourful T-shirts with the ISA '96 emblem
on the front and 'Taking the Dis out of Ability' on the back. In the
background, we can hear chanting and Jud talking through a
megaphone.*

**CHANTELLE**  Are we in the right place?
**JACKIE**       Yeah, I think so... it says opposite the sports centre...
*(reading)* We're with Group F and this is Coach Stop 4, so...
**CHANTELLE**  What?
**JACKIE**       Don't give me that. This secret present, what is it?
**CHANTELLE**  What's all that shouting?
**JACKIE**       Don't try and get out of it. It's some kind of demo.
**CHANTELLE**  Really?
**JACKIE**       Well, come on then...

**CHANTELLE** Oh Jackie I can't...
**JUD** *(voice offstage)* Jackie and Chantelle, this is the disability
  police... move away from that bus stop.

*Enter Jud. They freeze.*

**JUD**  Hey, Jackie, Chantelle! How you doin'?
**CHANTELLE** Who's that?
**JUD**  Jud.
**CHANTELLE** Jud?
**JUD**  The party.
**CHANTELLE** Oh right, yeah.
**JUD**  Obviously, I made a big impact on you!
**CHANTELLE** Sorry, I just forgot for a second.
**JUD**  Not surprised after that night. *(To Jackie)* What
  about you, have a good time?
**JACKIE**  Don't remember much about it.
**JUD**  Nor me. Why was I drinking that fucking furniture
  polish? *(They laugh)* How is Curtis... is he still alive?
**JACKIE**  Sadly.
**JUD**  I owe him one.
**JACKIE**  What's that about? *(points at his T-shirt)*
**JUD**  Oh this.
**CHANTELLE** What?
**JUD**  My T-shirt. It says, 'Taking the piss out of disability.'
  We're just trying to upset a few people. Didn't you hear the
  speech?
**JACKIE**  Was that you?
**JUD**  Me and a couple of the others.
**JACKIE**  We better go.
**JUD**  Anywhere good? *(Pause)* What? You're going on
  the coach trip, aren't you?
**JACKIE**  Just for a laugh.
**JUD**  Well, that was a waste of breath then, wasn't it?
**JACKIE** *(laughs)* We don't mind.
**JUD**  Don't you? You really wanna wear those T-shirts
  and get on a coach with a bunch of kids? Would you do it at
  home?
**JACKIE**  No.

| | |
|---|---|
| **JUD** | Exactly, so why do it now? |
| **JACKIE** | We ain't hurting anyone. |
| **JUD** | Only yourselves. |

**CHANTELLE**  Why are you so against it? Why did you bother coming, if you ain't going to enjoy it?

| | |
|---|---|
| **JUD** | We didn't come to enjoy it. We came to stop it. |
| **JACKIE** | Eh? |

**JUD**          We ain't here for the crack. You really think I'd be a part of this? Look, I don't want to give you a party political broadcast – have a look at that. *(gives them a leaflet)* There are enough of us to really do something. If we can upset an event as big as this, with all these VIPs, we've really achieved something.

| | |
|---|---|
| **JACKIE** | What are you gonna do? |
| **JUD** | We're gonna boycott the Gala. |
| **JACKIE** | What? |

**JUD**          Fucking right, we ain't gonna do it. We're gonna put a picket outside telling people not to go in and those that that do go in, ain't gonna see anything.

**CHANTELLE**  Then what?

**JUD**          Well, you've got to remember, there's gonna be loads of TV coverage because of the special guests, so we're gonna elect someone to make a speech stating our views. Can you imagine Kellerman's reaction? She'll be fucked and that'll be a first.

**JACKIE**      I wonder who's gonna make the speech?

**JUD**          No, that hasn't been decided yet. Besides it doesn't matter who says it, just so long as it's said. It could be one of you.

**CHANTELLE**  It won't be me.

**JUD**          No?

**CHANTELLE**  No way.

**JUD**          Why's that?

**CHANTELLE**  Cos I think it's really bad what you're doing. I think we're being treated really well. They're bending over backwards to do things for us.

**JUD**          I guess they are, and I love them for it. But I don't need to be told how unique I am. I'm quite happy being disabled, aren't you?

**CHANTELLE**  What? *(laughs)* What do you mean? No, I don't think so... I'm not ashamed but course I ain't happy about it.

**JUD** Maybe it's because no one ever allowed you to believe you could be. *(Pause)* Look I've got to go... I know you can't commit to it now... all I'm saying is – read the leaflet, think about what I've said and get back to me. You really ought to be part of it, we can't keep letting them get away with this crap, we don't need it.

**JACKIE** We've missed the coach.

**CHANTELLE** Oh no.

**JUD** There you are – you've just made your first political statement!

*He exits.*

## SCENE 8

*Jud is placing leaflets on the chairs and notice boards. Enter Jean-Marie Kellerman and Peter.*

**JMK** Have you cleared the passes for the White House visit?

**PETER** Yeah ,and if it rains – *(sees Jud)* Hi, everything alright there?

**JUD** Oh hi... actually I've been looking for a special arts person.

**PETER** That's me.

**JUD** I wondered if you could help me... it said in the brochure –

**PETER** On hand day or night.

**JUD** Good, that's great.

**PETER** What's your problem?

**JUD** Well, it's my friend's dormitory... she's in a wheel-chair.

**PETER** Sure.

**JUD** And whereas the pull bar above the bed is very useful for getting her into bed...

**PETER** Uh huh...

**JUD** The problem is, I keep banging my head on it when we're doing it doggy style... I wondered what you could suggest?

**JMK** *(sees notice board)* Is this an authorised display?

**JUD** Hi Jean, what do you think of the T-shirt?

**JMK** *(reads it)* Well, don't much care for it, to be honest.

**JUD**        Oh, why's that?

**JMK**        Let me guess, you're Jud Davies, right? *(He nods)* Well, young man, you've been causing quite a stir, haven't you? Many of the delegates have been rather upset by your leaflets and bullying.

**JUD**        We're only telling the truth.

**JMK**        The truth as you perceive it. *(looks at a leaflet)* I trust Mr Davies, you were democratically elected to the post of spokesman for the entire disabled population? Am I right, Peter, in saying that this complex is totally accessible?

**PETER**        Yeah, we have ramped or level entrances, Brailled signs, electric doors, induction loops, lifts to all areas, minicoms...

**JUD**        What's your point?

**JMK**        I guess I'm unclear as to what exactly you are campaigning against?

**JUD**        The way you're exploiting disabled people.

**JMK**        OK, look around you... do they look like they are being exploited, or do you see people having a good time?

**JUD**        No... I see a lot of people who think they're having a good time. *(They laugh)* Don't like being questioned, do you?

**JMK**        No, Mr Davies. I'll accept criticism and I'll accept that this festival is possibly not for you, but disability is a broad term and there are many less fortunate than you who don't have the same physical and mental abilities as you and have not enjoyed the luxuries of a good education or the possibility of a career. For those people, Mr Davies, I say that organisations such as ours, offer a great deal.

**JUD**        By brainwashing them with balloons? You do a lot more harm than good.

**JMK**        On the contrary, Mr Davies... you tell me you care about these people, yet you're willing to destroy, what may be for them, a once in a lifetime experience.

**JUD**        My point exactly, you want to give them one moment in a lifetime. I want to give them a lifetime worth having.

**JMK**        If you must be a martyr Mr Davies, why not find a cause that needs one?

**JUD**        You're so deep.

**JMK**          OK, I don't know what your plans are here, but I'm asking you nicely to stop, or I'm afraid you will be asked to leave.

**JUD**          Give us what we want and we'll happily leave.

**JMK**          Oh really? And what could I possibly give a rude, arrogant, self-opinionated, young man like you?

*Pause.*

**JUD**          Head?

*She storms out. Peter starts to exit, he stops at Jud, points a warning finger at him and leaves.*

**SCENE 9**
*A café in downtown Washington DC.*

**CHANTELLE**  Weird bloke, isn't he? I never thought he'd be like that.

**JACKIE** *(laughs)* It's interesting though, some of the things he was saying.

**CHANTELLE**  You think so?

**JACKIE**          Yeah, I'd never thought about it all like that.

**CHANTELLE**  You're not thinking of doing it, are you?

**JACKIE**          No, I'm not saying that... I'm just saying it was interesting.

**CHANTELLE**  I just think it's totally out of order. It's really ungrateful... like slapping I.S.A. in the face.

**JACKIE**          I might go to the meeting for a laugh.

**CHANTELLE**  You're on your own. Can you imagine what Fitzroy would say, after all the work he has put in?

**JACKIE** *(tuts)* Fitzroy.

**CHANTELLE**  What does that mean?

**JACKIE**          Nothing.

**CHANTELLE**  Didn't sound like nothing.

**JACKIE**          It doesn't matter.

**CHANTELLE**  If you've got something to say, you may as well say it.

**JACKIE**          Alright... why are you so worried about what Fitzroy will say? Don't you ever make a decision for yourself?

**CHANTELLE**  Of course I do, I'm just not into it, that's all. I think it's stupid just spoiling things for the sake.

**JACKIE**        And you're scared of what he'll say.

**CHANTELLE**  No I'm not. I respect what he says but I'm not scared of him.

**JACKIE**        You worship him.

**CHANTELLE**  I don't.

**JACKIE**        Not much.

**CHANTELLE**  If I do, it's because of what he's done for me.

**JACKIE**        Yeah? What's he done?

**CHANTELLE**  Well...

**JACKIE**        That much?

**CHANTELLE**  No, he's really helped me... Before, right, I didn't do anything. I had no black friends, I didn't dare go out 'cos I was so scared of people. I used to just stay at home the whole time... I think he's really brought me out of myself.

**JACKIE**        You shouldn't be feeling grateful. Half of those things you would've done yourself eventually. Just cos he was the first person to come along, it don't mean he's gotta be the last.

**CHANTELLE**  Maybe I want him to be the last!

**JACKIE**        Maybe you do, but I think he holds you back. You're bright, been to college... you're a strong woman, you could do anything with your life.

**CHANTELLE**  I'm doing it now.

**JACKIE**        You're doing what he allows you to do. He controls you like a puppet. You're his little show piece and people think he's so great, 'cos he's going out with a blind girl.

**CHANTELLE** *(upset)* That's not true. Most of the time he doesn't want people to know that I am. Who do you think you are anyway, dissing my man?

**JACKIE**        *Your* man.

**CHANTELLE**  What?

**JACKIE**        They way you two go on. *Your* man. *My* woman. It's pathetic.

**CHANTELLE**  I think you're really out of order... I love him, OK, and I'm sorry if this ain't the 'strong' thing to say but he wants me to marry him and I'm actually really happy about it. I don't care what you        think. If you don't like it, that's your hard luck!

**JACKIE**     Fair enough. I ain't gotta sleep with it. *(Silence)*

**CHANTELLE** *(softly)* I don't suppose you're sleeping with anyone?

**JACKIE** *(shaken)* What?

**CHANTELLE** I've never heard you talk about anyone.

**JACKIE**     So?

**CHANTELLE** Maybe you ain't got no one. Maybe you're just jealous of what me and Fitzroy have got.

**JACKIE**     Don't kid yourself. I ain't interested in no man, specially not him.

**CHANTELLE** I don't believe that... maybe it's true what they say about you.

**JACKIE**     What's true?

**CHANTELLE** Your being so mouthy and going on about being a tough woman or something, is just a big cover up.

**JACKIE**     For what?

**CHANTELLE** They say you're just frustrated that you can't get no man, so you act like you don't want one.

**JACKIE**     Rubbish! And who says I ain't got nobody? I haven't got to tell     you lot, my business. I could be seeing someone right now.

**CHANTELLE** Are you?

**JACKIE**     Why shouldn't I be?

**CHANTELLE** Dunno... they say it's 'cos of the way you look.

**JACKIE** *(stunned)* Do they? Well, who the fuck are *they* anyway? ...Let me guess – Fitzroy!

**CHANTELLE** I didn't say that.

**JACKIE**     You didn't have to... Well, he can just fuck off... what does he know about my life? He doesn't know me. He's got no business saying things about me... bastard! He can't talk about the way anyone looks.

**CHANTELLE** There's nothing wrong with Fitzroy.

**JACKIE**     Yeah right, and you'd know. You make me sick, you lot. You go on like you're so perfect, little miss fair skin, well you ain't all that... just 'cos you got guys sniffing around your tail the whole time, you think you're God's gift.

**CHANTELLE** I've never said that.

**JACKIE**     Good 'cos you ain't. 'Cos all those guys are just there feeling sorry for you – the poor 'sister' who can't see, and you play on it!

**CHANTELLE**  I don't.

**JACKIE**          Yes you do. I've seen you. The sad thing is, they're only telling you how pretty you are to get into your knickers 'cos they figure being blind, you can't be fussy. Ain't one of them got the guts to tell you what you really look like. *(Pause)*

**CHANTELLE**  Well, maybe they won't have to, for much longer.

**JACKIE**          How's that?

**CHANTELLE**  Forget it.

**JACKIE**          No go on.

**CHANTELLE**  Well, you don't know what my present is.

**JACKIE**          What – sight? What are you talking about?

**CHANTELLE**  It don't matter.

**JACKIE**          What's he gonna do, work a miracle?

**CHANTELLE**  Just get lost, Jackie.

**JACKIE**          Oh no! You idiot. You've let him talk –

**CHANTELLE**  It was my choice, Jackie!

**JACKIE**          Well then you deserve each other.

**CHANTELLE**  *(hurt)* Why are you being so nasty!

**JACKIE**          Me! I was talking about sticking up for yourself. It's you, who made it personal.

**CHANTELLE**  I was only telling you what people say.

**JACKIE**          Right, and I was just telling you what I see. *(Pause)* I'm going. What are you doing?

**CHANTELLE**  I know what I look like, Jackie.

**JACKIE**          Are you staying or coming?

**CHANTELLE**  *(softly)* I'm staying.

**JACKIE**          Fine! *(She exits)*

**CHANTELLE**  I know what I look like.

*Lights fade.*

## SCENE 10

*As lights fade up, we see a choir in silhouette. They swing from side to side, singing "This little light of mine".*

**SOLOIST**      This little light of mine I'm gonna let it shine
This little light of mine, I'm gonna let it shine
This little light of mine, I'm gonna let it shine
Let it shine, let it shine, let it shine.

CHORUS      This little light of mine, I'm gonna let it shine
This little light of mine, I'm gonna let it shine
This little light of mine, I'm gonna let it shine
Let it shine, let it shine, let it shine.

*Reverend Al Jeremiah enters.*

REV *(sings)* I love Jesus
CHORUS      I love Jesus
REV         Yes I do
CHORUS      Yes I do
REV         I love Jesus
CHORUS      I love Jesus
REV         How about you?
CHORUS      How about you?
ALL         I love Jesus, yes I do. I love Jesus, how about you?
REV         They love Jesus
CHORUS      We love Jesus
REV         Yes I do
CHORUS      Yes I do.
REV         You love Jesus
CHORUS      Yes you do
REV         I love Jesus
CHORUS      Yes I do
ALL         I love Jesus, yes I do. I love Jesus, how about you?
*(They chant)* H.O.W. A.B.O.U.T. Y.O.U.?
REV *(breathes in)* Oh yes! There but for the Grace of God, go I...
There but for the Grace of God, go I. Yes indeed, how many
times have you heard that said but never really thought about it?
We all know to whom that refers, but do we ever take the time to
do anything about it? No! It – is – not – enough to just feel sorry
for those people or to pretend they do not exist. If our Lord had
done that, a certain man would not have picked up his bed and
walked. Lazarus? Well, he would have stayed right there, in his
tomb. No, no, no, my friends, we should hold out an understanding hand to those who have been so cruelly afflicted. And *(points)*
yes, I'm not afraid to use that word, because an unfair affliction –
that's what it is. Now, I have to tell you, my critics, my doubters,
they come to my gatherings all over the world, OK, yeah, and sit

there at the back and shout, 'Heal me, cure me, make me walk, I dare you to try!' And to them, I say, 'Get Thee behind me Satan! Thou shall not tempt the Lord my God.' Some tell me, 'I don't want to be healed, I want to be like this, I'm happy the way I am.' And then like you, I would have to ask the question, 'Why?' 'I want to be handicapped.' How can that be? Yet this is what they tell me. Let me ask you, would anybody here like to have a cold? No. Toothache? Surprisingly, no takers. OK, lets blow the bank – what about – *(smiles)* a serious car accident, that left you paralysed and confined to a wheelchair? No. Of course not. So how can they be happy? It reminds me of when I was a boy, around ten years old and my Daddy bought me a bicycle. Now I loved that machine. I kept and cleaned it, took care of it so well that it lasted me 'till I was fourteen. Of course, by this time it was a little worn and rusty and beaten up but *hey* I adored it. All the other kids on the block were getting fancy new bikes with gears and so on but I wasn't interested. My old 'gusty' was all I wanted. Then one day I got home and right there on the porch was a brand spanking new bicycle – all shiny, soft saddle *and gears!* I stood and took one look at it and you know what I did? I got on old 'gusty,' rode down to the creek and tossed that old thing, right in there. *Of course*, I did and you know why? Because I realised what I was missing. Sure, I was happy with that old bike, but I was a whole lot happier with the new one. Yes, I was happy when I was a sinner, before I found God. Don't knock sight 'till you've seen a rainbow. Don't knock walking 'till you've run through a meadow. Don't knock hearing 'till you've heard God's words. Let's throw a few old bicycles into the river. Three days ago, a young man came to me at my office. He was from London; a little place called Bricks-on. (Brixton) He said, 'Sir, sir,' he said, 'You don't know me, but I've heard about your work. I've got a girl,' he said, 'who I love, and sir, I want to marry this girl.' He said, 'She is blind.' That young lady is here tonight. C'mon out here child. *(Chantelle enters stage left. She is very nervous. Nobody assists her. She has no feel of the space.)* It's alright. Don't be afraid, you're in the house of the Lord. What's your name child?

**CHANTELLE** *(quietly)* Chantelle.

**REV**            Estelle? Beautiful name, my wife's name...

**CHANTELLE**  Um...Chantelle.

**REV**  Oh, I'm sorry, forgive me child. Chant–elle.
*(To the congregation)* Let's raise the power of the Lord.
*(They sing louder)* Tell me – do you want to see?

**CHANTELLE**  I –

**REV**  Do you want to see all the beauty of God's earth?

**CHANTELLE.** ...well...

**REV**  I know you do. Stand with me, while I pray. All of
you, pray with me. Lord... Al Jeremiah, I stand here humble in
your presence with one of your children. A beautiful, young lady
to whom Satan has smote a vicious blow. Lord, I ask you to drive
out the evil, the sins of her father, the sins of her mother... she
asks you, she prays to you for forgiveness and the wretched life
she lived before, release her from this punishment, this darkness,
she wants to walk with you, she wants to walk in the light. She's
calling you Lord. I know you can hear her, *(To Chantelle)*, do you
believe in the Lord?

**CHANTELLE**  I –

**REV**  Tell him you love him. Tell him you want him in
your life.

**CHANTELLE**  I want –

**REV**  That's it child, cry out to the Lord, he is listening.

**CHANTELLE** *(nervous)* ...Fitzroy.

**REV**  The Lord is here. I feel his power in me.

**CHANTELLE** I want to go –

**REV**  Don't run from it child. Cast out Satan, cast out sin.

**FITZROY**  C'mon Chani, it's alright.

**CHANTELLE** *(frightened)* No.

*The chorus is going wild singing 'Amazing Grace.'*

**REV**  Sinner, come forward. Go child, and be in darkness,
no more.

**CHANTELLE**  No please... Fitzroy! *(screams)*

**REV** *(puts his hand forcefully on Chantelle's forehead. Makes a high
pitched scream)* WOOOOH! *(Chantelle appears to faint and falls
backwards. In hysteria)* Right there, is the power of the Lord!

*The chorus sings, as lights fade.*

## ACT TWO
## SCENE 1

*Fitzroy and Chantelle sit alone on stage. They are in a dormitory. Sunlight streams through a window. Chantelle sits on her bed. Fitzroy stands at the window.*

**FITZROY** *(tries to console her)* Chani... Chani... Listen to me, eh? Listen to me. It's alright, it don't matter. Just because it didn't happen this time, it doesn't mean it can't happen. Honestly, darling, you don't have to be upset about it. Maybe we just weren't strong enough in our belief... 'cos I know I had doubts in my mind, so maybe you did. I just know in my heart that it could work for you. We've just got to believe it... I'll tell you, next time I'm gonna stand with you and pray and we'll do it... Chani, trust me, we can beat this thing. *(Throughout this speech Chantelle remains completely silent, almost motionless, just gently rocking)* Chani... *(He tries to hug her but she puts her arms out to block him)* What's the matter...? *(She just shakes her head, speechless)* C'mon you can tell me. *(He tries to hug her again but she blocks him and shakes her head)* There's no point you holding it in. *(Pause)* I'm not arguing. I'm not. I've done told you it ain't your fault. *(Silence. She continues rocking.)* Eh, stop that now. C'mon stop it! Chani – say something, speak to me.

*Jackie enters. She notices the atmosphere.*

**JACKIE**         Sorry I just wanted my bag. I'll get it later. *(starts to leave)*
**CHANTELLE**  Is that you Jackie?
**FITZROY**       Yeah, it's OK, she's going.
**CHANTELLE**  No, I want her to stay.
**FITZROY**       Eh?
**CHANTELLE**  Tell her to stay.
**FITZROY**       But we're talking.
**CHANTELLE**  I want her to stay.
**JACKIE**         I'm still here... is there something you wanted to say?
**CHANTELLE**  Um...I *(Pause)* Fitz, would you get me a drink please.

**FITZROY**     What now? *(Chantelle nods)*
**FITZROY**     ....but we 're talking.
**CHANTELLE**  Please.
**FITZROY**     Right... OK *(He starts to leave)* Jackie, come here a
minute. *(He takes Jackie to one side)* Look, I heard you and her
had some kind of argument and she was saying you really upset
her or something.
**JACKIE**      It wasn't just...
**FITZROY**     Eh, I don't care what happened between you that's
your business, but I'm just telling you she's upset now so you just
take it easy, yeah? *(Jackie looks at him and says nothing)* You
take it easy, yeah!
**JACKIE** *(reluctantly)* Whatever.
**FITZROY**     Alright. *(To Chantelle)* I soon come back.

*He exits. Silence.*

**JACKIE**      Well... what did you want to say? I've got things I
wanna do.
**CHANTELLE**  Are you alright?
**JACKIE**      Yeah, why shouldn't I be?
**CHANTELLE**  Good.
**JACKIE**      Look, I ain't really into small talk right now, so if
that's all – *(She stops, Chantelle is sobbing)* What's the matter?
*(Tries to remain distant. Chantelle continues to cry.)* Look you
don't wanna take this thing too seriously... I ain't worried about
it. *(Chantelle sobbing becomes heavier. Jackie goes to her.)*
What, what is it, what happened? Tell me. *(Chantelle reaches out
for Jackie. Jackie hugs her.)* It's alright, it's alright I'm here...
**CHANTELLE**  He left me on my own... I was on my own up there.
*(sobs heavily)*
**JACKIE**      Sshhhh, it's alright.
**CHANTELLE**  He was just shouting with the rest of them... I was
so helpless...          I'm sorry Jackie.
**JACKIE**      No I'm sorry.
**CHANTELLE**  You can't imagine what it's like.
**JACKIE**      I can... I can imagine exactly what it's like.

*Chantelle continues to cry.*

**SCENE 2**
*Jud sits in the foyer. Enter Jackie.*

**JACKIE**          Hi.

**JUD**          Hi Jackie, you missed the meeting, you let me down, they were all expecting to see you.

**JACKIE**          Yeah I know, sorry.

**JUD**          What happened?

**JACKIE**          ....I just can't believe that fucking man!

**JUD**          Who?

**JACKIE**          Fitzroy... you know what he did, don't you? He took Chantelle to a faith healer!

**JUD**          What? Fitzroy did that? I didn't know he was into God, he doesn't seem the type. I mean he was pissed the other night!

**JACKIE**          That's 'cos he's a fucking hypocrite! It's totally messed her up, she could hardly speak, it's like she's in shock...

**JUD**          How was she when you left her?

**JACKIE**          Oh she was a lot better, but she didn't want to be left on her own, she was so scared she wouldn't let go of my hand till she fell asleep. That's why I missed the meeting, I couldn't leave her.

**JUD**          Course you couldn't. Look don't worry about it... listen, do you want to hear some good news?

**JACKIE**          Yeah go on. *(She sits)*

**JUD**          Well, basically, it's going really well, we've got four other groups involved, the Dutch lot are ninety percent on, and we've even got a couple of American delegates interested. On top of that at least two newspapers reckon they'll cover the story if it happens.

**JACKIE**          That's good.

**JUD**          The problem is we need to prove our credibility to the media so we thought we'd get a petition together, but we really need to          start getting the names down now so it would be really good if you guys could let us know soon. What's the hold up, you enjoyed the last meeting didn't you?

**JACKIE**          Even if I wanted to do it and I'm not saying I do, we'd still have to get the others involved including Fitzroy.

**JUD**          And you reckon he wouldn't be into it?

**JACKIE** Oh, what do you think after what I've just said?
*(Pause)*
**JUD** Alright.
**JACKIE** Sorry, it's just Fitzroy – he pisses me off.
**JUD** What is this big thing with Fitzroy? OK he's a bit off the mark but he's not that bad is he?
**JACKIE** You don't know him... he treats me like a little kid. Anyway, it's not just him, it's what he represents.
**JUD** What do you mean?
**JACKIE** It doesn't matter. I just can't get into that way of being, that whole small minded mentality...
**JUD** I don't get you.
**JACKIE** Well, it's all meant to be our culture isn't it? If you're black you dress a certain way, talk a certain way, think a certain way. I just can't get into that, it just don't fit me.
**JUD** Does it have to?
**JACKIE** Well, it ought to, because it's what I am.
**JUD** Well yeah, it is but that doesn't mean you've got to buy into a set of values that don't work for you.
**JACKIE** That's what I try and tell myself.
**JUD** And you're right to. Look, shut me up if I'm wrong but I get the feeling that maybe you're a little bit of a loner? *(Jackie sighs)* No, that's alright but the reason you feel like that is because you're trying to be something you're not. Look OK you're a black woman but that ain't all you are – from the day you were born right, the thing that set you apart from everybody else was your disability ...you feel alone because you don't fit into a certain culture but maybe that's because you're looking in the wrong place ...know what I mean?
**JACKIE** *(nods)* Yeah, maybe.
**JUD** Honestly Jackie, it's stupid to limit yourself by conforming. I mean what do you call yourself first, black or disabled? You've got to be where you feel comfortable.
**JACKIE** Yeah I know.
**JUD** Well, maybe it's time to move in a new direction. *(Pause. He puts his hand on her shoulder)* Eh, c'mon we got work to do. *(He pulls out a handful of leaflets)* We've got to work on the others and in the meantime you stop stalling, you know it makes sense. *(They collect their things)* Oh listen, if you're not

doing anything tomorrow night there's a load of us going into town, get out of this place. We're just gonna have a look round do a few bars ... get pissed, basically crips night out. Why don't you come along?

**JACKIE**        Yeah alright. I'll be into that.

**JUD** *(as they exit)* Bring Chantelle along, see if we can't cheer her up.

**JACKIE**        Yeah I'll ask her thanks.


**SCENE 3**

*A few days later. Fitzroy stands alone on stage. He is anxious, obviously waiting for someone. Enter Curtis.*

**CURTIS**        How is it every time I see you, you're looking for Chantelle?

**FITZROY**        I just wanted to know that's all. Is that a problem?

**CURTIS**        No, I don't know where she is. Am I her keeper?

**FITZROY**        Did I say that? *(Curtis looks around him)* What are you doing? What's the matter with you?

**CURTIS**        Nothing. It's these people... I can't even sit still for two minutes without someone wanting to push me off and give me a balloon.

**FITZROY** *(laughs)* They're just being friendly.

**CURTIS**        Nah man, I don't like it. I can't even sit and eat without someone wanting to help me.

**FITZROY**        Relax yourself, you just gotta get into it.

**CURTIS**        Like you? Getting into that JMK.

**FITZROY**        Hey, you know me. I ain't like that.

**CURTIS**        It's that Bible thing innit, Adam and Eve! That's where woman first start making trouble for man... her with the apple. He was a fool just like you, instead of the man drop two licks in her head and dash away, the apple, he stop there and lets her eat it.

**FITZROY**        Boy, you got to stop nyam so much chicken, it's affecting your head.

**CURTIS**        I'm serious, you keep following Jesus, see where it gets you. It may save your soul but you're gonna lose that nice woman.

*Peter and Jean-Marie Kellerman enter.*

**PETER**      Hey there fella, looking for some action? *(He grabs the back of Curtis' chair and starts to push him off)*
**CURTIS**     Look no... take your bloodclaart hands off me!

*They exit.*

**JMK**        Hi Fitzroy, glad I ran into you. How are you?
**FITZROY**    Alright thanks.
**JMK**        You lost someone? *(He doesn't hear her. Louder)* Fitzroy have you lost someone?
**FITZROY**    Oh no, I'm just looking out for Chantelle.
**JMK**        You mean she's left you on your own, is that wise! *(He laughs)* I think I saw her getting on the bus with some other UK delegates.
**FITZROY**    Sorry?
**JMK**        I think she's gone into town.
**FITZROY**    Oh.
**JMK**        I wondered if I might have a word, do you have a moment?
**FITZROY**    Sure. *(They go and sit.)*
**JMK**        OK well....
**FITZROY**    Oh...wait. *(He signs)* Hi, nice to see you.
**JMK**        And it's nice to see you too! That's wonderful, did you go to the group?
**FITZROY**    No, I just watched them, picked it up.
**JMK**        Great, how did it make you feel?
**FITZROY**    It's weird 'cos they seem so kinda laid back and the way they dress, they don't look, you know, they look really –
**JMK**        Sweet?
**FITZROY**    Yeah and then when they're talking... their hands... it's brilliant. They're just like a blur. There was a few of them who spoke like normal.
**JMK** *(laughs)* Did you speak with them?
**FITZROY**    No, I didn't want to and I couldn't understand them anyway.
**JMK**        Don't you think that's a shame? I know they'd like to meet you – this great dancer from the UK.

**FITZROY**       Yeah, but I'm not deaf.

**JMK**            No, you're not, you are hearing impaired.

**FITZROY**       That's right, I like that – hearing impaired.

**JMK** *(nods)* But I bet they'd still like to meet you. *(He laughs)* OK well, Fitzroy, I have to tell you that I.S.A. is selecting some of the outstanding delegates to sit with us on the main table at the Gala dinner... and I think I'd like to put your name down. Would that be alright with you?

**FITZROY**       Me?

**JMK**            Sure why not... what do you say?

**FITZROY**       Um yeah of course, I mean so long as you're sure and stuff, cos          like I don't wanna take some other person's place who deserves   it more than me. You know what I mean.

**JMK**            Yes, I know just what you mean, but having read about your work in England and now having met you, I think you're very deserving... so consider it done.

**FITZROY**       Thanks I'm really honoured.

**JMK**            Don't be, it's us who should feel honoured. I'm just wondering, have you heard anything about this so called boycott?

**FITZROY**       Boycott?

**JMK**            Yeah kind of weird isn't it? Apparently there's a group from the UK trying to jeopardise the Gala evening. Have you heard about that?

**FITZROY**        I ain't heard nothing about it. It's nothing to do with us, we're really looking forward to it.

**JMK**            But listen, we really do want to try and stop this nonsense. Will you do me a favour, and just have a chat to your group?

**FITZROY**       Yeah sure.

**JMK**            Oh that's great, thank you.

**FITZROY** *(repeat sign)* Thank you.

**JMK**            That's it.

*Lights fade.*

**SCENE 4**

*A karaoke bar. Loud music. Jud and Jackie are on stage. They sing to 'New York, New York' by Frank Sinatra.*

**JUD/JACKIE** *(sing)*
　　I'm gonna make a brand new start of it in old DC
　　And if I can be a crip out there, I'll be a crip anywhere
　　Its up to you Chantelle, Chantelle...
　　*(They kick their legs to the rhythm)*
**BOTH** *(sing)*　　Chantelle!

*Chantelle claps and cheers. They return to their table.*

**CHANTELLE**　That was great. You two were brilliant.
**JUD**　　　　Not me, it's her! Where did you get a voice like that from?
**CHANTELLE**　I know, I'm always telling her. You should have seen her at the talent night, she was great.
**JUD**　　　　You should do more of that, you don't wanna keep it in the closet. Is that what you're doing in the festival?
**CHANTELLE**　No, she hasn't got all her gear.
**JUD**　　　　Oh pity, that would have almost been worth seeing.
**JACKIE**　　I could always get an I.S.A. makeover.
**JUD** *(laughs)* You're kidding me, they don't really do makeovers?
**JACKIE**　　They do, it's in the information pack, 'Don't let disability be a barrier. If you want something extra 'special,' I.S.A. offers you the face and look you've always wanted.'
　　*(They laugh)*
**JUD**　　　　I dare you to have one done. I don't believe it... beauticians fucking body fascist, come the revolution they're against the wall, along with faith healers. You know why the church hates us so much – because we're an embarrassment to them, we're all supposed to be made in God's image so what does that make God? – A crip. *(Pause)* Hey, Chantelle.
**CHANTELLE**　Yeah?
**JUD**　　　　How many fingers? *(He holds up his palm)*
**CHANTELLE**　Eh?
**JUD**　　　　Didn't work then. *(They laugh)* This is what it's about. Wierd ain't it? When we're on our own we hate being stared at, but when there's a whole bunch of us I love it. *(He shouts across the club)* 'Oi there's pissed crips in the corner and you fuckers are scared.' Isn't it better not having to explain anything to each other, just feeling at ease.

**JACKIE**      Yeah, that's true.

**JUD**        See if we'd been allowed to put on that festival, it wouldn't be like that. In fact if we were given that amount of money to better our lives, we wouldn't be spending it in a festival, we'd be buying truck loads of cannabis and snorting coke. *(They laugh)* No seriously, we'd be sorting our inaccessible buildings, re-designing transport, pushing through legislation. That's how to improve our lives, not by ordering five thousand balloons and doing the hokey cokey. Peter Dwyer – I'd put him up against the wall and all. *(They laugh)* Alright, this is it, top ten... who are we gonna wipe out when crips come to power? We got beauticians and faith healers.

**JACKIE**      Doctors.

**JUD**        Definitely, same as faith healers. 'I can't cure you now fuck off!' ... Christmas.

**JACKIE/CHANTELLE**  Christmas?

**JUD**        It's the worst time. You spend the whole year building up your self-esteem, access, rights, liberty, feeling like you've achieved something, then you go home to your family and it's, 'Never mind, our Jud's funny legs, he's alright really.' And no one wants you to touch the babies. Yeah, families are definitely in. Who else?

**CHANTELLE**  Fitzroy's mother.

**JUD/JACKIE**  What?

**CHANTELLE**  Fitzroy's mother. I hate her, she's a witch. *(Jackie and Jud laugh)* You know what she did? Oh God, right, she took Fitzroy off on some prayer weekend, right. When he comes back he says we've got to finish, he says he's really sorry but it's over. I'm like, why? What have I done? He's almost in tears and tells me he loves someone else. I couldn't believe it, that's one thing I never suspected of him. So I'm crying now and I'm saying, why? Who is it? And he just won't tell me, he just keeps saying sorry and that he knows it's for the best. By now I'm really messed up, I've got a terrible thought in my mind of him with his ex girl friend or a different woman, then finally he breaks down and says, 'Chani... I love Jesus!' *(There is a silence. Then Jackie and Jud burst out laughing.)* *(Chantelle laughs)* Yeah, it's funny now, but at the time...

**JACKIE** *(laughter is out of control)* And this is the man you wanna marry? You should think about it.

**CHANTELLE**  Yeah, maybe...

**JUD**          Cab drivers, bastards, never turn up. 'Sorry not licensed for you lot.'

**JACKIE**      They never stop!

**JUD**          How many cab drivers does it take to change a light bulb?

**CHANTELLE**  Don't know.

**JUD**          'What all the way up there?!'

**JACKIE**      Careers teachers, 'We've got an opening in a factory testing light switches, you can do that with one hand.'

**JUD**          Social workers, 'Get rid of all that anger and bitterness, you're different but that's OK.'

**JACKIE**      Head teachers, 'Everybody, this is Jackie, now Jackie's only got one hand.' Don't fucking tell everybody! *(They laugh)*

**CHANTELLE**  I know one.

**JACKIE/JUD**  What?

**CHANTELLE**  Condensed milk in coffee.

**JUD**          Do what?

**CHANTELLE**  Fitzroy always makes it like that, I hate it.

**JUD**          That is obscene.

**JACKIE**      We need one more.

**JUD**          Oh right.

*Silence.*

**JUD/JACKIE**  ESTHER RANTZEN! *(They burst out laughing)*

**JACKIE**      That's it. I'm gonna get another drink, I'm celebrating.

**JUD**          Yeah?

**CHANTELLE**  What?

**JACKIE**      I'm in, I'm gonna do the boycott.

**CHANTELLE**  Jackie!

**JACKIE**      My mind's made up.

**JUD**          Brilliant. *(Jackie starts to get up)* No the drinks are on me, cocktails yeah?

**JACKIE**      Oh yes!

**JUD**              You up for it Chantelle? Who knows, I might be able to talk you into the boycott. God works in mysterious ways.

*Cross fade to evening recreation room. I.S.A. disco background music is heard. Fitzroy and Curtis stand alone. There are two balloons attached to the back of Curtis' chair.*

**CURTIS**        Why don't you just talk to her?

**FITZROY**      And say what? ...she knows where I am. I didn't tell her to go wondering off with other people. Chantelle must learn – she's in the wrong, not me. So it's for her to come to me.

**CURTIS**        You shouldn't play these games man, you're too old for that nonsense. Mess her about and you'll lose her.

**FITZROY**      What the hell do you know! You don't know nothing about relationships. When last did you have a woman?

*Fitzroy storms off. Silence. Curtis slowly exits. Outside. Late evening. Downtown DC. Chantelle and Jud enter.*

**CHANTELLE** *(laughing)* Jackie! Jackie. Where's she gone?

**JUD**              Oh god knows, I think she went off for a piss.

**CHANTELLE** Outside.

**JUD**              No, in the bar, back there.

**CHANTELLE** She's so drunk, she was knocking them back.

**JUD**              Yeah, she was a bit happy... you seem a bit better yourself.

**CHANTELLE** Yeah, I am thanks.

**JUD**              Did you have a good time?

**CHANTELLE** Oh yeah, I did. It was really great, I really enjoyed myself.

**JUD**              That's what happens when you get a bunch of crips together... even you seemed to be a different person tonight, bit more outgoing.

**CHANTELLE** That's 'cos I was drunk.

**JUD**              Or because you felt comfortable?

**CHANTELLE** You don't give up do you?

**JUD**              No.

**CHANTELLE**  All your friends, though, they all seem so into it... I don't know if I could be like that... wanting to be around disabled people all the time.

**JUD**   Why not?

**CHANTELLE**  I'd feel like I was stuck in the ghetto.

**JUD**   You're only in the ghetto if you feel disability makes you inferior and if you believe that you'll always be inferior.

**CHANTELLE**  But sometimes I want to be normal with normal people.

**JUD**   That will never happen, and what's normal? You went to that healer... Why? If you go there, you're saying there's something wrong, something that needs healing... there's nothing wrong with us.

**CHANTELLE**  Can you honestly say that you've never wanted to be normal?

**JUD**   I thought about it when I was a kid, but when I realised that's all I could do about it and Jim couldn't fix it, I gave up. *(Chantelle smiles)* I've got to tell you Chantelle... people, my friends, have died for this. It's not a fad, it's not going to fade away, it's a real struggle, a human rights campaign. That's what pisses me off about people who play the card, they come on marches, shout for rights, but when it suits them, when they think no one's watching, they play defenceless disabled people, 'cos they think it makes their life easier. But all it does is make it even tougher for the rest of us... no, I don't want to be so-called 'normal'.

**CHANTELLE**  Do many people play the card?

**JUD**   A lot more than will ever admit it.

**CHANTELLE**  I think I might do that.

**JUD**   Yeah, but you don't know any better. *(She cries)* What is it? ...Fitzroy?

**CHANTELLE**  Yeah and what you're saying... it's true but...

**JUD**   I know it's difficult, isn't it, I've been there. *(puts his arm round her)* Look, don't worry about Fitzroy, if he really loves you, he'll be there for you and understand, if he doesn't, then he's not the right one.

**SCENE 5**
*Rehearsal room.*

**FITZROY**      I don't believe this! What is it you're telling me? You've come all this way, practised all them weeks and now you don't want to do it?

*Jackie nods.*

**FITZROY**      Why?
**JACKIE**      I've told you.
**FITZROY**      No I ain't heard no answer, I've just heard a lot of chat about some back out.
**JACKIE**      Boycott. I've explained it twice.
**FITZROY**      Alright then I must be thick, 'cos it don't make any sense to me. Don't start with that oppression nonsense again.
**JACKIE**      It is... I just – can't explain it.
**FITZROY**      Because it don't make no sense.
**JACKIE**      It does to me.
**FITZROY**      No I'll tell you what makes sense. We were invited here by these people, they've paid for our flights, they've fed us, given us a bed, given us a chance to do something we could never have done...
**JACKIE**      We know all...
**FITZROY**      They've asked us to represent Black Britain and
that's          exactly what we're gonna do!
**JACKIE**      So you think.
**FITZROY**      So I know! ...Where's all this come from anyhow? A few days ago you couldn't wait to do it.
**JACKIE**      A few days ago we couldn't see it all for what it is.
**FITZROY**      No a few days ago you hadn't been talking to them people... yeah, you think I don't know... it's that same Jud guy, ain't it? I see a whole load of stuff... but you know what hurts me? It's not like he's a man you can respect and you lot were stupid enough to believe him.
**JACKIE**      Because you don't understand it.
**FITZROY**      I ain't got to understand it, people like him ain't got no use. They just wanna make a whole load of noise and upset people.

**JACKIE** Yeah and why?

**FITZROY** To get noticed.

**JACKIE** To get rights.

**FITZROY** Rights my ring piece. What rights is he after? Look you compare your life to other people's. Do you pay to get on a bus or tube, did you have to wait to get a council flat, you get into most things cheap, you even get given cars, there's people who'd kill to live like you.

**JACKIE** Human rights.

**FITZROY** You could give him more rights than the blasted queen, you think someone like him is gonna be happy? Never, he'd be lost, wouldn't know what to do with himself.

**JACKIE** That's what they said about us.

**FITZROY** No way, that's something different. This ain't got nothing to do with us. This is just white man's issue...

**JACKIE** What?

**FITZROY** Look, you know already how hard life is for black people. All them things you talk about, rights, equality, pride, we've been fighting for them things since way back, but we don't do it his way... if you're black you gotta play by their rules, work twice as hard as they do, do it five times better and that's when they sit up and respect you.

**JACKIE** And you think our show's gonna do that.

**FITZROY** Course, we gonna kill them with it. *(He laughs)*

**JACKIE** Nah, they're just gonna think, 'Ahh look at them, didn't we do well. Sad bunch of niggers'.

**FITZROY** That's Jud talking again.

**JACKIE** He's right and we don't wanna be a part of it.

**FITZROY** Hold up a minute who's this – we? You're not telling me that you're all into this nonsense. *(No one answers)* Oh Lord! Look you lot never even thought about any of this before... Alright I'm done talking, this thing stops right now! OK, it's finished, we're gonna do the show and that's it. *(starts to exit)* I'll see you later.

**JACKIE** It ain't as simple as that.

**FITZROY** What?

**JACKIE** It ain't that simple, we've discussed it.

**FITZROY** I don't give a damn what you discussed, there ain't gonna be no demonstration.

**CURTIS**      Yeah, but Fitz some of the things they're saying are
true.

**FITZROY**      Ah, shut up man, you can't even spell demonstration
never mind be a part of it.

**JACKIE**      You can't decide for us.

**FITZROY**      Can't I? I'm the leader. I need to be because you
people are all forgetting something – whilst you're there listening
to this guy getting head full of his politics, you're forgetting your
own people, the black people you're here to represent... are you
really prepared to let them down? Can't you see that this business
don't relate to you, there ain't one of you been oppressed by your
own people. Tell the truth has a black person ever done any harm
to you? *(Pause)* Exactly. They can't do enough for you, that's the
way we are and you know it. We don't need to go on marches
because we take care of our own. Don't forget who you are or
where you're from... Come Chantelle *(He starts to leave)*

**JACKIE** *(pause)* You think black people can only think one way?
And if we don't think like you, we ain't being black... who gave
you the right to dish out membership cards?

**FITZROY**      That ain't what I'm say –

**CURTIS**      You – you can't talk to me like that.

**FITZROY**      Eh?

**CURTIS**      See it ain't funny, you can't just put me down like
that.

**FITZROY**      C'mon Curtis, I was just fooling with you.

**CURTIS**      You're supposed to be my friend and you're treating
me the same as the other people, like I ain't worth shit.

**FITZROY**      C'mon Curtis man, I don't treat you bad.

**CURTIS**      Yeah you do... like I'm some kind of 'hop and drop'.

**FITZROY** *(laughs)* A what!

**CURTIS** *(serious)* Don't laugh at me man, it's true. There was this
guy in Jamaica right, they called him 'hop and drop' cause he had
a hunch and carried a stick for his limp. Everybody knew him,
they'd see him coming and shout, 'Hey hop and drop, wha'
'appen?' They didn't mean anything by it, that was just his name.
Hop and drop. He never paid them no mind, just went about his
business, just smiling at everyone... idiot. Then one day right, this
young girl got raped in the village. Everybody blamed him
because they said he must have been frustrated, all them years

without a woman. So some of the men, they went after him with knife and machete. Chopped him up – any other man they would have killed but 'cos he was a 'cripple,' they just took his good leg off so he couldn't get around to rape no one else. Course after that no one wanted to know him. *(Pause)* Frustrated! He was frustrated alright. One night he managed to get himself to the church in town, threw parafin on it and burn it down... killed himself. No one could work out why he'd done it, all those years he'd been such a nice man, so they said he was mad, that Satan took his mind... Bullshit, there weren't nothing wrong with the man. He was pissed off! ...You imagine in fifty years no one calls you by your name, just an insult, thinking you don't mind but that shit hurts, I'm telling you! That man, he took it, he took it all those years, 'cos he thought, 'They respect me, at least I'm accepted,' and look what they did to him.

**FITZROY**     Curtis, take it easy man, them names don't mean anything. It's just the way it goes.

**CURTIS**     Not for me! I ain't gonna have people shit on me. Respect me or fuck off. You're not doing me no favours by smiling at me and making jokes. I don't need you, I pick my friends. I don't care if you wanna cross the road when you see me... do it, it makes more room for me, *(He is in tears)* 'cos I'm a big man in here... you try and step on me and it won't be just your fucking church I burn.

*Pause.*

**FITZROY**     I didn't mean anything... my fight ain't with you.

**JACKIE**     That's the same supportive people you were just talking about. Now can you see my point.

**FITZROY**     I don't see anything... he's talking about the past. That ain't nothing to do with what you're saying.

**JACKIE**     So everything's fine now, we ain't got no problems?

**FITZROY**     That's not what I'm saying, I'm saying...

**JACKIE**     It's a white man's issue... what's white about standing up for your rights?

**FITZROY**     Nothing but...

**JACKIE**     And don't tell me we look after our own.

**FITZROY**     It's true.

**JACKIE**      Well, who the hell was looking after me 'cos that ain't my story. I know what he's talking about – the bullying, the teasing – I had it all through school and as a kid you can't understand it. You think, this ain't what my parents taught me, we're nice people. Everyday the different kids, the same jokes. You know I got quite practical about it, I knew they didn't like me so I'd go off and play on my own but they'd always hunt me down. Seemed whenever I got just a little bit happier about life, those kids would find me. You think, OK, kids will be kids, but the adults should know better, but I'd go to church on Sunday and see the same look on the adult's faces. I remember thinking if God created all man equal, why did he make me? And the answer wise sympathetic church-goers would give me, was that my parents had done some bad things in the past and this was God's punishment on them. Pray and I'd be forgiven... great, now will I grow an arm!And contrary to popular belief it didn't get better when I got older.  The kids just got more two-faced. In gangs, I was still 'hook arm stumpy' but get a few of them on their own and they wanted to experiment, get rid of their frustrations and I was always there for them. Don't be shocked. I was like any other kid, I wanted to be liked too. I could take them sticking their fingers up me and all the rest of it because it meant I belonged... it's ridiculous, I even made myself believe I was helping them, like a sort of mother figure... That's what made it even harder to take, when a group of older white girls trapped me in a classroom and forced me strip. I don't know why they did it... maybe by some kind of weird irony they were jealous of me. They tied my hand to a pipe and then called all the boys in to laugh at me, whilst I tried to get my clothes back on with my arm. The white boys I could handle. I could hit them, I could hate them but when the black guys stood there laughing with them, what was I gonna do? They're all grown up now, moved away, married, but I can't get rid of them because I still hear their laughing, when I pass a bus stop, when I go into a supermarket, when I go out. You know the laugh. I mean, you can be feeling a million dollars and you just hear it once and you know, you don't dare look back because you know it's you. Just the sight of those faces will destroy you for days and you've got to ask those *why* questions all over again.

**FITZROY**      It's not just the black people laughing.

**JACKIE**     But it's theirs that's hardest and hurts the worst... so don't expect me to embrace my wonderful people 'cos they ain't done fuck all for me. I'm a black woman and I love the fact that I am... I'm proud of my people but they ain't of me! They ain't proud of Curtis, they ain't proud of Chantelle, and they ain't proud of you, Fitzroy... Don't fool yourself, Fitzroy, you think because you talk and study your culture, that makes you a part of it? It doesn't – they decide... Oh yeah, sure they pity us and if one of us achieves something, we're a brother or sister but in between times you're just one of them funny people – a mumu.

*Silence.*

**CHANTELLE**  Do you want to go?
**JACKIE**     No, I wanna sort this thing out. *(To Fitzroy)* Can you honestly tell me you don't know what we're talking about, you've never experienced it?
**FITZROY** *(hesitates)* No... no, I haven't.
**JACKIE**     So it don't bother you when they call you 'deaf man'?
**FITZROY**    It doesn't bother me 'cos that's not what I am. I'm –
**JACKIE**     Like hell you're not. *(He starts to turn away)* Look at me Fitzroy. You know what colour you are but you don't know what you are...
**CHANTELLE**  Jackie.
**JACKIE**     If you could accept that, then you'd know what I was talking about... but you think you've got more in common     ith I.S.A. than you have with us, 'cos somehow you see yourself as a bit better than us. Our 'leader,' not quite as disabled... You say we're being led by a white man but it's not us rubbing up to that Kellerman woman.

*Enter Jud.*

**FITZROY**    You can talk all the nonsense you want. If you wanna do this        boycott shit you're on your own, 'cos the rest of us ain't having no part of it.
**JUD**        I think perhaps you ought to put that for a vote.
**FITZROY**    What?
**JUD**        I said you ought to take a vote.

**FITZROY**      Perhaps you ought to piss off and mind your own business.

**JUD**      Forever the democrate Fitzroy.

**FITZROY**      What did he say?

**JUD**      It just seems pretty straightforward. There's obviously some disagreement in the group and it's causing bad feelings, so the most sensible thing is to put it to the vote.

**FITZROY**      I don't see...

**JACKIE**      Why not? ...it's fair.

**FITZROY**      Because I'm the lead –

**JUD**      Is it that you're afraid you might lose?

**FITZROY**      I ain't afraid of nothing.

**JUD**      So let's vote.

**FITZROY**      Listen this ain't got nothing to do with you.

**JUD**      Oh I don't know... as it's me who's organising the boycott, I think I could probably argue that it's got a lot to do with me.

**JACKIE**      Let's vote, Fitzroy. *(Pause)*

**FITZROY**      Is that what everybody wants? *(No one answers)* See!

**JUD**      No one said they were against it.

**FITZROY** *(stares at him and kisses his teeth)* Let's vote.

**JUD**      OK – all those in favour of supporting the boycott. *(Jackie raises her arm)*

**FITZROY**      That's it then. *(He doesn't notice that Curtis also has his hand raised.)*

**JUD**      That's two for.

**FITZROY**      You can't vote. *(Jud points to Curtis. Fitzroy looks at him)*

**CURTIS**      Sorry man, you say he's talking rubbish, but he makes more sense than this badge and I ain't no hop and drop.

**JUD** *(quickly)* All those against.

**FITZROY** *(raises his hand)* Chantelle? *(She remains still)* You've gotta vote as well.

**CHANTELLE** I know.

**FITZROY**      C'mon then.

**JUD**      I'm not sure she's against it.

**FITZROY**      What are you talking about?

**JUD** *(softly)* Chantelle, what do you want to vote?

**CHANTELLE**  I'm not sure.

**FITZROY**  What did she say?

**JACKIE**  She said she's not sure.

**FITZROY**  What? What is this, just put your hand up.

**JUD**  That's not really how it's done mate.

**JACKIE**  You can't bully her into it.

**FITZROY**  I ain't talking about bullying anyone. I just wanna talk to her.

**JUD**  It's her decision.

**FITZROY**  Move yourself. *(He takes Chantelle's hand)* What's the matter with you?

**CHANTELLE**  Nothing.

**FITZROY**  Then why ain't you putting your hand up?

**JACKIE**  Cos she's got a mind of her own!

**FITZROY**  Is something upsetting you?

**JUD**  It could simply be that she wants to join the boycott.

**FITZROY**  Look whatever it is, we'll talk about it, we just gotta do this vote now. *(He tries to lift her hand, she resists)* Chantelle, this is important.

**JUD**  Tell him.

**FITZROY**  Tell him what?

**JUD**  That she's already agreed to take part, well practically, anyway.

**FITZROY**  No way! *(To Chantelle)* Is it true? *(She turns away from him)*

**JACKIE**  Yes!

**JUD** *(claps)*  Well done.

**FITZROY**  Wait a minute, don't bother start with that well done business. Chantelle, come here... what are you talking about? You can't be a part of this.

**JUD**  I thought we'd just established that.

**FITZROY**  Look, you just back off alright, 'cos I'm not talking to you... *(He turns to Chantelle)* So what are you saying?

**CHANTELLE**  I just think...

**FITZROY**  You mean to tell me, that you've gone off behind my back and discussed this and made a decision to follow some man you don't even know and you weren't gonna tell me about it?

**CHANTELLE**  It just...

**FITZROY**      Is that what you're saying? ...'cos I don't believe that after nearly two years together that can be possible... and now you're prepared to go against me in front of these people.

**JUD**      I don't think it's quite like that.

**FITZROY**      You move yourself. This is between me and my woman. *(To Chantelle)* ...is that what you're telling me?

**CHANTELLE**  Fitzroy...

**FITZROY**      Is that what you're telling me? ...'cos it seems to me, if that's what you're saying, then what you're really telling me is that this man's word means more to you than mine.

**CHANTELLE**  I...

**FITZROY**      And then what am I supposed to think about that? ...What does that mean? *(She doesn't answer)* Am I talking to myself here... what does it mean? I bring you over here, ask you to marry me and you spend all your time chatting to other people and shaming me in front of people... So what does that mean? ANSWER ME!

**CHANTELLE**  *(jumps)* What do you want me to say?

**JACKIE**      Leave her, Fitzroy.

**JUD**      You don't have to say anything, it was a democratic procedure and you've simply responded the way you felt best.

**FITZROY**      Who are you? Who the hell are you telling her what she can and can't do.

**JUD**      Who are you?

**FITZROY**      I'm her fiancé?

**JUD**      Oh, I forgot, that gives you parental control...

**FITZROY**      What?

**JUD**      It... don't matter, forget it.

**FITZROY**      I'm waiting for an answer Chantelle.

**JUD**      C'mon mate, leave it, you can't agree on everything.

**FITZROY**      Don't put your hand on me... Chantelle? You better answer me or the way I'm feeling, I reckon we just better forget about this engagement thing.

**CHANTELLE**  Fitzroy...

**JUD**      Don't you think that's going a bit over the top?

**FITZROY**      Shut up.

**CURTIS**      Come on, Fitzroy, you don't need this.

**FITZROY**     What I don't need is my friend turning his back on me. Is that what you want? ...Is that what you want? *(He takes her by the shoulders.)*

**CHANTELLE** *(shrugs)* Whatever.

**FITZROY** *(stunned)* What did you say?

**CHANTELLE**  Whatever... if that's what you want.

**FITZROY**     You don't mean that... you can't mean it, you're just saying it because... *(shouts)* What's the matter with you, what are you doing this for! *(Jackie moves to comfort Chantelle)* You move away from her! She don't want you. It's you who started this. *(pointing at Jud)* It's the two of you that put all this fuckery in her head. *(goes to Chantelle. Softly)* That's all this is, you've just been listening to him chatting his white man business. This ain't you talking.

**JUD**             Isn't that racism?

**FITZROY**     What?

**JUD**             Nothing.

**FITZROY**     Look, I don't know what it is you keep saying but I'm             telling you now, I've had enough of your jokes and yourlong word shit. You can fool her with it, but not me.

**JUD**             Perhaps that's because she can understand them.

**FITZROY** *(stares at Jud for a moment)* Chantelle, are you gonna side with this man against me?

**CHANTELLE**  It's not like that.

**FITZROY**     Yes it is, like that... I'm telling you, it's like that! Look, I'm giving you a chance. You can change your mind now and stop this or you can stay here with him. It's up to you... but if you stay, you can forget about everything.

**JACKIE**     That's fair.

**FITZROY**     Shut up.

**JUD**             You know what you've been feeling, it's a chance to do something about it.

**FITZROY**     You shut your mouth... *(Long pause)* ...that's it, now I'm going... are you coming?

**CHANTELLE** *(shakes her head)* I can't.

**FITZROY**     Alright... good. You stop with him, all of you carry on, follow the white man 'cos you see me, I don't business... I don't business. I know my mind... fuck it... fuck all of you... Chantelle you know how much I love you.

**JUD** *(tuts)* I thought you loved Jesus?

*The others try, but cannot suppress their laughter.*

**FITZROY** *(laughs)* You know, you're too funny. *(approaches Jud)* You're too – *(suddenly hits Jud hard across the face)* FUCKING FUNNY *(He hits him again twice, knocking him to the floor).*

*There is total confusion. Chantelle screams at Fitzroy to stop. She tries to break them up. Jackie pulls her back.*

**CHANTELLE**  Stop it!
**FITZROY**      I warned you didn't I? Told you to stop. *(hits him again)* Now you see what you've done. I'm a Christian. *(He kicks him)* A God fearing man. *(kicks him again)* You see how scared I am. *(He kicks him)* Terrified. *(kicks him)*
**JUD** *(in pain)* Jesus.
**FITZROY**      Yes my son. *(kicks him)* Go on laughing, boy... laugh now. *(kicks him)* Laugh now!
**CHANTELLE**  Fitzroy!!

*Jackie and Curtis manage to pull Fitzroy back.*

**JUD** *(struggles to his feet in pain)* Bloody ignorant bastard.
**FITZROY** *(moves towards him)* Yeah, that's me.

*Jud quickly exits.*

**FITZROY**      I'm ignorant, dark and fucking ignorant.

*He picks up a chair and hurls it across the room. Chantelle screams. Fitzroy's anger is now at himself, he pushes a table over. Chantelle terrified, tries to get out of the room. After an undignified effort, Jackie grabs her arm and guides her.*

**CURTIS**      Fitz... Fitz...

*Fitzroy ignores him and picks up another chair. Jackie beckons Curtis to get out of the room. They exit.*

**FITZROY**     I don't... business... *(throws the chair)* I don't
fucking business. *(He sits staring at the floor. Long pause.)*
Fuck it!

*Lights fade.*

**SCENE 6**
*Jean-Marie Kellerman in a large black leather office chair.*

**JMK**          You mean they're really serious about this thing?
**PETER**        It appears so, and he's got a fair amount of support.
*(hands her a petition)*
**JMK**          How many here?
**PETER**        Fifty-two I believe.
**JMK** *(hands it back to him)* Get rid of that. OK... this thing has gone
far enough. *(She dictates a memo to an unseen secretary)* Be sure
and mark this urgent Mary. *(She smokes a cigarette using a
holder)* OK. *(dictates)* "To whom it may concern, *(Pause)* In the
light of the current dissatisfaction felt by a tiny faction of the part-
icipants it has come to our knowledge that some kind of a boycott
or demonstration is being planned for ISA Gala 96. Though ISA
does not take this threat seriously we feel however it is important
to state the following: Should any delegate decide to take part in
the proposed boycott or any similar demonstration, ISA will consider this a breach of the 'good will' contract previously agreed.
Therefore, the participating group would be required to repay all
monies donated by ISA for flights, accommodation and all meal
allowances. ISA fully recognises and supports the right to free
speech but wishes to stress that money raised by ISA is done so to
enhance the lives and give opportunities to those with disabilities
and not to fund political protests..." *(Pause)* Let's see what Mr
Davies does with that. Ungrateful little shit!

*Blackout.*

**SCENE 7**
*Lights fade up on Jackie, Chantelle and Curtis. They are in
rehearsal. The recreation room.*

**CHANTELLE**  It's just not working Jackie.
**JACKIE**        It is, we've just gotta keep going at it.
**CHANTELLE**  It's too late, we don't even know what we're doing.
**CURTIS**        She's right it's just a mess.

*Enter Jud.*

**JUD** *(shouts to someone offstage)* Whatever... do what you have to
    do, just don't let them move us from the main entrance... You
    know what that bitch has done, she's got a load of no neck
    fucking neanderthal security guards to 'shift' us from the main
    entrance. We're allowed to demonstrate but in the middle of a
    fucking car park at the back of the building... No chance! We
    ain't moving. Anyway, I've come to round up the reinforcements
    ... you ready?
**JACKIE**        Oh right I – we thought it was cancelled.
**CHANTELLE**  We were just trying to get something together.
**JUD**            How do you mean?
**JACKIE**        For the Gala.
**JUD**            You mean you're going ahead with it, dropping out
    of the boycott?
**JACKIE**        Yeah I know.
**JUD**            Not, you lot as well... you gotta be kidding me, why?
    The Dutch group left. *(Pause)* ...because of that pathetic memo?
    ... no way! That's – it's nothing, it's just something she's cooked
    up to try and scare us... it's an empty threat, she can't possibly
    carry it out.
**CHANTELLE**  Yeah but...
**JUD**            But what? ...what can she do? The money's already
    spent. Come on guys you're not really giving up on me are you?
**JACKIE**        We don't want to.
**JUD**            Course you don't.
**JACKIE**        We have to.
**JUD**            Well, that doesn't sound like the Jackie of two days
    ago... eh. And you Chantelle, c'mon!
**JACKIE**        We can't Jud.
**JUD**            What's the problem?

**JACKIE**       What she said... we come from a little community centre. If I.S.A. got heavy about the money, we'd close down, we ain't a funded organisation like you.

**JUD**            We've been through that – the chances of her doing anything are next to nothing. Look, I'm taking the same risk.

**CURTIS**       Yeah, but you're not black.

**JUD**            Do what? Oh c'mon change the record... you're not gonna hide behind that are you? Get a grip will you, the fact is there's disabled people out there now, trying to do something and they need your help. Colour ain't got nothing to do with it, we're all in the same boat. Race isn't an issue in disability politics. It's about being there when it matters... don't let them win this.

**CHANTELLE** We still want to be part of it.

**JACKIE**       We're just gonna do it a different way.

**JUD**            And you think going out there is going to help? C'mon, people will be arriving soon. *(pause)* Curtis, my man, let's go, eh. *(Curtis shakes his head)* Oh for fuck's sake, what is it with you lot? They can't hold you responsible for the money – it's not you that's liable, it's the organisation – the leader, it's Fitzroy's problem, not yours. Shit, they're starting to move us now... are you lot coming or not? *(They don't answer)* Please! *(no answer)* Fine, you hide behind your excuses, we'll fight, we'll do all the work and you can reap the benefits. See ya! *(starts to leave)* But you know, the one thing that pisses me off about all this, that really surprises me is that you'd have thought that being black and disabled, you'd have more reason to rebel than anyone else. You've got double the cause, but instead you're running scared, you're... you're letting yourselves down. *(starts to leave)*

**JACKIE**       Eh, wait. Is that right? Since when did black people need lessons from a white man on how to rebel?

**CURTIS**       Tell him.

**JACKIE**       Read your history, we've been doing it since time.

**JUD**            But not now?

**JACKIE**       No, because we can't be that selfish.

**JUD**            And I am?

**JACKIE**       I mean one minute Fitzroy's your disabled brother, now you're happy to drop him in it.

**JUD**            What's the sudden loyalty to Fitzroy, a couple of days ago you were at his throat.

**JACKIE**     Because he was wrong!

**CURTIS**     Don't get confused man, it don't matter what he's done, I'd take him before you, every time.

**JUD**     Why's that, because he's your friend or just because he's black? How hypocritical can you get, I'm sorry but my feeling is, you side with the enemy, you die with them, whether you're black, green, yellow or red. Don't let colour cloud your judgement.

**JACKIE**     Don't let it cloud yours! You're talking to us like we just wandered off the plantation, like we don't know our own minds. Just because you think our music's great, vote labour, wanna save the rainforest and got gay mates, you think that makes you immune to being a racist. Well, you watch yourself because you're getting damn close.

**JUD**     Well, that's rich coming from you, Jackie. A few days ago, you weren't sure you wanted to be black.

**JACKIE** *(pause)* You bastard... I didn't say that.

**JUD**     That's how it sounded. *(Pause)* So that's it... I'm a selfish racist. *(Pause)* Is that what you all think? *(Pause)* I don't believe this... you're so wrong... you're all missing the point.

*He exits.*

**JACKIE** *(angry)* Why didn't you two say anything! Have I always got to do it? I'm sick of wet nursing you two. Right, I know what I'm doing and I'm going on there tonight, I don't care what you do, you can suit yourselves. *(starts to exit)*

**CURTIS**     Jackie.

*Lights fade.*

**SCENE 8**
*Sound effect of applause. It is the Gala evening, the atmosphere is one similar to that of the 'Oscars' only on a much smaller scale. In the blackout, an announcement is heard.*

**ANNOUNCER** Ladies and gentlemen, I.S.A. welcome you to GALA 96. Tonight is indeed a 'special' night because this evening, we the able-bodied take a metaphorical back seat and

allow the disabled to take the wheel, as we sit back and admire
the talents, pay tribute and salute our disabled friends. Ladies and
gentlemen, your host for the evening from the motion picture, "I
danced with Helen Keller," star of TV and film, Hollywood's own
William Foster!

*Loud applause. Cut to video of William Foster. Cross fade to
Chantelle dance. Chantelle performs a solo dance piece (to 'I wish'
by Nina Simone). It is a strong, emotional and extremely physical
piece. When the dance is complete there is a snap blackout. Lights
fade up. Backstage Jackie applauds. Chantelle enters. Followed by
Curtis.*

**CHANTELLE**  Was it alright?
**CURTIS**  Wicked!
**PETER**  Did you enjoy it?
**CHANTELLE**  Yeah...Yeah I did. I really enjoyed it.
**PETER**  Your friends are over there.
**CURTIS**  She was really good.
**PETER**  Curtis you're on.
**CURTIS**  Backside! *(He exits)*

*In the background we hear rap music.*

**CHANTELLE**  Good luck Jackie... hurry up, Curtis has gone on.
I can't believe I just did that, I was so nervous before, but it just
all went away. I felt brilliant, all those people... listen, I'm really
sorry I made all that fuss, I was just scared, I really didn't think
I could do it without him... but I did, I'm really glad we changed
it.
**FITZROY**  Chani.
**CHANTELLE**  We didn't think you wanted to do it, didn't think
you were coming.
**FITZROY**  No I wasn't really interested. I didn't come for that, I
was just watching, let you guys get on with it.
**CHANTELLE**  We really wanted to do your act but –
**FITZROY**  But you're glad you changed it. *(Silence)* No, you...
you looked good up there... you wouldn't have known it was
supposed to be both of us... you were... *(Pause)* Are you alright?

**CHANTELLE**  Yeah.

**FITZROY**  I had to go off, chill for a bit, you know, sort my head out... um... um Chani... I'm sorry about what happened, fighting that guy and everything.

**CHANTELLE**  That's alright.

**FITZROY**  I just lost my temper.

**CHANTELLE**  It dosen't matter.

**FITZROY**  I think I just got a bit scared you know, that you and well... you just took me by surprise you know, I didn't know what was going on. *(Pause)* Anyhow, I think it's best that we both forget it, yeah? *(Silence)* Chani, I think...

**CHANTELLE**  I don't know.

**FITZROY**  Don't start that up again. You worry me when you do that, it's like I don't know you... now I'm saying that I'm sorry and didn't mean all them things I said about us breaking up.

**CHANTELLE**  I'm not bothered about what you said.

**FITZROY**  Then what is it? *(She shakes her head)* Chani, tell me yeah, I can't –

**CHANTELLE**  You – you said it was good, my dance.

**FITZROY**  What? ...yeah, it was.

**CHANTELLE**  I don't know whether it was or not... but I really enjoyed it.

**FITZROY**  That's good.

**CHANTELLE**  ...and maybe it was because I was doing it for myself... on my own.

**FITZROY**  OK, that's alright, whatever you want to do, I'll help you with it, you know that.

**CHANTELLE**  I – I don't want help.

**FITZROY**  Alright, whatever, let's just sort this thing out.

**CHANTELLE**  It's not gonna work.

**FITZROY**  Don't be saying that, course it is, it was working before... you were happy.

**CHANTELLE**  I thought I was.

**FITZROY**  Oh Jesus, what? What is this?

**CHANTELLE**  I don't know... what would you say, if I said I didn't want to see –

**FITZROY**  What?

**CHANTELLE**  Because that's how I felt when I went to that Healer.

FITZROY     I only did that for you.

CHANTELLE  I know but it's got me confused. I couldn't work out why I was so scared.

FITZROY     I shouldn't of pushed you.

CHANTELLE  No, I wanted to do it... *(Pause)* I've always wanted to see, but when that man was trying to take my blindness away from me, I didn't want to let go, I couldn't say yes because...

FITZROY     Don't say that.

CHANTELLE  It's true. It's you who needs me to see Fitzroy, not me.

FITZROY     Don't Chantelle, you're just upsetting yourself.

CHANTELLE  I want you to love me as I am.

FITZROY     I do, I just want us to be together properly.

CHANTELLE  That's what I mean. You can only see it as a problem.

FITZROY     How else must I see it?

CHANTELLE  I don't know, but I don't want to think like that. I can't, not now.

FITZROY     Chantelle...

CHANTELLE  I don't want to go back to all that.

FITZROY     All what?

CHANTELLE  Being owned by you.

FITZROY     What? I don't own you.

CHANTELLE  You do! You're always telling me what I can and can't do, what's right for me, what's the right way to think. I know you only do it to help me and I'm really grateful but...

FITZROY     I don't want you to be grateful, I just want us to stay together, you mean everything to me.

CHANTELLE  I know but we can't hide behind each other.

FITZROY     I don't understand what you're saying. I'm not hiding.

CHANTELLE  You are Fitzroy, we both are. We're scared of what's out there, you won't admit it. That's why it hurts you so much when it happens, you need me because everyone got to respect a man who's good enough to be with a blind woman and no one canget at you... I'm sorry, I half wish I didn't feel like this and thateverything could be alright.

FITZROY     It can. *(She shakes her head)* Oh god this... no this ain't right, this don't make sense, it's wrong... this thing was

important to me you know, all I was... I wanted us to do
something out there tonight, something strong, show people I was
just trying to make you lot proud of yourselves, Jesus! ...I know
what I am, Chantelle, I ain't an idiot, I know how it is... that's
what I mean innit, where am I gonna find someone else? *(He
starts to cry)* I ain't proud, I'll beg you...

**CHANTELLE**  Don't Fitzroy.

**FITZROY**       Alright, just answer me straight. *(Pause)* OK, I don't
care if the answer's 'yes', I just want to know – is it Jud? Are you
saying all this because you want to be with him? *(Pause)*

**CHANTELLE**  Fitzroy... No, I don't want him... I love you.
*(Fitzroy moves forward. He hugs her. They kiss for a moment.)*
*(She moves her face away)* No Fitzroy...

**FITZROY** *(persists)* Please Chant –

**CHANTELLE**  No Fitzroy, stop! I don't want him but I don't want
you either. I don't want anyone... I'm sorry...

*Silence.*
*Lights fade.*


**SCENE 9**
*Jackie enters (to the sound of "Respect" by Aretha Franklin), she
mimes and dances to the song, impersonating famous female soul
singers.*

**JACKIE** *(during the music break, slight USA accent)*
Hello D.C. Wooah! I'm feeling hot tonight... oh yeah. How you
all doing? Woooh! *(Music ends)*
Thank you, Miss Aretha Franklin,
Well, here I am and I ain't taking no prisoners! Well, what do you
think? An improvement eh? Well, I got myself an I.S.A.
make over, isn't that something, they really know their stuff.
Well, I have to tell you I'm really happy to be here tonight. I've
been called all kinds of stuff in my life, I've been called nigger,
I've been called bitch, I've been called slag, but it's OK now,
because I'm 'special'! ... and that's the worst thing I've ever been
called. You know, there are some people outside who didn't want
to be a part of this evening and I'm sure they want to know why I
came out here tonight... Miss Kellerman, you say you believe in

the right to free speech... well, I'm taking it, so this goes out to you, blue eyed, pale skin, ironing board backside straight up, straight down no frills, no thrills Miss six o'clock figure Kellerman. WE DON'T DIG THIS SHIT! OK, you heard it here first, and straight from the horse's mouth! Well now, I see a lot of famous people here tonight, important people, big profiles, oh yeah! Well, I've sat on bigger than that! Don't look so innocent you can't fool me, some of you kinky fuckers are into this stuff, know what I mean? *(She makes an obscene gesture with her arm)* Yeah, look at you squirming in your seats, you know who you are, don't you? ... laughing in the streets, jerking off in your bedrooms. Who would be a woman today, huh? Who would be a black woman today? Who would be a black disabled woman, who would be me? Anybody out there screw a black disabled woman? C'mon don't be shy ... no? Well, my uncle has many times. Uncle Benji, what can I say about him? ... how can I describe him? ...he was a damn fool and I mean stupid, if you don't believe me, I'll tell you how fool he was... him and his wife were obviously having some trouble in bedroom – he couldn't get it up basically, so she told him to go to the doctor. So after a lot of persuading he went, because you know how our black men are, they're proud... Anyway, when he came back from the doctor his wife saw him coming down the street and the man was dressed up in suit and tie, top hat, the whole business and his wife said to him, *(Jamaican accent)* 'Benji, wha' happen why you look so?' and Uncle Benji said, *(Jamaican accent)* 'Well the doctor tell me I'm impotent, so I must dress important.' Oh yes, that was Uncle Benji. He was my favourite, he always made me laugh and what a man love soup. Every time I'd see him, he'd be going home for soup. 'Me fancy a little soup today'. Even on Sunday he'd say to his wife, 'But you can't put a little to one side'. When he couldn't get his soup he'd get really upset so he'd say to me, 'Come Jackie,' we'd go to bottom of the garden to my dad's shed, and he'd say, 'Now this is our special soup, go on Jackie stir it up.' But it was difficult for me because I couldn't get hold of the zip, but he'd always help. 'That's it baby, stir it good, stir it, stir it... don't spill it now! Drink it up, don't waste the special punch, don't waste it.' *(She is crying. She shifts)* Anyway... years later, they gave me a metal hook, you know to grip things and I always thought... come Uncle Benji, let me mix you one fucking soup now. I told my mother about it but she said I was lying,' What man would want you?' What with that and all the teasing ridicule I went through, I thought, how can I embrace my wonderful people after what they've done to me? *(Pause. She sings slowly and emotionally)* What... you want... baby, I got it... What you need baby, I got it... all I'm asking is, give a little RESPECT, when I come home baby R.E.S.P.E.C.T., that is what you give to... me. *(Pause)* People ask me why I'm so bitter, what do I want? ... there's your answer. Hey, but that's over now, right? Because finally you guys like me, I've come out here tonight, I've achieved something and that makes me acceptable. Well, tell me something will you please? ...what the hell did you ever achieve in order to be accepted? ... *(calmly)* but now I'm allowed in the club after twenty-five years, I'm finally in with my brothers and sisters, but you know what, until you change your attitudes, we're gonna have to stay distant cousins because I – we don't want you any more than you want us... I'm glad you liked our little performance and I'm pleased to know you like me... but fuck you, fuck you all because you're too late! *(She pulls off her wig)* I don't want your applause, I don't want your appreciation, I don't want your sympathy ...you're too fucking late.

*Pause. She walks offstage, leaving the spotlight to shine on her disgarded wig and microphone.*

**SCENE 10**
*Fitzroy is on the phone.*

**FITZROY**      There is... there's always someone there... sorry? Hello, what? ...I can't ...I can't hear you, look, I just wanna talk to my mother. *(He slams down the receiver)*

*Enter Jean-Marie Kellerman.*

**JMK**          Hello Fitzroy.
**FITZROY**      Oh, ... er hello ... look about what happened ...
**JMK**          Don't say another word ... actually it was quite entertaining .... I rather enjoyed your fiancée's little dance

number, it looked like she was having a good time and that's always great to see.

**FITZROY**   Yeah. *(Pause)*

**JMK**   How is Jackie?

**FITZROY**   OK, I think.

**JMK**   Oh good .... poor thing, she really looked upset on there tonight. It's annoying you know, because the speakers went down at that point and we really couldn't get a lot of what she was saying. I think perhaps she should talk to someone, you know...maybe get a little bit of help, she really does seem very confused and under a lot of stress. *(Pause)* Well, I've got to go.

**FITZROY**   Look I'm really sorry we didn't do our piece, I –

**JMK**   Please Fitzroy, don't apologise. I've spoken to my colleagues and we've agreed there are to be no repercussions on you or your group. You really mustn't feel badly about this whole business. It was quite clear to me that you didn't instigate it.

**FITZROY**   Yeah?

**JMK**   Of course... someone like you would never be behind a radical     outburst like that. *(She smiles)* I really must get to the dinner,     they'll be wondering what happened to me.

**FITZROY**   Yeah, it won't take me two seconds, I'll just get changed and I'll be right there.

**JMK**   Oh, you know Fitzroy, I gave it some thought and I decided it would be a real shame to break up your group, it being your last night and all. So I've arranged for you to sit at your own table, I thought you'd be more comfortable there, am I right?

*Pause.*

**FITZROY**   Sure .... yeah, thanks.

**JMK**   OK, well you have a great party and a safe flight. *(She holds out her hand)* It's been wonderful meeting you.

*Fitzroy slowly shakes her hand. She exits. He stands motionless for a while. Then he attempts to clear the stage, eventually he sits heavily on the steps. Long pause. Slowly he wipes the white make-up from his face, as the lights fade.*

*The end.*

## Ray Harrison Graham

Trained at Webber Douglas Academy. As resident Writer/Director of the *Pegasus* Theatre Company, he wrote his first two plays *A Way of Life* and *YOP*. Four years later, his widely acclaimed play *Gary*, won a fringe first at Edinburgh, prior to a West End run.

His other plays include: *Lost in the Night,*(Tour) *Spirit of a Clown, The Dreamcatcher,* (Unicorn Arts*), Question of Colour.* (Basic Theatre Co.)

His first Television Drama *Strong Language* was nominated for a BAFTA and won prizes at the Turin Film Festival and the Japan Prize. For his second drama *Dream On*, based on his early childhood, he finally won a BAFTA and also the Royal Television Society Award. Most recently, he has been writing and directing the second series of *Rush,* his ground-breaking new drama for Channel 4.

# Fittings: The Last Freak Show

## Fittings: The Last Freak Show.

For me, *Fittings* began on a sunny day in 1996, when Garry Robson, Jenny Sealey, Caroline Parker and I were working on a play for Special Schools. Garry and I got talking about Chang and Eng Bunker, the original Siamese twins, about whom I'd written a play. We both revealed a fascination with the whole subject of freak shows. It seemed to be a subject whose time had come again – with the current obsession with the body in all its forms and the prurient fascination with the minutiae of other people's lives. But this show would never have been what it was without the generous opening up of the actors from Grae*ae*, who showed me their family album.

**Mike Kenny**

The play began life originally as a fusion of theatre and a visual art exhibition. Working with the co-director of our company, Felicity Shillingford, and with the support of North West Arts Board and The Arts Council of England, we developed a work in this style that initially explored the fusions of steel, skin, latex and leather – the 'fittings' that many disabled people use to help them negotiate their way around what is largely an alien environment. From this, it became clear that an everyday experience for many disabled people, is to be stared at – in someone's wonderful phrase, 'Me and Madonna get looked at when we walk into a room' – from there it was a short roll to consider what it was like to be exhibited, and from there a minor lurch to reclaim from the dustbin of history what was one of the few job opportunities for crips in past times – The Freak Show.

Freak Shows, with their combination of dead and alive exhibits, feisty theatricality and the questions they raised about voyeurism and power, were the ideal platform for the work. Then to make all our dreams come true, we needed a lovely company with touring experience to work with; enter stage left Ms Sealey and the hordes of Grae*ae*, and then a lovely writer to help the spirit become flesh; enter stage right Mr Kenny. The rest, as they say, is history and reclaimed and reinterpreted history at that. Reflect and enjoy.

**Garry Robson, Artistic Director, Fittings mma.**

# Fittings: The Last Freak Show

## Mike Kenny

This play was first performed on 17th June, 1999 in a tent at
Staunton Country Park, Havant, Hampshire with the following cast:

| CHARACTERS | CAST |
| --- | --- |
| **Gustav Drool** | Garry Robson |
| **Christian** | Jamie Beddard |
| **Avia** | Lisa Hammond |
| **Aqua** | Karina Jones |
| **Hans** | Caroline Parker |

Directed by Jenny Sealey & Garry Robson
Designer Felicity Shillingford
Lighting Designer Ian Scott

*Note:*
*The play is intended to reproduce the atmosphere of an old touring
Freak show. It toured in a large tent and was accompanied by an
exhibition of work by Felicity Shillingford. The 'freaks' themselves
were presented as living exhibits, much in the way that they would
have been in the days of Barnum and Bailey. They were their own
acts. 'Fittings' uses this and deconstructs it for our times. The
exhibits look back at the spectators. In this case the acts were the
biographies of the characters and were worked on with the actors
who played them.*
    *To further blur the edges between artifice and reality, there was a
pre-show outside the tent, encouraging the audience in. The stage
was also the backstage.*

**ACT ONE**
*Sound of a fanfare.*

**GUSTAV**      Ladies and gentlemen, what we are about to show
you is not for the faint-hearted. Let me emphasise that this is the
final, positively the *last* tour of the *last* official freak show on the

face of this planet. In this tent, I promise you, wonders and
marvels. There are monsters and prodigies – creatures who live in
the shadows, outside the limits of your imagination. No fakes, No
fiddles, no forgeries and no farting about. Just bona fide freaks,
madam. *(He introduces the freaks)* Catch it while you've still got
the chance – we may not be here long. Who needs a hall of
mirrors, when you've got us? Catch a view of your perfect world
in the mirror of our imperfections. Don't worry. We won't bite
you, (though we may give you a nasty suck.) Did I say suck? Do
you want to touch my internal organs miss?
*(Inside the tent, Gustav sings/speaks)*

SONG: SPARTA *(partly spoken)*
Oh I started out in Sparta
And I'm getting to the end
The detritus that you call scum
I number them amongst my friends

Yes, you can kill the messenger
If you don't like what he says
There's no need to ask permission
It's a very long tradition
I'll think you'll find
No one will mind
Or try to bar your way

.

But when I turn up as messenger
Before my message's said
I'm just about to say it loud
I've always liked to work a crowd.
They say, no fear
Don't want to hear...
Invariably, I wind up dead

How's it going?
It's going pretty fine.
You show me yours
Before you get a look at mine.
You can come in through the front
Or I can sneak you round the back

Take a look at me
What d'you feel about what you see
Maybe before you go
You'd like to know the things I know.

**GUSTAV**   It's been a long time coming but we're drawing to
the end. (The detritus that you call scum, I number them amongst
my friends.) I was born in a far off place and time in Sparta. In
my day, if you didn't like the message, you'd kill the messenger.
No unions, see. In my case, they didn't like the look of the
messenger. *(Pause)* 'Oi, ugly! You can't have anything to say,
that we want to hear. – Die.'
They didn't want to hear my message, so they exposed me at birth
on the chill, chill hills of my homeland. *(Pause)* But I came back.
In Rome, they threw me to the wolves. Lions was for Christians.
To cut a long story short, and not wanting to rub your noses in it –
I've been enslaved, incarcerated, mocked and ignored. I've been
experimented on, sterilised and gassed and I'm currently gazing
through the bars at the paint cracking on orphanage walls from
Bow to Beijing. I guess you could say I was pissed off... and I
still haven't got to give me message. *(Pause)* Well this is your last
chance. This is the message. But it's in code. *(Pause)*
Look this way. *(To the freaks)* Alright, you lot. I'm paying you.
Earn it. *(To Avia)* You're going to have to fly. For real. New
Year's Eve.

**AVIA**      No.
**GUSTAV**   Work with me.
**AVIA**      That's private. It's not for sale.
**GUSTAV**   Then hatch an egg.

*Sound of another fanfare.*

**GUSTAV** *(introduces Avia)*
Ladies and gentlemen and fellow sufferers. Rest your head in the
bosom of the clouds and let your fears flutter away. I am proud –
no – deeply honoured to present to you the delights of seven
continents. The Mistress of the Skies – Part Woman, Part Bird.
Before your very eyes she will soar unaided across the roof of the
tent, twisting and turning as she pirouettes through her kingdom.

The Kingdom of the Air. Finally to rest, hovering inches before
your eyes. Ladies and Gentlemen. I give you the Feisty, Fantast-
ical First Lady of the Air. Avia – the Bird Woman.

**AVIA** *(perched on a swing in a giant bird cage.)*
Well, the name's Jane.
Avia's a stage name.
Surprisingly.
There's not many Avias where I come from.
Council estate.
Youngest of five.
My mother always used to call me her little sparrow.
I was beloved.
Then at puberty I started getting bumps.
Two at the front and two at the back.
I thought – What!!?
My brother always said I couldn't tell my arse from my elbow
I thought they were tumours –
I was going to die.
I couldn't ask...
Things you don't talk about in a freak's family:
Births, Marriages and Deaths
They're all dodgy areas.
Birth: 'Oh my God, what did I do wrong? If I hadn't had that fag,
took that pill... Will it live? Depends on what you call living.'
Marriage: 'You mean they have sex...? Children they can't see?
How will they find them? Got no hands... changing nappies –
Nightmare.'
And Death: Well, you know... *we* die.
Nobody else does, apparently.
Anyway, I started bleeding. I'd been warned about this. But –
from my *shoulder blades*?
What was I going to do? Stuff my bra with bog roll and put it on
backwards?
So I thought I'd have a butchers.
I climbed up on the dressing table, turned my back to the big
mirror, and looked in my make up mirror. Sure enough – blood.
But not a lot. And sticking out of the middle – a feather!
I wasn't going to die. I was going to fly.
Well, it was three months waiting for them to grow and a lot of

hard flapping before I got off the bed. I'd be crashing into walls and sweating. My sister would be shouting: 'Mam, our Jane's at it again!' Me mam would run in and shout to me dad. 'Des, give us a hand with Jane. She's fallen out of bed again.'

Of course, the day came when I got stuck on the top of the wardrobe. Me mam looked at me. 'How did you get up there, our Jane?'

'I flew, Mam.'

'Don't take the piss. You're covering up for one of your brothers aren't you?'

'No, Mam.'

Then she was off. 'Who left Jane on the wardrobe? It's not funny. You'll be laughing on the other side of your face. Have this.' Smack. 'Do you want another one?' etc.

Anyway, they put me back to bed. Me mam gave me a kiss. And I said, 'Mam... Can you leave the window open? It's a bit hot.'

'Of course, lovey', she said.

And as soon as the door closed, I threw back the covers and I was flapping. Out through the window and soaring out over Norris Green – well, not soaring exactly... I'm not a Golden Eagle, and I was red in the face with the effort. But I was flying and I was out. I was looking in through all the windows. I knew who was doing what – and who with...

It was fucking fantastic!

It was like watching *Eastenders* with the sound turned off.

Well I was hooked. I was there every night. Flapping. I had shoulder blades like a brick shit house. *(Pause)*

Then one summer night... I seen Brenda at the pub shagging Norman from number four for the umpteenth time when her Sid was on an away quiz night and I thought: 'I've been given the precious gift of flight and what am I doing with it? I'm watching others living their lives.' And I caught a whiff of vanilla essence from the biscuit factory. And I thought: 'I don't want to be watching – I want to be living. And you can watch me if you like. For money. I'm off.'

I tagged on to a group of Canada Geese who were heading South for the winter... I was shagged out by Thornton Heath, but it was a start... *(descends from her cage and starts to take photographs of the audience.)* This isn't the only string to my bow.

In my spare time I'm doing a PhD in Freakology.
Roll up, roll up! In the old days there were five basic classes:
Your natural freaks – midgets, pinheads, bearded ladies and the
like...
Your self-made – tattooed men, jolly fat people etc.
Novelties – snake charmers, contortionists...
Exotics – you don't get many of these, these days They used to
get Inuit and parade them around. People get out more and telly's
put a stop to it.
And fakes – (That mermaid is a fake)
I'm wondering about additions – the ones due to medical fuck-
ups... And the ones due to social fuck-ups – nuclear fall out etc.

*Gustav is looking worried – he's looking at the books. Avia is still
taking photos.*

| | |
|---|---|
| **AVIA** | What you looking at? |
| **GUSTAV** | You need a new act. |
| **AVIA** | What's wrong with you, shit face? |
| **GUSTAV** | Money. |
| **AVIA** | Need help spending it? |
| **GUSTAV** | Not enough of it. Now shut your ugly trap. Let me think. |
| **AVIA** | He loves me really. Look at me. Smile *(She takes a photo)* I think you fucking broke it. Bastard. |
| **GUSTAV** | Shut up. What are you looking at? |
| **AVIA** | I wish I knew. |
| **AVIA** | Where are we going then? |
| **GUSTAV** | Up our own arses. |
| **AVIA** | Again? |
| **GUSTAV** | We gotta do something or we'll fold. This'll be the last one. |
| **AVIA** | You've been telling them that for years. |
| **GUSTAV** | Yeah, well this time, it's true. They don't approve of us. We're exploitative. They aren't coming any more. I'm thinking of heading for the Millenium Dome, might pick up a bob or two. What you think? |
| **AVIA** | What? You've seen the best that humankind can offer – now come and feast your eyes on the alternative. |

GUSTAV    It won't be enough. Anything else you can do?

AVIA    What do you suggest?

GUSTAV    You're not scary enough.

AVIA    I scare Christian.

GUSTAV    Bambi would scare him. But *they're* (the punters) not scared of you. They're sorry for you. You're not freaky enough. You're not. We're competing with Jerry Springer.

AVIA    I'll show them the family album.

GUSTAV    I'm trying to keep this show on the road and all you've got to offer is the family album?

AVIA    They love it.

GUSTAV    They don't. It's shit.

AVIA    It's full of freaks.

GUSTAV    No offence, love, but... you see one, you've seen them all. We need something fresh.

AVIA    That's Aqua's province. Flipper the Slapper.

*Sound of another fanfare.*

GUSTAV *(introduces Aqua)*
Fresh from the darkest depths of the Ocean. A Flower from the deepest pools of our Forbidden History. The Eternal Temptress. The Siren call to man's most primitive desires. Mothers, daughters, wives – lock up your husbands, brothers and sons. For tonight. For one night only... A soupcon of disgust and desire. A beautiful woman's naked body joined to the slender slitheriness of a fish's tail. *(Pause)* Men – she will be your downfall. Beware our own babe with a tail. I give you – her slipperiness. Aqua. Princess of the Deep.

AQUA *(lying in a large aquarium. She's clearly drunk)*
I'm Aqua, Princess of the Ocean, found washed up on a beach where a handsome fisherman found me, kissed me and my tail disappeared.
On land I can walk.
A drop of water will restore my tail
(Gustav thought of that.)
He's got an eye for a good tale. (tail.)
My father was a sailor
And my mother was a seal

And that's why I drink like a fish.
So...
Me.
Only child. Family – religious nutters
I was twelve... got pregnant...
Only found out when I miscarried...
Mother screamed.
Father beat me.
The devil had entered me.
They bound my legs together
Dumped me in the canal.
*(Pause)*
I lived.
Woke up in hospital.
All over the tabloids...
'The Mermaid Girl.'
My dad was the dad.
They banged up my mum and dad.
Oh god, I've got to get a new story...
Am I boring you?
 I'm certainly boring me.
So...
Gustav saw my picture in *The Star*.
Came to see me.
Gave me a job.
And a new family.
He was my new dad...
Same as the old dad...
So here I am
I sit in a tank.
I dance around.
I have an hour or two
Then Gustav lines them up
To come and discover the treasures of the deep.
I suppose I could run away
But every time I try
Gustav throws water on my legs
And it turns into a tail again.
*(Pause)*

I'm your ideal woman –
Piss on me and I'm flat on my back.

**AVIA**     I knew it.
She's a metaphor
I can't stand metaphors.
You are not a freak.
A real freak.
You're a metaphor.
I could see it coming a mile away.

**AQUA**     Oh and you're not, I suppose?

**AVIA**     No way. I'm not a metaphor.
I'm a phenomenon.
You see, you can go either way with me.
Physical state outside –
Could be evidence of evil within –
Richard the Third
Rumpelstiltskin
Or holy fool
Quasimodo.
But then, I've got wings.
I can fly.
Am I an angel?
More spiritual than you lot?
Just visiting?
Feel the breath from my fluttering wings, then I move on.
Stick that lot together and you're spoiled for choice.
I'm a star.
You cannot view me metaphorically without getting in a right old
shit-hole of a state.

**AQUA**     What about those wings? Aren't they metaphorical?

**AVIA**     What do you mean by that?

**AQUA**     Well I've never felt the breath from them.

**AVIA**     At least, I've got an act. You've just got a couple of
episodes of *Eastenders*.

**AQUA**     At least, mine's true.
*(She sings)*

SONG: THE REAL ME
When I was a little girl
When I thought I'd start to grow
And my mother promised me
Somebody would love me so

They would see the real me
There would be no need to hide
There'd be someone who would find
The person that's inside.
When you take a look at me.
What is it you think you see?
Do you think you'll ever find
The person that's inside my mind?

I don't want to hurt your feelings
Please don't take this personally
There's no question that I love you
But I don't think you're right for me.

What do you think about my size
My hair, my hands, my legs, my eyes?
Am I as beautiful as her?
Are there bits you would prefer?

Now I know my mother lied
There is just nowhere to hide
It's okay, you won't hurt my pride
There's no person that's inside

This is me – the one you see
I won't fall apart you see
You won't have to pick up the pieces
And I won't take it personally.

What you get is what you see
You're looking at the real me.
What you get is what you see
You're looking at the real me.

**GUSTAV**     Right, you lot. I've sold your bodies to science. I
didn't get much for you. And I'm changing the show. We'll make
more money if they laugh at you. I need you to be victims. Aqua,
can you stumble around and bump into things?

**AQUA**     Why?

**GUSTAV**     You're supposed to be blind, act like it.
*(To Christian, who has emerged from his box; a large, travelling
trunk with a distorting mirror inside. The image in the mirror is
Gilbert, Christian's twin.)* You – sick boy. What do you do?

**CHRISTIAN**     I wobble.

**GUSTAV**     You wobble? Anyone can wobble. Dribble too.
What about Gilbert? What's he do?

**CHRISTIAN**     He looks after me.

**GUSTAV**     Is he your appliance? *(He does something
disrespectful to Gilbert.)*

**CHRISTIAN**     Don't.

**GUSTAV**     Oooh. That got a reaction *(He does some more.
Christian starts to get really upset. After a while he stops.)* Oh yes
we can use that. They'll turn out for that. Kick away the crutch.
Stamp on the specs. Hide the batteries for your hearing aid.
Puncture the tyres on your wheelchair. Paint your white stick
black. Rust up your callipers. Oh yes... *(Turning to Avia.)* And
you. You're out.

**AVIA**     What?

**GUSTAV**     Since when has deafness been your particular
impairment? Get out. You're sacked.

**AVIA**     I'm top of the bill.

**GUSTAV**     I can't afford you. On your way.

**AVIA**     But... You can't. Where would I go?

**GUSTAV**     Not my problem.

**AVIA**     Please... don't do this. Don't. How will I cope? How
will I manage? Don't do this. You can't do this. Who will sort my
medication? Who will change my colostomy? Who will lift me up
the stairs? Don't–

**GUSTAV**     Get your ugly face out of here.

**AVIA**     I'm begging. Please don't. Please...
*(We take this to a horrendous and uncomfortable extreme. Then–
Avia suddenly snaps out of grovelling and weeping.)* Was that the
sort of thing you had in mind? Victim stuff?

**GUSTAV**     Oh, she's good. She's good. Oh you nearly had me going there for a minute.

**AVIA**          What do you mean, *nearly*? I'm not the star of this show for nothing.

**GUSTAV**     That's exactly what I meant. It's in the circus spirit. The wobble on the high-wire, just to let the punters know how dangerous it is. You'll have them weeping. They'll love it.

**AVIA**          No way. I'm not doing that. You expect me to do that in front of people? How degrading is that. I'm not doing that. I'm an *artiste*. Anyway, I've laid an egg. I'm going to be a mother. You can't throw me out. I've got statutory rights.

**GUSTAV**     Well you'd better come up with something quick, or you'll be out on your boneys, up shit creek, looking for a paddle shop.

*Hans enters. (This character has functioned until this point, as an observer and signer for the group. Now she begins to sign her own tale. It is voiced over by Gustav. The others talk over this. She cannot hear and is not distracted by them.)*

**HANS** *(signing)*/**GUSTAV** *(translating)*
I didn't always dress like this.
The first thing I remember wearing was my grey school skirt.
Part of the uniform.
But I don't remember much.
Somebody said to me recently...
If you can't remember your childhood, it must have been happy.

*The others start talking simultaneously, led by Avia.*

**AVIA**          I wish somebody would put the kettle on. This is so boring.

**CHRISTIAN** Sssssss...

**HANS/GUSTAV** It must have been – happy...

**AVIA**          She can't hear me – what's the odds?

**HANS/GUSTAV** Normal. If happy *is* normal. I'm not sure.

**AQUA**         Do you fancy her? ...

**HANS/GUSTAV** So, I was a good girl with good parents...

**CHRISTIAN** No.

**HANS/GUSTAV**  Father went out to work in a shop. Mother stayed
at home. In a house.

**AQUA**          Do you fancy me?

**HANS/GUSTAV**  The house was in a village. The village was in a
valley.

**CHRISTIAN**  No. Shut up.

**HANS/GUSTAV**          It had a church. A school. A shop. One
street. A Post Office...

One day I went to sleep and I had a dream

But I don't remember going to sleep

And I don't remember the dream.

The next day

I got up

Got dressed

Went downstairs

Had breakfast

Went to school

Couldn't speak

Couldn't hear...

**AVIA**          She can speak. She can, she just doesn't feel like it.
She goes for the sympathy vote.

**HANS**          But I hope it will be different for my baby. *(Pause)*

**AVIA**          What? What did you say?

**HANS**          I thought that would make you sit up.

**AVIA**          Say that again

**HANS**          You understood the first time, shit face.

**AVIA**          You're pregnant?

**CHRISTIAN**  What? What are you talking about?

**AVIA**          Who's the father?

**CHRISTIAN**  What? Father? What?

**HANS**          God.

**AVIA**          God?

**CHRISTIAN**  You've seen God's penis?

**AVIA**          God doesn't have a penis. He rains down radiant
white light on you.

**HANS**          How would you know?

**AVIA**          I've had him.

**HANS**          You're a liar.

**AVIA**          I am not. I am not a liar. I've had him. And his dad.

**HANS**          My baby will be born on the stroke of midnight as
we enter the new millenium. He, she –
**AVIA**          Or it–
**HANS**          Will be the beginning. The future. *(She leaves)*
**AVIA** *(shouting)* I *have* had him. And he was crap. Fuck me – she's
been working on her act.
**CHRISTIAN**  It must be Gustav.
**AVIA**          What?
**CHRISTIAN**  The father. It must be Gustav. Because it's not me.
**AVIA**          It's Gustav's idea alright. Virgin birth on the stroke
of the millenium. It's brilliant. The millenium baby, born in a tent
outside the Millenium Dome.
**CHRISTIAN**  Is that possible?
**AVIA**          Of course it is. They can do anything these days.
She'll be on every front page.
She'll top the bill... She'll top the bill!
And all she is, is *deaf.*
I'm not having a crap act like that topping my bill.
Marry me. We'll have a big do.
I'll bleach me plumage.
**CHRISTIAN**  I don't want to marry you.
**AVIA**          You'll have to. I'm not having her pushing me off
my perch.
**CHRISTIAN**  But I don't love you.
**AVIA**          You could learn to.
**CHRISTIAN**  Where do you learn things like that? They don't
have evening classes for love.
**AVIA**          They will soon.
**CHRISTIAN**  I couldn't marry you. I know you too well.
**AVIA**          Where do you get these outdated ideas?
**CHRISTIAN**  But I want somebody normal.
**AVIA**          What?
**CHRISTIAN**  I want to marry somebody normal.
**AVIA**          Are you saying I'm not normal?
**CHRISTIAN**  You're a bully. That's an indicator of damage. It's
not normal.
**AVIA**          It is where I come from.
**CHRISTIAN**  Have you tried therapy?
**AVIA**          Oh God.

**CHRISTIAN**   The father?

**AVIA**         Son and holy fucking ghost.

**CHRISTIAN**   That's blasphemy.

**AVIA**         So are we, in some people's eyes. Marry me. You'll feel the benefit.

**CHRISTIAN**   I'll think about it.

**AVIA**         Good.

**CHRISTIAN**   And I'll talk to my therapist about it.

**AVIA**         I'll take that as a yes then.

**CHRISTIAN** *(talks to his mirror image)* Gilbert – Avia wants to marry me. I don't think she loves me. And I don't think I can take her home to meet mother. She's so common.

I've been doing therapy lately

I've done all sorts.

I've located my inner child

But it won't speak to me.

I mean. Nobody's right are they?

Lately, I've been locating my inner cripple.

I haven't told Avia because she'll think it's metaphorical.

It isn't.

My therapist says, you've got to look past the outer casing to see the real person.

The therapist helps find the true you.

I mean you might be a paraplegic, but the inner you, might be totally paralysed.

There's a woman in my group who's partially sighted, but her inner self is profoundly deaf.

I can't decide about me.

What do you think, Gilbert?

I think, maybe I was in a head-on collision with my parents and I was the only survivor. I'm an inner amnesiac.

*Gustav and Aqua enter.*

**AQUA**        So what did you do to deserve this?

**GUSTAV**      What do you mean?

**AQUA**        In a previous life. Your Karma. It must have been something pretty bad, eh?

**GUSTAV**     Well, I'm not sure. I've been regressed a couple of times, but the evidence is conflicting. I was Atilla the Hun in one previous life, but another clairvoyant I met in a pub in Plaistow said it's an established fact that Atilla came back as Mother Theresa.

**AQUA**     That's not what Glenn Hoddle thinks.

**GUSTAV**     Fuck me, what did he do to deserve his destiny?

**AQUA**     Hitler?

**GUSTAV**     At the very least.

**AQUA**     My mum thought I was a blessing. A challenge sent only to the very good. She thought this was maybe my last time round before Nirvana.

**GUSTAV**     Well... It takes all sorts doesn't it?

**AQUA**     No.

**GUSTAV**     Erm. Have you ever thought about getting married?

**AQUA**     Who'd you have in mind?

**GUSTAV**     I just thought it might be good for the show. A millennium wedding.

**AQUA**     Who?

**GUSTAV**     It works for the Royal Family.

**AQUA**     Are you asking?

**GUSTAV**     *Me?*

**AQUA**     I see. Wrong question. How much?

*Sound of another fanfare. Christian is in his box. Avia and Aqua open the door of the box.*

**GUSTAV**     Ladies and gentlemen. You have seen the Beauty, now dare you see the Beast. At birth, so fearful his poor twisted body was locked away and buried deep in the bowels of the earth. Spewed out by a landslide, this twisting, tumbling terror was exposed trembling to the ravages of light. We found him cowering in the caves of Macedonia and bought him here today for you. Dare you face him? He lurches, he leers, he dribbles, he drools. Ladies, don't' get too close. Many a poor woman has been seduced by his fiendish charm. Friends, with some trepidation, I present The Master of Manipulation. His Royal Jellyness.
*(He finishes his act and wobbles to a halt)*
Sorry... I've just finished wobbling... I'm wobbled out...

I'll be alright tomorrow.
It makes me feel sick. Me and him.
Gilbert and Christian.
We were born
35 years ago.
Out of the same womb.
Twins. Identical.
Mum and Dad.
Well-to-do.
Big House.
Middle class.
I like being middle class.
Four years old.
Me and Gilbert were going different ways.
He was walking.
I was wobbling.
He was talking.
I was wobbling.
He walked and talked.
I wobbled and wobbled.
I got used to it.
Mum and Dad didn't.
One day,
The plague and the circus came to town.
The circus took me.
The plague took mum and dad.
That's what we in the business call, irony.
I got me first box.
It was a bit too little.
Because I was growing.
On the side, it said
Wobbly Bits Galore.
I'd lie there.
People's faces all around
Looking down at me.
I'd wait...
Then I'd fucking wobble
I'd smash the box to smithereens.
I was getting through a box a week.

They'd have to reinforce them.

The MD – the woman before Gustav

(I can't remember her name)

When the people weren't looking, at night – she'd teach me how to wobble better.

I built up me range.

When I started, I just used to do angry wobbling.

But I learned to do funny wobbling.

They'd piss themselves.

Sad wobbling.

I can make them feel real sorry for me.

Not a dry seat in the house,

That was a joke.

Gustav says I shouldn't try to do jokes. He says I'm shit at them.

I like doing guilty wobbling, but I have to be careful with that one because they don't come back and if Gustav catches me he kicks me. He's got a boot with studs on.

(It's no surprise is it? You can tell just by looking at him, that he's an evil bastard. I always hoped he'd surprise me with a heart of gold but he never has.)

'They're bored' he shouts. 'Wobble better.'

Then he'd kick me.

Sometimes I wouldn't get fed.

But this isn't a hard luck story.

I got on well with the others.

My best friend was this bloke with no legs.

He ran away.

See... I'm not as bad at comedy as Gustav says.

Gilbert was always there for me.

He'd tell me what was going on at home.

Funny things about chimney sweeps.

Yeah, chimney sweeps.

Come tomorrow, I might tell you...

Or I might not. *(Pause)*

They made me a bigger box.

Wobbly Bits – (No longer Galore)

I'm not sure if I prefer being galore

Or not galore.

Gilbert went away.

He went away...
He went away...
But he never went away for me.
He's in the army now.
I'm stuck in a box.
He's fucking shooting people.
He's a major. (I call myself a miner)
Because I'm deep.
Not because I'm under-age.
A little joke between us.
A woman came and looked at me last week
She said, 'What do you do for sex?'
I said, 'Not have it.'
I think she liked my wobbly bits.
But it's not strictly true.
Gustav sometimes slips me in the queue for the mermaid.
I used to love her.
I don't now.
Well, she's a slag, isn't she?

*Avia comes to look at Christian.*

**CHRISTIAN**   Are you deconstructing me again?
**AVIA**   No. He doesn't like it.
**CHRISTIAN**   You are, I know you are. Well... fucking don't.
**AVIA**   I'm not. I wouldn't. I love him.
   But he loves the mermaid. Sad isn't it?
   He could be the wind beneath my wings.
   But he wants to be the current between her fins.
   It's a human tragedy.

*Christian approaches Aqua.*

**CHRISTIAN**   Aqua. Let's get you a new story.
**AQUA**   What?
**CHRISTIAN**   Well, what's wrong with you?
**AQUA**   Dunno... Background of sexual abuse...
   Parents beat me, then tried to kill me...
   Splashed all over the tabloids... prostituted...

**CHRISTIAN**   I hope you don't mind me saying so, but it's all a bit old hat. Everybody's bored of all that. They get enough of that at home. Erm, you can't see very well can you?

**AQUA**            So?

**CHRISTIAN**   Well, you could have mystical inner powers.

**AQUA**            I haven't.

**CHRISTIAN**   You can't see their faces, but you can see their souls. Their auras... You can read minds.

**AQUA**            Oh, I can do that.

**CHRISTIAN**   You can? What am I thinking?

**AQUA**            You're thinking... you fancy me. You're wishing you didn't. Now you're wondering if I know when Gustav slips you in line with the others after the show.

**CHRISTIAN**   That's amazing. How do you do that?

**AQUA**            Now you're wondering, if you were any good.

**CHRISTIAN**   Was I?

**AQUA**            I'm not telling you.

*Gustav alone.*

**GUSTAV** *(looks at himself in a mirror)* You ain't getting my story. 'Beauty is truth, truth beauty. That's all you know on earth. And all you need to know,' mate. 'S'alright, you have my permission to stare... You've paid your money... You'd probably stare anyway, wouldn't you? Whether I gave you permission or not. A freak show is a safe place. When the punters have gone home, who cares if you've got one leg more or less? The more the merrier. And we're free to hate each other if we want to. *(Pause)* I love this show. They're my people. But it won't last. Times change. There was a time we got called monsters, from the Latin monstra... to warn, show, or sign. We were up there with unicorns... Now we're errors. Mistakes. Blunders. Nobody's going to pay to look at that... I'd rather be a monster. *(He sings)*

SONG: SCHADENFREUDE
Come on in and see the show
Take the weight off your plates
Let your worries go.

Feeling down?
You won't when you've employed ya
Schadenfreude.

My misfortune makes you rise
I can see it in your eyes.
Make the most of it.
Can you get any paranoider?
Schadenfreude.

There's always one worse off than you.
With any luck there might be two
Feeling better?
In here you can't avoid the
Schadenfreude.

It's a feeling you can rely on
Better than drugs or a shoulder to cry on
It's easy
Wish it on someone who's annoyed you
Schadenfreude

The Germans have a word for it.
But not one for the opposite.
Think about it
Be careful or it can destroy you
Schadenfreude

We have never-ending stocks
Leave when you like there are no locks
You won't offend us
Look at me – I've got two cocks.
Ooops, I think I've just enjoyed a
Little bit of Schadenfreude.

| | |
|---|---|
| AQUA | I wonder about the baby. Will it have a tail? |
| AVIA | I could pass on my knowledge of thermals. |
| AQUA | You could teach it to wobble. |

**CHRISTIAN**    I don't think it can be taught. You have to be born
  wobbling.
**HANS**         Tell us a story. I can't sleep.
**AVIA**         A new one.
**CHRISTIAN**    No, not a new one. New ones wake me up.
**AVIA**         Tell us the one about the big house. I want to update
  my list.
**CHRISTIAN**    Tell us a story. I can't get to sleep.
**AQUA**         Right...Get comfortable.
  I don't mind being in a goldfish bowl.
  I won't say I like it but I am used to it.
  People watching me.
  Life's always been a bit of a one way mirror... *(Pause)*
  I went to this place. It was a big house...
**CHRISTIAN**    With gardens all around.
**AQUA**         Yes. With gardens all around.
**CHRISTIAN**    And sunny all the time.
**AVIA**         Oh for god sake, shut up.
**AQUA**         Who's telling this?
**CHRISTIAN**    Sorry.
**AQUA**         I met a woman. She said, 'I want to learn what it's
  like to be like you. I want to be you.'
  I said, 'You mean swap?'
  She laughed. I don't know why.
  The rate science is developing these days
  I don't know what's possible and what isn't.
  Apparently that, isn't.
**CHRISTIAN**    Except in the imagination.
**AVIA**         Or fiction.
**AQUA**         'No', she said, 'I want to become you, in the sense
  that no one can tell the difference.
  I said, 'Go away.' She didn't. She just watched me. (Her eyes
  were too close together, but she was very beautiful)
  There were lots of people in this place
  And they all had people watching them. We'd just wander about
  being watched all the time.
  Sometimes the woman would say,
  'Let me watch you drinking a cup of lapsang souchong.'
  And I'd have to do it till I was sick of the bloody stuff,

'Or let me watch you having a bath,'
'Or let me watch you losing your temper,'
I said, 'I already am.'
She said, 'That's not very interesting,'
So I kicked a few chairs.
She seemed pleased
So I threw one out of the window.
Even better.
She said, 'Tomorrow I want to watch you eating oysters.'
I said, 'I don't eat oysters. I don't like them.'
She said, 'I need to watch you eating them.'
So next day, I didn't turn up.
I tried to get away and I came to a place, a part of the building
where people were walking around on their own
Nobody watching.
It was quite a shock. They looked almost naked.
A nurse stopped me.
'Who are they? Why is nobody watching them?'
But she wouldn't tell me anything.
So one night, I didn't take the tablets
I pretended to sleep.
I had to pretend well
And for a long time
The woman was watching me.
But at last
She went
And I thought to myself as I slipped down the corridors that
maybe I could be pretty good at pretending to be me too.
I got to the West wing
I went along the corridor trying the doors
Most of them were locked.
Finally I found a door.
It wasn't.
'Who's there?'
There was somebody in the bed.
A man.
I stepped into the moonlight so that he could see me. I showed
him I couldn't hurt him.
'Get me out of here. Get me out of here.'

'Who are you?'
'Don't you know me?'
I shook my head.
'I'm Daniel Day Lewis. Surely, you must know me. Someone
must remember.'
I shook my head.
They steal people's souls here.
Dustin Hoffman's in the next room and Bobby De Niro's the
other side of him..
*Bobby*... So I knew he was the real Daniel Day Lewis. An
impostor would have called him Robert.
'Get us out of here.'
I said, 'I'll see what I can do.'
And I left the room, and closed the door.
I noticed that someone had left the key in the lock.
'That was careless,' I thought.
So I turned it.
Better be safe than sorry.
I woke up late the next morning.
There was the lovely woman
Watching me doing late waking.
I said, 'What did you say your name was again?'
She said, 'Gwyneth Paltrow.'
'That's an unusual name,' I said.
She smiled and nodded.
I watched her.
The particular angle of her head, the drop of the gaze.
I tried it out in the bathroom mirror later.
And when I collected my Oscar some months later, she was the
one person I omitted from my thank yous, but I did hope they'd
given her a nice room in the West Wing.
Daniel and Dustin and Bobby all hugged me at the party after-
wards. I gave them that particular smile, and as I did, my gaze fell
on Matt Damon. What a sweet boy.
He came over.
'I'm playing a retard in my next movie,' he said and he asked me
about my research.
So, of course I gave him the number of a certain large house.
'I said, 'You should call.'

He said, 'Thanks.'

And as he crossed the room, I watched him.

**AVIA**        Lovely arse that boy.

**AQUA**      Yeah. He's still on the death list.

**CHRISTIAN**  Who've we got now?

**AVIA**        Tom Cruise.

Dustin Hoffman.

Robert de Niro.

Al Pacino.

Daniel Day Lewis.

Woody Harrelson.

Helena Bonham Carter–

**AQUA**      All those who died of cancer for their art–

Debra Winger.

Meryl Streep.

Susan Sarandon.

Ali Mcgraw.

Julia Roberts.

Shirley Maclaine.

**CHRISTIAN**  She didn't die.

**AQUA**      No, but she let her roots show.

**CHRISTIAN**  Chuck her in then.

*They gradually drift off to sleep.*

**AVIA**        Val Kilmer.

**AQUA**      What's he doing?

**AVIA**        Blind.

**AQUA**      He's shit anyway.

**CHRISTIAN**  Kill him.

**AQUA**      Yeah. Kill him.

**CHRISTIAN**  Robson Green.

**AVIA**        *What?!!*

**AQUA**      Say it's not so.

**CHRISTIAN**  Yeah. Robson Green. Tragically blinded in a car
accident. Two part drama. *(They start giggling.)*

**ALL**         Kill him. Yeah, kill him etc.

**AVIA**        That only leaves Richard Gere.

**AQUA**      Richard Gere?

AVIA            Yeah...
CHRISTIAN   Richard Gere, the last actor in the world?

*There's a bit of a pause, then they all start laughing.*

AVIA            Oi, Gilbert!
CHRISTIAN   What?
AVIA            I'm not talking to you. I'm talking to Gilbert. Tell
your brother he can wank on me if he likes.
CHRISTIAN   Fuck off.
AVIA            Did somebody speak? Oi Gilbert. Tell your brother
I'm going to think about him while I have a wank.
CHRISTIAN   You wouldn't.
AVIA            I already have, pal.
CHRISTIAN   Was I good?
AVIA            I'm not telling you. He feels about deconstruction
pretty much the way I do about metaphor.

*Avia comes over to him.*

GUSTAV       Do us a favour.
AVIA            What is it?
GUSTAV       Let 'em wank on you.
AVIA            Y' what?
GUSTAV       Just a few of them. After the show.
AVIA            Let 'em wank on me?
GUSTAV       Yeah. We'll clean up.
AVIA            Will we? Fuck off.
GUSTAV       Go on. You can keep your eyes shut.
AVIA            You let 'em wank on you.
GUSTAV       I would.
AVIA            Would you fuck, as like... Fuck off.
GUSTAV       I would. I have. Well, when I was younger. They
drank champagne out of my boot. But I'm past my best.
AVIA            And I'm in my prime?
GUSTAV       Go on. You don't have to touch. Or look. You just
have to be.
AVIA            I'm an artist.

GUSTAV    Well, pretend to enjoy it. We're talking survival
here. Give the people what they want.

AVIA    No.

GUSTAV    Just think about it.

AVIA    I'm going to have trouble thinking about anything
else. Now fuck off.

GUSTAV    You think you're so interesting people are going to
want to come and look at you doing nothing?

AVIA    I may be ugly, but I'm not stupid.
And I know what people come here for.
They don't come to look at me.
They come for me to look at them.
It's the Medusa stare –
They want to survive it.

GUSTAV    That's it. I'm closing the show. Disbanding the club.

AVIA    What?!

GUSTAV    I'm closing the show.

*We see a side show, slide show begin.*

AVIA    Right. Since that's that... I'd like to say...
It's not a club. It's a family.
In that you don't have a choice who you get stuck with.
You may have very little in common
And you may hate their guts
But they're still family.
And you stick up for them.
Switch the lights off.

*We see a slide show of classic and famous freaks. (This depends
slightly on the availability of images.) There is an element of
improvisation in the reactions of the actors who talk about the
images as of old friends, or family members.*

*SLIDE ONE*

AVIA    Everybody said she was such a nice woman, but I'm
here to tell you different.

GUSTAV    I always liked her.

**AVIA**          You never knew her. And that husband of hers. Under the thumb, or what? We always said they should be doing a different act. The Two-faced woman and the Spineless man.

*SLIDE TWO*

**AVIA**          Little Sheila. We used to get her into the pictures as a half. But if there was an X she wanted to see, she always carried her passport. She had the dirtiest mouth of anybody I've ever known.
**CHRISTIAN**  Even you?
**AVIA**          Watch it, shit for brains, I'll send the boys round.
**AQUA**          What happened to her?
**AVIA**          Opened a café in Florida.
**AQUA**          Get away? (No?)
**AVIA**          Yeah. Dropped in on her once. She still made the worst cup of tea I've ever tasted. Though I'm reliably informed she gave good blow jobs.
**CHRISTIAN**  Really?
**AVIA**          No. How would I know? Nobody tells me anything. I've got a mouth like the Mersey Tunnel.

*SLIDE THREE*

**AVIA**          Aw. She was German and went back at the start of the war
**CHRISTIAN**  What happened?
**GUSTAV**      Auschwitz.

*SLIDE FOUR*

**AVIA**          Chang and Eng Bunker and their kids. Now, Chang was a tea-totaller and Eng loved his fags and beer. It used to cause such fights. They used to knock seven colours of shit out of one another. 'You'll kill me, you bastard,' Chang would be shouting. I'm amazed they didn't kill each other. One of their descendants was in *Reservoir Dogs*. Sharp businessmen, both of them. Died rich.
**CHRISTIAN**  They kept slaves.

**AVIA**       So? Everybody did.

**CHRISTIAN**  I disapprove of it.

**AVIA**       Disapproval... It's not up there with passion, jealousy, love and hate is it? You couldn't write an opera about it. Why did she throw herself off the battlements? Because they disapproved of her. I expect Chang and Eng could live with your disapproval.

**AQUA**       Disappointment. You could fill an opera with disappointment.

**AVIA**       I wonder if I can catch it on the wedding photos?

*The Maladjusted Marriage: a ceremony takes place between Aqua and Christian's mirror image, Gilbert.*

**GUSTAV**     As Captain of this frail craft, I welcome you here today for the union of Aqua and Gilbert. There aren't as many of you as we were hoping for... we'll put that down to the recent decline in spirituality – I thought *Hello* magazine might pay us a visit. *(Pause)* We call upon you people here present to witness the marriage of Aqua and Gilbert. A triumph of romance over reason. The victory of love over capital. The union of the blonde and the bland. They, like others who have gone before them, are going to need your help. The voyage ahead may be stormy. Very stormy...

**AVIA**       In your dreams Gustav, do you walk without your sticks?

**GUSTAV**     I always thought that *this* was the dream. Please don't tell me I'm wide awake.

**AVIA**       Gustav?

**GUSTAV**     What now?

**AVIA**       Is there a secret that you could find out that would truly shock you?

**GUSTAV**     Try me.

**AVIA**       I've got a secret. I've decided to tell it to you.
I've never told anybody...
But I don't want you finding out from somebody else.
It's this –
Some days, not every day,
(I want to emphasise that.)
Not every day,

But some days...
I don't like being me.
GUSTAV      That's it?
AVIA        That's it. Better than lap-dancing, isn't it?
GUSTAV      I'm not shocked. I'm not even surprised.
AVIA             No. The shocking thing is how hard it was for me to
tell you. You'll have to marry me now.

*The clock begins to chime midnight.*

HANS *(uses her voice for the first time)*
I was pregnant but I'm not any more.
I had a termination.
The results of the CVS revealed a hormonal abnormality.
The extent of the impairment was unknown.
I was offered counselling but they emphasised that the decision
was mine.
So I took it.
It didn't take long...
I just felt that the quality of life...
The quality of his
Or her
Or its life...
My irregular circumstances...
A kid on the road...
I mean – the Millennium Child –
He'd have to be perfect, wouldn't he?
The child's father was, in fact, God.
He came over me in a shower of light.
I was chosen,
But I couldn't bear the consequences,
So I made my own choice.
Do you think Mary might have made the same choice if it had
been available to her?
*(During this, all the company leaves the stage.)*
Ladies and Gentlemen –
I'm not clairvoyant
But I can predict the future –
This is what it will look like.

*The cast has all left the stage. The stage is empty.*

**HANS**     Perfect. The end.

*The actors return to take a curtain call and then leave the stage again.*

**GUSTAV** *(getting another show together)* Cheer up. Look, it's not all gloom and doom. I'm negotiating a fly-on-the-wall docusoap. We'll have to stop Avia swearing. There's always going to be freaks – The Gulf War, Chernobyl – we'll get a few out of Kosovo... Medical advances... we're just going to have to look a bit further afield for them. Maybe we can get a clone? Get a sheep? Tell them it's Dolly... Course you'll have to take a cut...

*Blackout.*
*The end.*

## Mike Kenny

Mike Kenny is probably best known for his plays for children. *Stepping Stones* won the Writers' Guild Best Children's Play Award in 1997. In 2000, he was the first ever recipient of the Arts Council of England's Children's Award, for his children's plays. He lives in Leeds, with the actress Barbara Marten and their three sons.

# Into The Mystic

# Into The Mystic

My illness began around the time of the Gulf War. While generals disabled their enemy's command and control structure, a doctor told me that my own command and control structure was also being disabled – from within. The 'war' inside me was 'biochemical'. It 'took no prisoners'. Thus I entered the strange world of Disease As Metaphor.

Years passed. The metaphors of battle were replaced by the metaphors of religion. Unable to treat me, let alone cure me, doctors talked of my 'suffering', with my health being 'beyond redemption'. Unconsciously following the rules of Disease-As-Metaphor, they seemed to cast me in a Three Act narrative, wherein (Act One) The Victim is disabled. In Act Two, The Victim fights back. Act Three sees The Victim transcend his incurable affliction, to reach a state of wisdom and empowerment... only to die before the final curtain.

I didn't like that ending. I was sick of playing a noble victim. So I dropped the part and limped out of hospital. When I was strong enough, I picked up a pen, recast myself as a writer. *Into The Mystic* subverts the clichés of Disease-As-Metaphor the only way I know how: by telling the untold story of a disease, which truly IS a metaphor. In dramatising this mystery I hope to rewrite its message for myself, and for everyone.

**Peter Wolf**

*With thanks to: Leona Heimfeld, Cherry Cookson, Tom Ryan, Julia Parr, Jonathan Meth, Mark Ravenhill, Jenny Sealey and all her great company.*

# Into The Mystic

## Peter Wolf

This play was first performed on 31st January 2001 at Studio 2, Riverside Studios, Hammersmith, London with the following cast:

| CHARACTERS | CAST |
| --- | --- |
| **Robbie** | Simon Startin |
| **Chris** | Amit Sharma |
| **Jade** | Pamela Mungroo |

Directed and designed by Jenny Sealey.
Lighting Designed by Ian Scott.

*'In order to be made whole, we must first be broken...'*
                                                    - St Thomas Aquinas

| *Time* | The present. |
| --- | --- |
| *Place* | A Northern town. |

**SCENE 1**
*A&E cubicle. Chris and Jade burst in, she with a gashed wrist.*

| JADE | Guuh – |
| --- | --- |
| CHRIS | Here. |
| JADE | Guuuh – |
| CHRIS | Look away. |

*Jade obeys. Chris injects her wound.*

| JADE | Bitches. |
| --- | --- |
| CHRIS | What? |
| JADE | Behind KFC. |
| CHRIS | Hold still. *(He cleans Jade's wound.)* |

JADE          "Give us everything," says Chief Bitch. They have
     machetes, I have nothing – except onion rings and a Diet Pepsi. I
     don't think that's what they meant. But I gave it them anyroad.
     Actually I threw it. Onion rings bounce off. Diet Pepsi's a hit...
     l take my chance and run. Into dusbins. Wanker.
CHRIS         Am I hurting you? *(He stitches Jade's wound)*
JADE          I feel nothing. "Ten pence? She's nothing," says
     Bitch Number One, "but we cut her anyhow." I say why, when
     I'm skint and nothing. Because she says she wants to see what my
     insides look like. And everyone laughs. Even me... close my eyes,
     I still see her, axe rising, then with all her power she brings axe
     down and –
CHRIS         Machete.
JADE          Uh?
CHRIS         They had machetes. You said –
JADE          Axe machete it's all GBH.
CHRIS         But you just / said –
JADE          Hey: I'm The Victim here.
CHRIS         Last week they had machetes, week before they had
     machetes – why axes suddenly?
JADE          The blood I – got freaked I – calling me a *liar?*
CHRIS         Jade I call you what I called you last week.
JADE          Sod you. Screw you.
CHRIS         A hurting person, in need of –
JADE          Cold bastard. Doctor Fridge.
CHRIS         And now the abuse.
JADE          No. Tonight, tonight I choose to forgive. He's
     overworked. We forget. 30 hour shifts freeze the brain. My poor
     man in white. Thank you. For being here. Under the sign of the
     Red Cross. Thanks for existing.
CHRIS *(writes)* ...you could stay and rest.
JADE          In Casualty?
CHRIS         Yes. No. A different ward.
JADE          It's Monday – got to work.
CHRIS         Fine.

*Chris hands Jade a prescription, along with a card.*

CHRIS         Pills for infection, you know the deal...

JADE          And a card.
CHRIS          A self-help group. At least, think about it. Tonight's
wound is your deepest yet. Soon you'll nick a jugular. What then?
*(A pause. Jade leaves. Chris uses the phone.)*
Psych Wing? *(pause)* Dave, where were you? *(pause)* Hm? Nuh I
messed up. *(pause)* She won't volunteer. *(pause)* Next Monday as
ever... could you have someone ready for her this time?

**SCENE 2**
*Jade's place. She's watching an operation on TV.*

TV *(voiceover)* '...though a painful incision, if the wound is cleanly
made and properly dressed it should soon heal into a scar.'

*Robbie enters. He's facially disfigured.*

ROBBIE          Nurse?
JADE          Who's asking.
ROBBIE          Said on the door.
JADE          It would: Monday night I work from home, rest of
the week I'm at college if you must know.
ROBBIE          Whoa, she's hot.
JADE          Access Course. Feng Shui. *(smokes)* What do you
do?
ROBBIE *(declines cigarette)* When.
JADE          Whenever.
ROBBIE          I follow you.
JADE          Uh?
ROBBIE          You have a follower.
JADE          ...since when.
ROBBIE:          18.05 hours left hospital. 18.20 caught a 51 bus.
18.35 to *Superdrug* for nine kinds of medicine.
JADE          Twelve.
ROBBIE          Herbal crap don't count.
JADE          ...a medicine head. You like hospitals too?
ROBBIE          Outpatient. Need injections regular.
*(He gestures at his damaged face.)*
JADE          Problem skin.
ROBBIE          Yeah. Problem.

**JADE**          Seen worse.
**ROBBIE**      Where, roadkill?
**JADE**          A&E if you must know. Sister Jade McNaught, Casualty. Like on TV. It's heavy but hey: we save people. My surgeon is Dr Christopher Howell. I'm under him. Fact I got this *(her wound)* while he amputated the leg of a toddler. Didn't hurt. It were life or death. Do you watch?
**ROBBIE**      Television's evil.
**JADE**          I mean when they shoot you. With a needle. Full of wonder drugs. *(switches off TV)* Or do you look away.
**ROBBIE**      Make like it's not me. Then it hurts less bad.
**JADE** *(pours drink)* I must try that.
**ROBBIE**      Yeah, shot up I pretend I'm someone. A victim of cancer. A psycho. Robbie Williams.
**JADE**          A psycho. *(offers drink)* Come to see what my insides look like?
**ROBBIE** *(ignores drink)* Jade, I'm the opposite of psycho, I'm here about love...
**JADE**          A fuck's 20. 30, I fuck you dressed as a nurse. 40 buys a fuck dressed as a nurse plus a Diet Pepsi enema, wicked bubbles and froth… *(drinks)*…for 50 quid up front I pull off this dressing, you fuck the lips off my brand new gash–
**ROBBIE**      How much for love.
**JADE**          Fuck love.
**ROBBIE**      Fuck *love?*
**JADE**          Men used to prefer blondes, now they prefer wounds, okay?
**ROBBIE**      I weep for you Jade.
**JADE**          Deal with it.
**ROBBIE**      Selling yourself.
**JADE**          Move on.
**ROBBIE**      Lying she's a nurse, and Angel–
**JADE**          Mondays only – once week revenge on this cunt of a body, screw every penny from it, then one day you watch: I'm talking laser surgery, removal of scars till I'm perfect. So virgin get it quick before I'm out of your league and BEAUTIFUL. *(Pause.)* UGLY FUCKER, GET IT UP! *(Pause.)* Am I not... good enough?

*Robbie makes to leave.*

**ROBBIE**     We were meant to kick out as friends. That were the
plan. Till I blew it.
**JADE**     Maybe we could... be... friends. Maybe I'm alone
since Mac died.
**ROBBIE**     He your pimp?
**JADE**     My computer.
**ROBBIE**     I'm sorry. I'm Robbie.
**JADE**     Williams?
**ROBBIE**     Robbie Friend.
**JADE**     Okay. And what do friends do?
**ROBBIE**     Dunno... talk and dance and that.
**JADE**     We could talk about favourite hospitals. For a price,
of course.
**ROBBIE**     ...I paid already. In grief.
**JADE**     Friendship costs more than sex.
**ROBBIE**     But less than love, right?

*Robbie gives Jade money.*

**JADE**     Oh you're my friend Rob... sure you're not up for a
quick blow job and have done?
**ROBBIE**     Tonight the blow job's on *me*.

*He puts a CD in Jade's machine.*

**JADE**     Uh?
**ROBBIE**     A blow job of the mind...
*(He plays the CD: dance music, over which he karaoke-raps.)*
we whack it up and we jack the vibe
we jam till dawn harmonic supahigh
pop the pill is sugar only
free our soul no guns drugs money
cos sinning is illing unhiphophappy
spiritual living's our holychemotherapy
*(CD Chorus)* yo we are the club club club pure ecstasy
*(over CD chorus)* Friend I saw you and I saw you was
lost. At Club Pure Ecstasy we work undercover, befriend and

save lost souls through the, like, Wages of their Sin. Tonight I buy not the flesh or owt bur your soul... feel a higher love kicking in. Non-sex type love. Peace and love type love. Raise up ands blow your mind with God's– (*Jade retches.*) Whoa...

**JADE**          Oh, what –

**ROBBIE**        I'll fetch a Kleenex.

**JADE**          I'm okay, it's cool –

**ROBBIE**        But you still need saving – for my first convert I get a gold cross –

*Jade vomits.*

**JADE**          What's happening?

**ROBBIE**        I'll come back. With friends. And a Kleenex. And we'll dance to the Lord –

*Jade vomits on Robbie. He flees.*

**SCENE 3**

*An overflow corridor in A&E. Chris speaks into a dictaphone.*

**CHRIS**          ...Cubicle 9, pulse 146 bp 111 over 78, patient semi-conscious, breath laboured, GP informed but no history, patient awaiting transfer to Ward H... cubicle 12...
*(pulls back a curtain to reveal Jade lying on a trolley.)*
...ohhh twice in four days?

**JADE**          Five hours waiting, nurses giving me crap –

**CHRIS**         We're busy.

**JADE**          There's a Patient's Charter –

**CHRIS**         Yeah, even for patients from hell.

*Jade retches. Chris pulls away her blanket, revealing a wound in her side.*

**JADE**          Wait I must expl –

*But Chris probes her wound. She shrieks.*

**CHRIS**         It's weeping. Matches did it? Cigarette lighter?

JADE        I don't smoke.
CHRIS       Look away. (*Jade doesn't look away.*) Jade I said –
JADE        I'm innocent of this wound. This is new. This wound
  is not me –
CHRIS       Fine.

*Chris injects Jade. She doesn't look away.*

JADE        You don't believe me.
CHRIS       But I do: you meet a guy. Behind Kentucky Fried.
  Turns nasty. You lob a chicken wing at him. It flies off. So
  instead of pulling out his machete, no his *axe,* to hack you open,
  the bastard gets out his thumb, gives you the most wicked
  Chinese burn.
JADE        Met a guy, yeah. Made friends. Then he did. He did
  it. Doctor, he did this with *words. (Chris bandages Jade's
  wound.)* Oh. Right. Break open the Elastoplast...
CHRIS       Surgical dressing.
JADE        ...dunno what First Aid course you took but
  Elastoplast's useless against words, yeah? Unless you tape up that
  bastard Robbie's mouth–
CHRIS       I refuse to have this conversation.
JADE        Please you must / believe –
CHRIS       Three years I'm in Casualty – words never hurt /
  anyone.
JADE        Well, I've been in Casualty all my life but never /
  for–
CHRIS *(leaving)* I'll phone someone / okay?
JADE*(hyper)* He he he opened his mouth and his words cut like
  power-drills, corkscrew my gut, barbed wire skull and pain such
  such pain –
CHRIS *(intervening)* Calm it.
JADE        Guuh...
CHRIS       Can you breathe yet?
JADE        Course I can breathe... I'm fucking talking.
  *(Chris releases Jade.)* Patient talks... doctor never listens. Cold as
  coke.
CHRIS       I listen. Every Monday the same shit.

JADE           That other shit, that Monday shit, that shit's shit I
confess: but this is Friday, why'd I make shit up on a Friday?
Think I got no life, no better shit to do come Friday than make
shit up when I should be partying and having fun like normal
people? I mean, watch the adverts, you don't see them scarred to
fuckery by words...

*Chris finishes up.*

CHRIS          Outpatients. Monday next. Earlier if it whiffs. They
can also check my stitches from last Monday, tastefully hidden by
gloves I remark...
JADE           You care then.
CHRIS          ...about...
JADE           My choice of glove.
PARAMEDIC *(off)* Doctor?
CHRIS *(off)* Uh-huh. *(to Jade)* OD. Cubicle 9. Bad. She's young.
*(Jade rises to leave.)* ...see you next Monday then, if not before...
next Monday, we get back to normal okay? Deal with the / under-
lying–
JADE           Oh this is farewell doctor, for real this time...
CHRIS          Then get real and out of denial before you turn into a
Munchie.
PARAMEDIC *(off)* Chris?
CHRIS *(off)* Yo. *(To Jade)* Munchausen Syndrome. Mean anything?
JADE *(memory)* Munchausen Syndrome By Proxy: to wound others,
then heal them for kicks.
CHRIS          I'm talking straight Munchausen, the urge to self-
inflict, in order to grab attention and be cared for. Modern
epidemic: blame the NHS: however gross a patient's self-harm,
there's always someone like me on call to try make it better again.
And again... reading of our new burns unit, one guy fed the cat,
rang 999, and set himself on fire... two years it took Martin to die.
As a student I'd peel off his scar tissue. The agony. I never saw
anyone so happy. His parting words – through what charcoal
remained of his jaws: 'Don't cry. I'm blessed by your sainted
hands.' *Sainted?* I laughed. He didn't. The End. Does this ritual
sound familiar?
PARAMEDIC *(off, urgent)* Doctor Howell –

**CHRIS** *(off)*   I'm with a PATIENT.
**JADE**            Munchie...
**CHRIS**           Can't go on like this, can we. Has to be done tonight.

*Chris hands Jade a sheet of paper, and a pen.*

**JADE**            So... if I sign... you treat me?
**CHRIS**           If you sign you are taken in.
**JADE**            By you?
**CHRIS**           For assessment.
**JADE**            Just you I mean. *(hyper)* Me in bed and you in white
with knives and gleaming needles and that that that face full of
grace keeping ghosts away –
**CHRIS**           Yes. That's exactly what happens during assessment.
**JADE**            ...it *is*?
**CHRIS**           And why we must take you in.
**JADE**            ...we?
**CHRIS**           Yes.
**JADE**            As in you and me?
**CHRIS**           As in us, yes.
**JADE**            As in *just* you and me.
**CHRIS**           Yes. More or less.
**JADE**            ...*not* just you and me.
**CHRIS**           Absolutely. As part of a... team thing.
**JADE** *(reads paper)* Who's 'Professor Lukic'?
**CHRIS**           Dave... heads the team.
**JADE**            Department?
**CHRIS**           Massively respected –
**JADE**            The shrink department?
**CHRIS**           Knows all about you –
**JADE**            Professor Psych Psycho of the Psych Wing.
**CHRIS**           Jade I'm a butcher not a shrink –

*Jade rips off a glove. In the palm of her hand, a weeping hole.*

**JADE**            Think a shrink can cure this? *(She pushes Chris's
pen into her hand. It stands up.)* What am I becoming.

**SCENE 4**

*Jade's place. Robbie comes in with a bunch of flowers. Looks around Puts a CD in Jade's machine. Checks her ansafone.*

**ROBBIE'S VOICE** *(bleep)* Hi. I'm a prick. Could we um, like, start over?

**HOSPITAL VOICE** *(bleep)* This is Professor Lukic again –

**JADE** *(enters)*   ...How did / you get in –

**HOSPITAL VOICE**   It really is most important I / speak to –

**ROBBIE**     Who's Professor–

*Jade mutes the ansafone with heavily bandaged hands.*

**JADE**        Out.

**ROBBIE**     Listen, I'm a prick: when you puked I freaked.

**JADE**        And why did I puke in the first place.

**ROBBIE**     Same as everyone. When I am beheld. *(offers flowers)* Friends?

**JADE** *(can't hold them)* Ohhh find a vase... *(Robbie roots about.)* Just keep everything shallow this time. No deeply hidden shit to set me off.

**ROBBIE**     I vow to be a total airhead.

*Jade swallows pills and drinks.*

**JADE**        Where'd you go, anyhow. Last week. After our –

**ROBBIE**     Nowhere. Ethiopia. With the Club. This village we sponsor used to grow food, now grow flowers for *Asda*. Then *Asda* pulled out. So everyone had to eat the flowers. Not me. I went without. I starved in Ethiopia. For *you*.

**JADE**        Storming.

**ROBBIE**     Yeah?

**JADE**        That's... deeply shallow.

**ROBBIE**     Some African's tight on us for bringing ghetto blasters when all they lack is grain. Brother Paul – our leader – tells'em mellow: pray for summat loud enough and it will come to pass. So whack up the volume, get down on them knees, get saved. It's how you look at stuff. Even Third World stuff's curable if only we 'Smile& Think Positive. *(beat)* See?

**JADE** *(smiling)*  What.
**ROBBIE**          A smile's the best medicine.
**JADE**            This is a Prozac smile. Strictly chemical.
*(Robbie finds a jar for the flowers.)* Anyroad, smiling and
thinking positive hasn't stopped *you* looking ugly as fuck.
**ROBBIE**          Thank you for sharing your thoughts with me.
**JADE**            Robbie, will you piss off with this positive shite, it's
unnatural.
**ROBBIE**          Unnatural's them.
**JADE**            Uh?
**ROBBIE**          Bandages, frigging bandages –
**JADE**            So. *(drinks)* Am I a Munchie? Am I?
**ROBBIE**          Dunno the name but I been there. Years ago. After
the attack. Domestos, wire wool... anything to, like, burn out all
memory of my... this... *(gestures at his disfigurement.)*
Bro' Paul reckons we hurt our bodies when our souls have no
past... she's smiling again.
**JADE**            That word. Soul.
**ROBBIE**          Brother Paul / says –
**JADE**            Doesn't exist Robbie. The Soul. The Past. Deep
things. Shit that meant stuff... it's over. Move on. *(drinks)* Time to
dumb back down and have fun okay?
**ROBBIE**          'Storming'.
*(He triggers the CD: 'Don't Believe A Word' by Thin Lizzy. He
and Jade must shout to be heard.)* Nan left me her CDs.
**JADE**            Sound prehistoric.
**ROBBIE**          She called it Rock Music.
*(They laugh. Robbie dances. Jade laughs at him.)*
Here. *(Robbie puts his hands on the CD speakers.)* Go on.
**JADE**            Nuh my hands –
**ROBBIE**          It's fun...
*(Jade drinks, then copies Robbie with her damaged hands.)*
Feel owt?
**JADE**            A buzz, or is it chemical... *(drinks)* Pernod on
*Prozac*. Fuck, I'm spaced...
**ROBBIE**          Push harder.
**JADE** *(obeys)* ...hey ...something...
**ROBBIE**          Yeah?
**JADE**            His voice . The singer.

| | |
|---|---|
| **ROBBIE** | Phil Lynott. |
| **JADE** | He's well rocking. |
| **ROBBIE** | He's dead. |

*(Jade pulls her hands from the speakers. Robbie lowers the CD volume.)* There. Proof.

| | |
|---|---|
| **JADE** | Back off Robbie. |
| **ROBBIE** | What's dead never truly dies. |
| **JADE** | A trick – |
| **ROBBIE** | His voice still echoes. |
| **JADE** | Tosser the past is dead. |
| **ROBBIE** | Though we deny it, we still feel that vibe. |
| **JADE** | Goodbye Tortured Man – |
| **ROBBIE** | He's in this room... and he's *alive.* |
| **JADE** | No. |
| **ROBBIE** *(grabs her)* | Embrace – |
| **JADE** | No. |
| **ROBBIE** *(clutches her)* | Embrace the Lord – |
| **JADE** | No. |
| **ROBBIE** *(rubs against her)* | Embrace your Lord Jesus Christ. |
| **JADE** | No no no no – |

*(Robbie kisses Jade. The CD shorts, sparks, dies into silence.)*

**ROBBIE**    Whoa. My first... I – I never... Holy Spirit I guess. Here. With us. Vivid. I felt it felt you felt... Like heaven. ...don't weep Robbie. Think Positive. I think, I just got my first gold cross... How was it for you? Sister? Smile. You just got saved.

*Jade smiles. Her smile trickles blood.*

**SCENE 5**
*A hospital washroom. Chris, besuited, grooms himself in the mirror. Robbie bursts in, hands bloody. Chris instinctively plunges Robbie's hands in a sink, and begins rubbing at his disfigurement.*

| | |
|---|---|
| **CHRIS** | Where is it. |
| **ROBBIE** | Ow. |
| **CHRIS** | The wound – can't find your – |
| **ROBBIE** | This is how I *am*, right? My *face,* okay? |

*Chris releases Robbie. They look at Chris's bloodied suit.*

**ROBBIE**      Whoa! (*Now Robbie tries to clean Chris up.*)
**CHRIS**      You should be downstairs.
**ROBBIE**      I came upstairs.
**CHRIS**      A&E. Ask for Dr Ekoku.
**ROBBIE**      Not *me*, Doc. The emergency's Jade McNaught.
**CHRIS**      ...who... (*looks at the blood*) ...then ...she was right?
No Munchie. Or fantasy. You exist. Fine: another diagnosis
trashed... so what was it this time, hard man. Axe? Machete?
**ROBBIE**      Huh?
**CHRIS**      She believes you do it with words.
**ROBBIE**      Reckon I cut her or summat?
**CHRIS** (*dials phone*) I know you do it with knives and acid. Where
is she.
**ROBBIE**      You got me bang wrong.
**CHRIS** (*on phone*) Security.
**ROBBIE**      So why's a hard man begging your help eh? Iceman?
If I can't tell you everything about Jade... I'll tell everyone else.
**CHRIS** (*checks watch*) You have one minute.
**ROBBIE**      She's at her place, I pray over her 24-7, useless: Bro'
Paul's no help neither – says Smile, God's the Father of Love, of
Peace and, like, Healing. This he can't handle. (*the blood*) This –
this medieval shit. Every time I try to save her it only makes her
worse.
**CHRIS**      Look, whatever drug you're on–
**ROBBIE**      It's called religion doctor, I'm a religion user.
**CHRIS**      Whatever, take her to Casualty so Dr Ekoku can
patch her up and refer her / to–
**ROBBIE**      She said you'd say that.
**CHRIS**      She would: I'm sorry to tell you, Jade has a very,
well, tragic syndrome called –
**ROBBIE**      Munchie.
**CHRIS**      Yes.
**ROBBIE**      She said you'd say that an' all.
**CHRIS**      Look – I'm not being clear –there are
**ROBBIE**      Channels.
**CHRIS**      Channels. Ways of
**ROBBIE**      Doing things.

CHRIS        Doing things.
CHRIS        It's out of my hands, Jade's been referred –
ROBBIE       To what.
CHRIS        Professor Lukic, who keeps trying to –
ROBBIE       You're referring.
CHRIS        Yes.
ROBBIE       To Professor Lukic.
CHRIS        He's a brilliant –
ROBBIE       You're referring Professor Lukic to Jade.
CHRIS        I – I'm referring Jade to Professor Lukic.
ROBBIE       I'm lost.
CHRIS        This is what we call a referral.
ROBBIE       If that's a referral, we have a problem.
CHRIS        Why.
ROBBIE       Jade referred to Professor Lukic as a *shrink*. She
    doesn't need a shrink, she needs emergency bloody First Aid.
    From you. She wants you only Doc. No one else may touch her,
    because she is hallowed. By ME. Understood?
CHRIS        That bad then?
ROBBIE       If we wait any longer she'll –
CHRIS        What.
ROBBIE       She'll be –
CHRIS        What. Dead? What
ROBBIE       Worse.
CHRIS        Worse than dead? Surprise me.
ROBBIE       She'll be damned. (*Silence.*) Unless we get Jade well
    enough, to repent, as – as Satan's whore she goes to hell.
    (*Silence.*) Hell's red Doctor. All mouth and bloody teeth. And hell
    will eat my Jade sure as a pitbull ate my face. See, you don't
    believe in hell like I don't believe in pitbulls. They were banned
    remember. Weren't meant to exist anymore. Just because we...
    (*sob*) ...don't believe in summat... (*sob* )...don't mean it can't rise
    up and rip us apart.

*Chris's bleeper goes off.*

CHRIS        I must go.
ROBBIE       I don't care.
CHRIS        ...why me?

| ROBBIE | Jade thinks you care. |
|---|---|
| CHRIS | I'm caring, sure: I'm a carer – |
| ROBBIE | A carer. |
| CHRIS | Professionally. |
| ROBBIE | But not *actually.* |
| CHRIS | Really, I do, I care for all my patients. |
| ROBBIE | If she's patient she'll wait forever right? Till there's |

flames in her mouth and her eyes weep fire –

**CHRIS** *(checks watch)* I'm late. For the enquiry. Into the girl.
Overdose. Friday last, my shift, Cubicle 9. We were busy. I
missed her symptoms. And now she's in a state. A persistent state.
A Persistent Vegetative State.
*(He composes himself in the mirror.)*
Leave the address downstairs. I'll be over for Jade when – if – I
can. If I'm still a doctor that is. After the enquiry.

**ROBBIE**      I'll pray for you.

**CHRIS** *(leaving)* There is no God you know. Only DNA. And luck.


**SCENE 6**
*Jade's place. Lying on a sofa, bloody and filthy, she watches a talk
show with the sound turned down. She lipsyncs a woman on TV.*

**JADE**      Hey Montel. *(pause)* For sure. *(pause)* Sure it's way
tough on me, but if my story can touch one hurting person out
there – *(She lipsyncs a girl.)* 'Mum I'm not angry or anything. I'm
cool... but you want me to kneel at the feet of The Tortured Man
and whenever I do, it hurts...'

*Robbie enters with a Superdrug carrier bag.*

| ROBBIE | ...you spoke. |
|---|---|
| JADE | TV. |
| ROBBIE | Praise the – |
| JADE | Hey it was only – |
| ROBBIE | Volume's off, it's your mouth Jade, speaking like |

*words* again... *(switches off TV)*

**JADE** *(dawning)* Wow. Language.

**ROBBIE**      Yeah. No more blood or puke. *(cleans Jade's face
with wet-wipes from the carrier bag.)* Keep on.

| | |
|---|---|
| **JADE** | Uh? |
| **ROBBIE** | Use it. Speak. Or lose it again. |
| **JADE** | Say what. |
| **ROBBIE** | Say what you want to say. |
| **JADE** | Can't. |
| **ROBBIE** | Why. |
| **JADE** | My head. The voices. |
| **ROBBIE** | Saying what. |
| **JADE** | You don't want to know. |
| **ROBBIE** | Talk out the evil, Jade. |

**JADE** *(hyper)* Voices won't let me say what I want to say – too much pain – on cold grey rock the red blood weeping –

| | |
|---|---|
| **ROBBIE** | She's going weird again. |
| **JADE** | Never... |
| **ROBBIE** | You're going weird again. |
| **JADE** | Nevermore... |
| **ROBBIE** | Then say what *I* want you to say. |
| **JADE** | ...like what. |
| **ROBBIE** | Owt. Summat positive. Make summat up. |
| **JADE** | Robbie is the North's greatest lay. |
| **ROBBIE** | Yeah, yeah... now say what I want to *hear*. |
| **JADE** | You want me to confess. |
| **ROBBIE** | I wish you to get better. |
| **JADE** | You want me to repent. |
| **ROBBIE** | I'd like you to be well. |
| **JADE** | You want me to take the fall for us fucking each |

other's guts out.

| | |
|---|---|
| **ROBBIE** | She's talking sick again. |
| **JADE** | You want me to kneel and lick your – |
| **ROBBIE** | Is this the voices? Or is this Jade? |

**JADE** *(hyper)* Voices bleed a waterfall onto desert sand that burns with such... such ...longing ...for *who I might have been...*

*Silence.*

| | |
|---|---|
| **ROBBIE** | Fair enough. |
| **JADE** | Hey. |
| **ROBBIE** | I'm not very clever. I'm really not very clever. |
| **JADE** | You asked for talk, you wanted me to – |

**ROBBIE** *(grabs her)* All I want is for you to be SAVED ... ready?
**JADE**          Later.
**ROBBIE**          Now.
**JADE**          Something's changed.
**ROBBIE**          Think positive.
**JADE**          Inside.
**ROBBIE**          Think legs.
**JADE**          Coming out.
**ROBBIE**          Then let rip: if we can't talk out the evil we must *walk* it out, think movement Jade.
**JADE**          Please just hear out / my –
**ROBBIE**          Think: 'Hallelujah, this time I STAND!'
*(He hauls Jade to her feet. She takes a step.)* Mercy! The Cripple rises again. Sure as Christ cured lepers –
*(A squirt of diarrhoea. Jade crumples. Robbie ransacks his carrier bag.)*
*Wet-wipe. Elastoplast.* Cotton wool. *Germolene. Kleenex. Tampax.* Bib... *(He re-counts) Wet-wipe. Elastoplast.* Cotton wool. *Germolene. Kleenex. Tampax...* forgot the nappies.
**JADE** *(weak)* Use *Kleenex.*
**ROBBIE**          I'll GET them, okay? *Superdrug* 're open till –
**JADE**          Stay home. It's theft.
**ROBBIE**          What's another crime? More punishment eh? Already broke my vow to Brother Paul about Sex Before Marriage, and here are we, living in SIN and SHIT –
**JADE**          So use *Wet-wipes.*
*Robbie attacks the dirty sofa with a wet-wipe.*

**ROBBIE**          Crap, *Wet-wipe. Wet-wipe,* crap. Crap, *Wet-wipe Wet- wipe Wet-wipe* What's wrong with her who is she where's her grace? *(He stops attacking the sofa.)*
...*Superdrug* recognise my arse: I'll try *Mothercare.*
**JADE**          You're not my mother, Robbie.
**ROBBIE**          Right. I'm your carer. I care and I care.

*Robbie exits. Jade picks up the TV remote from her diarrhoea, channel surfs, finds a soundless talk show. A woman weeps.*

**JADE** *(lipsyncs)* 'She was our only child Montel. Brought up normal. Prayers at bed. Sunday Mass. Everything in order. And then her confirmation. Should've seen her dress. My husband called her his blessed virgin angel. Then she knelt at the cross. Kissed its feet. Wet her confirmation dress. Bled all over the altar. *(Chris enters unseen, a white hygiene mask over his face.)* The shame. I lost control. Wanted her to suffer like us. But her father took my only child away.' *(Chris pulls on surgical rubber gloves.)* Why is there no order?

*Chris wields a pair of surgical shears. Jade freezes as he snips apart her filthy clothes and bandages.*

**CHRIS**        What a mess. They did it. On full pay. 'Pending Disciplinary Action' ...patient ODs, doctor gets suspended... 1 mean you were there that night: chaos. How could I know the girl in Cubicle 9's diabetic?

**JADE**        you came

**CHRIS**        A conspiracy of course... there's A&E staff snuff a child a month and get promoted. And now loving each moment. Of the trashing of Dr Howell.

**JADE**        he came

**CHRIS**        Can't have you *both* on my record, another screw-up like Cubicle 9, I'm toast... Doctors, eh? Specialist this, consultant that, hooked on detail, never kick back to view the full picture... I've had it with fragments Jade... need your whole person laid bare because this shit means something...

*Chris pulls Jade clear of her cut-up rags.*

**JADE**        my saviour...

**CHRIS**        Jesus Christ.

*As Chris carries Jade away her whole body is exposed: the side wound is deep and raw; holes in both hands and feet.*

## SCENE 7

*A derelict building littered with syringes, used condoms, porn.*
*Outside: sirens and flashing lights. Robbie enters breathless,*
*clutching a pack of Huggies. He hides. Siren and lights fade. Robbie*
*stands up to find a syringe embedded in his knee.*

**ROBBIE**     Shoplifter. Criminal. Victim. Freak. *(mantra)*
Pretend you're someone else Pretend you're someone else
*(He pulls the syringe. It stays embedded.)* Smile. Think positive.
Think Club Pure Ecstasy. Pretend you're someone else, someone
good, then it can't hurt. *(pulls syringe. It won't budge. It hurts.)*
Pure Ecstasy? What're we *on*? Like: hello pricks, welcome to
Planet Fistfuck, wake up to the... pain. Yeah. Pure pain. Pure
religion. Yeah. Religion's pain, pure as this... place? This, this
what-they-used-to-call CHURCH. *(looks around)* See?
Dickheads? Pure religion. Built in brick. Opposite of clubbing.
Fun. Soft things. Bro' Paul were wrong – religion's a hard bastard:
square, uncool, lonely, dark, forgot, condemned, but REAL. As
PAIN. So get real, uh? Prickhead frown. Frig fun. Frig ecstasy.
Think negative for once. *(mantra)* Don't pretend you're someone
else Don't pretend you're no-one else. *(He pulls the syringe hard.*
*It comes out.)* ...cah! *(He kneels to pray.)*
Lord, who puts thorn in flesh
As punishment and that
Here in your house
You, like, cleanse me with pain
*(His bad knee gives, and he pitches forward into the litter.)*Huh?
*(He brushes litter from a yellowing, coverless book.)* 'The Old...'
Ha ha. *(blows dust)* 'The Old Test...' *(flicks through)* ...and it shall
come to pass... when the vir-gin com-eth forth...' Ha ha. *(flicks)*
'...unto the thick darkness... clothed in a vest – a vesture dipped in
blood, and his name is called The word of God...' God's word? In
my hands? Whoa. *(flicks, stops)* 'Rise up and be transformed.'

## SCENE 8

*Chris's place. He's on the phone and the net: his PC monitor shows*
*medical close-ups of gaping wounds.*

**CHRIS**          Prozac 50. Valium. *(Pause)* Oral uh-huh: and
Morphine. *(Pause)* 10. *(Pause)* Er, shots. Hold them for Chris,
A&E. I'm due at hospital now so... *(Pause)* Chris. *(Pause)*
Howell. *(Pause)* And? *(Pause)* Look, I can still give drugs, I'm
suspended, not struck off.

*Jade enters in a wheelchair. She's heavily bandaged, plus an
eyepatch. Chris hangs up the phone, clicks off his PC monitor.*

**JADE**          Saint Christopher.
**CHRIS**         Me?
**JADE**          In bed. You open my lips. And in the hole you push
a finger – no, a wafer – and it melted and I am healed.
**CHRIS**         ...dream on.
**JADE**          Uh?
**CHRIS**         That was the last Valium I fed you. You should be
dead to the world. *(takes her pulse)* How do you feel.
**JADE**          I feel wheelchairs are the perfect height for blow
jobs, so talking to your crotch is screwing with our doctor /
patient relationship. *(Chris sits at Jade's level with a stethoscope.)*
Anyroad I'm sorted.
**CHRIS**         Inhale.
**JADE**          Found the cause. Of everything.
**CHRIS**         And out.
**JADE** *(obeying)* I'm talking L...S...E...
**CHRIS**         S.L.E.'s auto-immune. Body rips itself apart like a
wolf attack – Lupus in Latin. Systemic Lupus Erithrea. You
tested negative.

*Chris takes Jade's blood pressure.*

**JADE**          Nuh *L.S.E.* – Low Self Esteem Chris... I mean, all
week you' ve taken the piss out of me.
**CHRIS**         Uh-huh.
**JADE**          And the shit. And the blood.
**CHRIS**         Relax your fist please.
**JADE**          And sweat. And skin. And hair. And who can forget
my smear?
**CHRIS**         Okay chill...

**JADE**     But each test came out negative. So, it's official. I'm
   Jade Negative. So there's nothing wrong, right? Except I hate
   myself. Test positive for just one thing: Negative Body Image.
   Well sod that Montel... *(TV voice)* Hi. I'm Jade Positive. Birth
   sign Cancer – the crab not the disease. Got one?
**CHRIS**     Birth sign? Caesarean.
**JADE** *(TV laugh)* Nowadays I'm treated private, 24-7. He only takes
   the piss because I'm *worth* it... yeah... *(begins unwrapping
   bandages)* I'm Jade Positive and I love myself... look... *(She can't)*
   Dare you girl: be positive. *(sob)* With a healthy beautiful Body
   Image –

*Chris injects Jade: she shrieks.*

**CHRIS**     Sorry, Jade. Sedative.
**JADE** *(deadpan)* Ow.
**CHRIS**     You used to feel nothing.
**JADE**     You used to be gentle.
**CHRIS**     Yeah, before your flesh turned into pizzacrust.
**JADE**     Now you're hard eh.
**CHRIS**     Only a jab.
**JADE**     One cold hard prick.
**CHRIS**     And now the abuse. *(packing up)* Just like Casualty.
**JADE**     ...you wouldn't.
**CHRIS**     Hn?
**JADE**     If I wake up in hospital I'll top myself.
**CHRIS**     I thought you loved yourself.
**JADE**     Fuck off. *(Pause. Chris makes to leave.)*
   Um don't fuck off. Till I crash?
**CHRIS**     I'll be late for my hearing.
**JADE** *(hyper)* But when I'm alone the moon turns red and butchers
   come with with hammers and ten inch nails –
**CHRIS**     Nails?
**JADE** *(pause)* Said needles.
**CHRIS**     You said hammers and *nails*.
**JADE**     I said... hammers and nails.

*Silence.*

**CHRIS**          Fine. *(checks watch)* I stay till you crash, if you answer my questions. Deal?

**JADE**          Actually I'm better now. You can go and –

*Chris hits a button on his PC. Files print out.*

**CHRIS**          1: Is there a History? Maybe, but the patient won't admit it. 2: A Trigger? Robbie Psycho. Absolutely. 3? Medical Evidence. The killer... the body never lies does it, you can't cheat biology: when the map of a victim's wounds equal those on the dying body / of –

**JADE**          Dying.

**CHRIS**          Let me finish –

**JADE**          I am.

**CHRIS**          Not yet, listen –

**JADE**          He did.

**CHRIS**          ...he?

**JADE**          I am cos he did.

**CHRIS**          ...are we *getting* somewhere?

**JADE**          Who cares I'm dying.

**CHRIS**          That's only the / drugs –

**JADE**          He died I'm dead / okay?

**CHRIS**          *He* you say, / He –

**JADE**          Him. Father.

**CHRIS**          ...of course I see that: He goes by many names yes Jade: Father Son and Holy –

**JADE**          Dad. Dad. *(hyper)* Under the sign of the Tortured Man you and Mum drink the wine eat the bread call me your blessed virgin angel... 1 know you must confirm me to to to save my soul but Daddy please it HURTS... you pray I bleed you kiss I kick you fall on the chapel floor cracked rib –

*Jade spews blood. Chris intervenes. Jade resists.*

**CHRIS**          – come on –

**JADE**          – guuh –

**CHRIS**          – why are you –

**JADE**          – DNI –

**CHRIS**          – Jade I – where did you –

**JADE**          His chart *(gasp)* they write *(gasp)* Pneumonia DNI
DNI –
**CHRIS**         Breathe!

*Jade obeys. Her gasps subside.*

**JADE**          ...so they Did. Not. Intervene. One less hospital bed
wasted. Dad were fifty-eight. Cause of death? Life. Quality of.
Had he lived he'd have none. Sure he'd have life, but the wrong
Quality. That's what they said. The doctors. Patrick McNaught
DNl... he died for my sin, right? Under the sign of the red cross.
Mother cried, I bled and bled. Under the sign of the Tortured
Man.
**CHRIS**         Listen to yourself.
**JADE**          For what?
**CHRIS**         Diagnosis.
**JADE**          Of what...medical murder?
**CHRIS**         RELIGION. *(Silence. Chris speaks into a
dictaphone.)*'Patient's history confirms... all this... it's caused /
by –
**JADE**          But I'm atheist.
**CHRIS** *(into dictaphone)* Patient in denial about her twisted faith,
her subconscious morphing of father's spiritual and genetic –
**JADE**          FUCK FAITH! I believe in TOSS ALL, which
means I'm NORMAL okay? Modern like EVERYONE ELSE.
**CHRIS**         Yeah? My family didn't believe in medicine, only
prayer. When I became a medic they trashed their belief. In *me*.
**JADE**          ...Jehovah's Witness?
**CHRIS**         Close. The name of my wound is Christian Scientist:
what's yours, Catholic?
**JADE**          Feng shui if you must know. I'll finish college, go
professional –
**CHRIS**         Feng shit. Religion Lite. Get real Jade, out of denial,
face up to –
**JADE**          Dr Hard. Dr Ice.
**CHRIS**         Hard's Robbie. Religion Heavy. No Feng Shui for
him: hard as your Dad, is he?
**JADE**          As your prick Chris. *(Silence.)* Hard on my thigh
Chris. *(Silence.)* Since you injected me... *(Chris switches off his*

*dictaphone.) That it? You a meat freak? Guts sex you up? That why you took me in? And fuck with my head? So you can fuck with my head? That your religion is it? (Jade rips off her eyepatch, revealing a punctured forehead weeping into a bloody eye.)* Come worship. Fuck with my head big time. Like you always wanted. Ever since hospital... hey: Casualty must be heaven, one endless snuff movie, so do it sick fucker make it terminal. *(Chris backs off from Jade.)* Wow.

| | |
|---|---|
| **CHRIS** | Jade. |
| **JADE** | Terminal. |
| **CHRIS** | Jade – |
| **JADE** | Injection... |

*Jade somehow rises from the wheelchair, grabs the phone.*

**CHRIS**        I wouldn't do that.

*She dials the phone, voice blurring.*

| | |
|---|---|
| **JADE** | ...what did you spike me with. |
| **CHRIS** | Sleep. Rest. |
| **JADE** | What did you SHOOT me with? |

*Jade talks down the phone with growing disability.*

**JADE**        999 It's HIM Doc-tor DEATH Play-ing GOD. *(Jade falls. Chris catches her.)* devil... I thought you... my saviour...
**CHRIS**        A thought is just glucose plus oxygen. Let it go.

*Jade slumps lifeless. Chris wheels her away.*

**SCENE 9**
*Flashing lights. An ambulance passes. By a large red cross and a road sign pointing the way to 'Emergency,' Robbie waits at a bus stop, reading his book. Chris enters, trying to light up.*

**ROBBIE**        Friend. *(Chris sees Robbie, wishes he hadn't.)* Outpatients me. Need injections regular. You?
**CHRIS**        Meeting. Management.

**ROBBIE**          Here? *(He lights Chris's cigarette.)* Give you cancer,
mate.
**CHRIS**          Really? That's me damned.

*They laugh.*

**ROBBIE**          Cancer's good for the soul as it happens. The agony
right? Makes victims humble. Like my Mam. Till doctors go
wreck it with painkillers.
**CHRIS**          Medics eh? Intervene, not intervene: each way we're
shafted.
**ROBBIE**          Vegetable was it?
**CHRIS**          Hn?
**ROBBIE**          Your meeting. About the, like, girl you turned into
a—
**CHRIS**          The girl in Cubicle 9? She's awake in fact.
**ROBBIE**          Whoa.
**CHRIS**          Upgraded from vegetable to animal. Last week she
had the IQ of a cabbage. Today? Brain of a snail. Given time who
knows? She might even regain the intelligence of a *Westlife* fan.
**ROBBIE**          …a miracle then? Praise the Lord.
**CHRIS**          Praise Intensive Care
**ROBBIE**          Ah it were prayer got you through.
**CHRIS**          I don't pray Robbie. Only blaspheme.
**ROBBIE**          I mean mine, in Church: down on them knees in the
porn and smack. All to save your arse, which means you owe me.
Yeah. You owe me Jade... *(Silence.)* Last night I switched to
*Burger King*. First in how long. Took a bite: chucked it. Weren't
the meat though, burgers can't change... but I have Doc. Normal
me. As of whenever I am transformed and ready for Jade. *(Chris
stubs his cigarette to go. Robbie blocks his way.)* Wanted help not
theft –
**CHRIS**          She was too far gone, you were the trigger for –
**ROBBIE**          Gone aye: 8 days, 5 hours, 23 minutes.
**CHRIS**          I took a professional decision to –
**ROBBIE**          Screw her. *(Pause. Chris tries to light up. He can't.)*
…where is she, your place?
**CHRIS**          Around.
**ROBBIE**          Round here?

| | |
|---|---|
| **CHRIS** | Around about here. |
| **ROBBIE** | Outpatients? General Ward? A&E? The Morgue? |
| **CHRIS** | Confidential. |
| **ROBBIE** | Where's that. |
| **CHRIS** | A doctor – patient thing. |
| **ROBBIE** | Whoa... you got a Thing? |
| **CHRIS** | Yes. No. A relationship. |
| **ROBBIE** | So… was a Thing, now a Relationship? |
| **CHRIS** | Of *trust,* yes: a thing – a confidential relationship of– |
| **ROBBIE** | 'Your Trust In Our Hands.' |
| **CHRIS** | Well, that's our hospital mission statement. |
| **ROBBIE** | Maybe your trust's a cover, to like wipe out us |

crippled and that...

| | |
|---|---|
| **CHRIS** | Robbie. Get therapy. |

*Chris exits.*

**ROBBIE**          …therapy's talking, right? Instead of needles right? Hung round here that long waiting for you to turn up I kind of did. Got it. Therapy.

*Chris enters.*

| | |
|---|---|
| **CHRIS** | You *talked* – |
| **ROBBIE** | About me. And thou. And my Jade. |
| **CHRIS** | ...told a cop? My boss? |
| **ROBBIE** | Him aye. |
| **CHRIS** | –but I just – at the meeting – he said nothing about – |
| **ROBBIE** | He's bang wild, pal. |
| **CHRIS** | Shit. *Shite.* One mistake and – |
| **ROBBIE** | Two mistakes: *(counts)* Cubicle 9, Jade McNaught – |
| **CHRIS** | Haven't I paid enough? |
| **ROBBIE** | Not for murder. |

*Flashing lights. An ambulance glides past.*

**CHRIS**          Okay: over there, top floor: tell my boss you're wrong I'm no Harold Shipman okay: all I did to Jade was –
**ROBBIE**          Not her. Third mistake. We killed someone older.

**CHRIS**    ...we –?

**ROBBIE**    US! Or have you conveniently forgot?

**CHRIS**    Killed who? Fucking WHO? Robbie – headcase – who've we trashed if not Jade?

**ROBBIE**    Our FATHER. *(sob)* You and me. *(sob)* And the moon turned red. And sickness came. And pitbulls. And crack. And now the reckoning... 'Cos maybe he weren't extinct all along, only watching us piss on his grave, waiting for us to find him again... oh we try. Surf websites: blank. Cruise brothels: dick. Check out jail: zero tolerance. Dance clubland dry, no action... so me. I do. I dare. I look in the mirror. *(He claws at his disfigurement.)* Uglybug. If HE exists how dare HE curse ME with this... this... GOD you CUNT.

*(Far away, briefly, a siren wails.)*

Then. On my knees. I look down. *(He flicks through his book.)* ...He's well in command... think He care if I've a face like a butcher's shop? He's the future pal. Back from the past in a blaze of sirens from the sky... the Father we killed but couldn't kill is HERE, and mad as owt, and He says peace and love? They're over. Party's over. Last time we blew it. This time it's personal. He's talking hardcore faith for a hardcore age and we must be pure. And moral. Are you with me?

**CHRIS**    It's over.

**ROBBIE**    Such is the test. The Old Test. Brother, do you test positive? Will you give me Jade?

**CHRIS**    I'm not your brother.

**ROBBIE**    Reckon?

**CHRIS**    Jade's beyond you now.

**ROBBIE**    Fair enough. *(He hits Chris with his book.)* 'He shall be driven from light into darkness. Repent. His remembrance shall be driven from the earth. Surrender to the Almighty!'

*Siren: an ambulance screams past. Chris grabs Robbie's book. They fight. It rips. As Robbie gathers its pages, Chris floors him, by chance.*

**CHRIS**    Shit. *(He drags Robbie into the shadows.)* It's your appendix. Too much *Burger King*. Eat bark, dung, anything primitive. *(thunk)* Mm: neck damage also. From gravity, and walking upright... in fact there's trauma way down to the coccyx. *(thunk)* The what?

**ROBBIE**          Ughh...
**CHRIS**           The *what?*
**ROBBIE**          ...cock-six...
**CHRIS**           Last bone of the spine, feel it? *(thunk)* Bible basher? *(thunk)* Why does it prove we're apes and Darwin rules and your book lies?
**ROBBIE**          Urghhh
**CHRIS**           Because the COCCYX *(thunk)* is what's left of our TAIL...

*Chris comes out of the shadows. Robbie doesn't.*

**CHRIS**           Day we met, upstairs from Casualty, I'd just pushed a baby's eye back in its head with my thumb and a plastic spoon. Her *eye* Robbie... *(dials mobile)* Kid's Mum says – kisses my hand, says – GOD is a DOCTOR. *(on phone)* Ambulance? Some crip hit a road sign. I came the Samaritan. *(pause, laugh)* Weirdest thing, you'll find him right outside your –

*From behind, Robbie presses a gold cross to Chris's cheek. He speaks on Chris's mobile.*

**ROBBIE**          Fake call. He got it wrong. Gambled against the resurrection. *(hangs up)* 'He that reproveth God, let him answer it.'

*Robbie pulls Chris into the darkness behind the sign.*

**SCENE 10**
*Chris's place. Jade lifeless in bed, full of tubes and wholly bandaged, even her eyes. A doorbell buzzes. Jade goes into spasm, blindly hitting Chris's remote. His TV plays a DVD, out of focus.*

**TV CHRIS** *(as voiceover)* Subject sedated.
**JADE** *(blind)*    ...Chris?
**TV CHRIS**        Condition extreme.

| | |
|---|---|
| **JADE** | Doctor – |
| **TV CHRIS** | Treatment unlikely. Prognosis unknown. Diagnosis |

unbelievable...

*Jade peels the dressings from her eyes – just as what could be her own naked body comes into focus on-screen. Unconscious and profoundly mutilated. Jade watches TV. Robbie enters, watching only Jade.*

| | |
|---|---|
| **ROBBIE** | Whoa. |
| **JADE** | Yeah. |
| **ROBBIE** | So? |
| **JADE** | So what? |
| **ROBBIE** | So...what is this? |
| **JADE** | What is this what. |
| **ROBBIE** | *This*. What I'm looking at. |
| **JADE** | Celebrity Makeover. Mystery Guest. They take |

someone normal, change her into someone famous, then everyone tries to guess who: only some people know already, so they better shut the fuck up.

**ROBBIE**    Frig TV Jade. I watch reality. And out here in reality *you look Iike* –

**JADE** *(looks at him)* You look older. Jacket maybe. Next?

**ROBBIE**    ...next...

**JADE**    The label. We are what we wear, right? My label's *Body Shop* if you must know. I model their designer bandages. These 're hand-made. By lepers. In Sodom.

**TV CHRIS** *(voiceover)* Subject: delusional fantasist. History: Religious abuse. Gentlemen, she denies the past, only for it to be reborn in her flesh...

**ROBBIE** *(looks at TV)* Who – ha ha – that looks like –

**JADE**    SHUT THE FUCK UP! *(She hits the remote. The screen goes blank. Silence.)* Doesn 't fit. The image. All wrong.

**ROBBIE**    Reckon.

**JADE**    Bad buy. Return it.

*Jade gestures at Robbie's jacket.*

**ROBBIE**    ...oh, uh, jacket? It's borrowed.

JADE          You're dead then.
ROBBIE        Eh?
JADE          He'll gut you, the owner, you marked it, don't look
    at *me,* check out that... stain, Robbie, there, on the arm –
ROBBIE        Water.
JADE          It's red.
ROBBIE        Wine.
JADE          You don't drink.
ROBBIE        *He* did. The owner. The ex-owner. He smoked he
    drunk he whored he blasphemed –
JADE          It's blood.
ROBBIE        Jade it's whachacall... inherited.
JADE          Someone left you his *blood*?
ROBBIE        His jacket.
JADE          Shed it quick or it hijacks you possesses your / soul -
ROBBIE *(counts)* Jacket, mobile, plus you of course: Iceman's
    earthly possessions. His image – now *mine.*
    *(lights one of Chris's cigarettes.)* TV included.
JADE          ...television's evil.
ROBBIE        So said Robbie Soft. *(smokes)* Robbie Hard says
    Evil is Live backwards. Either way I can take it.
JADE          Yeah? Lived is Devil backwards, can you take that?
ROBBIE        You're talking Dr Devil, sure I took him.
JADE          You did?
ROBBIE        Got Biblical on his arse. Sin by sin.
JADE          You did him.
ROBBIE        Lust Pride Greed Wrath Mindless Frigging Violence
    now he's sorta kinda ever so slightly DAMNED.

*Robbie advances on Jade.*

JADE          Fuck off. I'm sick.
ROBBIE        *Were* sick now you're on video: this shit *means*
    summat –

*He triggers the remote. The body on TV is now clearly Jade.*

TV CHRIS *(voiceover)* – fessor Lukic, members of the Hospital
    Trust, let me put my career in turnaround by proving what you

see... is one hundred per cent Stigmata. To begin with her crown of thorns –

*The TV shorts, sparks, and goes blank. A long silence.*

**JADE**        Not me.
**ROBBIE**    But the picture.
**JADE**        The Tortured Man up there.
**ROBBIE**    What it shows...
**JADE**        Is not me.
**ROBBIE**    Under them bandages.

*While Robbie pumps the TV remote, Jade pulls out her tubes.*

**JADE**        Get real Jade.
**ROBBIE**    Ohhh it's a *test* right? The New Test...
**JADE**        Out of denial.
**ROBBIE**    Like do I worship her arse? Or burn it?
**JADE**        Take control. Embrace the Grace.
**ROBBIE**    Choose right I'm saved, wrong I'm damned. *(trashes TV remote)* Christ I need the FULL PICTURE –

*Jade pulls at her catheter. Screams. Robbie pulls out Jade's catheter... tubeless but still bandaged, she rises.*

**JADE**        Okay. Full picture. I am the full picture... think. Robbie? The trashing of Dr Howell's remote. The trashing of Dr Howell's jacket. The trashing of Dr Howell... it's cool. So chill. *(She kisses Robbie's hand.)* You are...forgiven.
**ROBBIE**    Yeah?
**JADE**        Everything: ozone, landmines, mad cows, Jill Dando, anything... even though you turned me from a Munchie into... into *this*... wow: I regain the power to forgive.

*Jade kisses Robbie's forehead.*

**ROBBIE**    Didn't hurt.
**JADE**        Storming.
**ROBBIE**    ...so where is it.

**JADE**          Huh?

**ROBBIE**        The pain.

**JADE** *(blurt)* Everywhere, don't ask: when I said I felt nothing I was
lying, I feel everything, like the the the Tortured Man... I must
take it: He did. With the power to forgive comes the cost of of
*having* to forgive... all of it. The world's guilt and shit. I must
take it. Like He did. Though it hurts...

**ROBBIE**        ...so can I have some.

**JADE**          Of what.

**ROBBIE**        Pain.

**JADE** *(laughs)* You have enough. *(Jade kisses Robbie's disfigurement.)* Smile, Robbie: you're healed.

**ROBBIE**        ...so quick?

**JADE**          Your pain is mine now: you're free.

**ROBBIE**        How easy.

**JADE**          Yeah at last I was... good enough.

**ROBBIE**        Right modern.

**JADE**          Now uh... get my wheelchair eh.

**ROBBIE**        Too twenty-first century.

**JADE**          We can do it. Just rush me to Casualty and –

**ROBBIE**        Need more pain not less.

**JADE**          Hey I won't last the night without / medical –

**ROBBIE**        Salvation needs damage Jade... like how can we be
saved... unless we suffer?

**JADE**          With love.

**ROBBIE**        Fuck love.

**JADE**          Sure. I was there. But now –

**ROBBIE**        Fuck love you said –

**JADE**          That was the sick me, the dead me, now I'm arisen –

**ROBBIE**        Red mouth, your teeth, you said –

**JADE**          Love's blood Robbie... it flows from our wounds
regardless as the stars...

**ROBBIE**        Fuck love you said. Fuck love snarls God.

**JADE**          Listen listen He speaks to me right? He says we can't
fuck love only cherish –

**ROBBIE**        See you said what God growls and God barks fuck
Love cos GOD is DOG backwards... *(He shows his gold cross.
Jade recoils.)* ...tore off my modern face when my modern ears
wouldn't heed his old hard soundbite: *(barks)* NO PAIN NO

GAIN NO PAIN NO – (*He kneels on the upturned blade of the cross.*) …cah!

*Jade breaks for the door. Crumples in agony. Robbie crawls toward her. They struggle.*

**ROBBIE** CHRIST. I. NEED. YOUR. PAIN –

*The bandage rips from Jade's head, revealing a crown of holes in her skull, plus the shadow marks of an early beard...*

**JADE** accident
emergency
how did this happen
once l was young
lived only for the light
and the promise of tomorrow
then yesterday
from the shadows came
the agony
father why
to be made whole
must we first be broken?
**ROBBIE** *(kisses her feet)* I'm sorry.
**JADE** ...Father you have cursed me with the incurable
disease of being human
**ROBBIE** *(kisses her knees)* Forgive me.
**JADE** I crossed the desert sand
I found the promised land
I dignified the weak
I turned the other cheek
I threw the rich men out
I made the downtrod proud
**ROBBIE** *(kisses her thighs)* Blessed virgin angel –
**JADE** daddy WHY HAST THOU FORSAKEN ME?
*(Robbie kisses Jade's crotch. Jade wets herself. And Robbie. He tears away her wet bandages, revealing a Christ-like androgyne riddled with stigmata.)*

el eloi avinu
lama sabachthani
hosanna hosanna hosanna

*As Jade repeats the mantra, Robbie finds Chris's lighter fuel.*

**ROBBIE**        'God hath delivered me to the ungodly.'
*(As Jade repeats the mantra Robbie pours the fuel over Jade.)*
'Turned me over into the hands of the wicked.'
*(As Jade repeats the mantra he pours fuel over himself.)*
'My face is foul with weeping
And on min eyelids is the shadow of death.
For wrath bringeth the punishments of the sword,
That ye ma know there is a judgement.'

*As Jade repeats the mantra Robbie flicks Chris's lighter.*

**JADE**          hosanna hosanna hosanna

*Robbie is still flicking the lighter, as Chris enters.*

**CHRIS**         Beautiful.
*(To dictaphone)* 'Stigmata update: get this?
She looks like Christ crucified because she *is*.
From Saint Francis onward, some freaks react so deeply to the
crucifixion it possesses them. Literally. No fraud no ketchup
gentlemen: it only needs a trigger to –
**ROBBIE**        Bastard you're DEAD – *(He rushes Chris. His bad
knee gives way. Jade speaks in tongues.)*
**CHRIS**         Hear her? Jade is not Jade now, only the host of her
disease.
**ROBBIE**        LORD SHOW THYSELF.
**CHRIS**         Robbie you did this. Just like her Dad.
**ROBBIE**        HERESY STRIKE 'EM DOWN –
**JADE**          guuuh –
**CHRIS**         Breathe! *(He slaps Jade. Silence.)* …better?
**JADE**          I'm dead
**CHRIS**         Not quite.
**JADE**          you crucified me

**CHRIS**        The name of your wound is psychoneuro-
immunology.

**JADE**        ... psycho...

**CHRIS**        The memory / sound / image of bad faith hardwired
in your primal brain.

**JADE**        ...my voices...

**CHRIS**        Once triggered, they blast your nervous system
which in turn somehow makes your immune system misfire and
burn these same hardcore images in your flesh.

**JADE**        ...why...

**CHRIS**        Well, you 're ill. Add history. And religion. The SM
mind-fuck of praying to an image of crucifixion for years when
you were young.

**JADE**        ...but my wounds –

**CHRIS**        Are real.

**JADE**        Are Christ's wounds.

**CHRIS**        Not quite. He was *roped* to the cross.

**JADE**        But the nails –

**CHRIS**        The nails, the hammer and nails are a Catholic myth
Jade, never happened.

**JADE**        BUT THE SPIRIT OF CHRIST IS WITHIN ME.

**CHRIS**        Jesus is alive okay. In your immunology.
*(To dictaphone)* Christ as medical affliction? The Vatican hid
their own research. I found it. So here we are at the death of faith,
ahead of the pack... just. Gentlemen I name this disease Immuno-
Stigmata: Howell's Syndrome. Thank you.

**ROBBIE** *(wrecked)* Dr Devil.

**JADE**        – Robbie –

**ROBBIE**      – here –

**JADE**        –help me –

**ROBBIE**      – how –

**JADE**        – pray for me –

**ROBBIE**      – yes –

**JADE**        – save me –

**CHRIS**        He can't. But there's a clinic. Private. They take
samples. DNA. The code of life within us yeah? Each program
longer than eight hundred Bibles. This clinic deal in futures.
Okay? Their pitch: if Immuno-Stigmata's weird enough to burn
thoughts into your flesh, what if spliced into the DNA of, say, a

cancer victim? Some day tumours could explode with one
positive thought, a prayer... I send this film to the clinic tonight,
tomorrow we go there.

**JADE**          ...I'd be cured.

**CHRIS**         You'll be loaded.

**JADE**          And cured?

**CHRIS**         You *are* the cure.

**JADE**          ...but not cured?

**CHRIS**         Immortal. Your immune system at least.

**JADE** *(beat)* I'm incurable.

**CHRIS**         You are... beyond cure... I'm sorry. But your DNA
could live forever, zapping illness and disability like a, well,
miracle.

**JADE**          You sell my body? To someone else. They use it. To
wipe out the crippled?

**CHRIS**         Jade our genetic saviour. *(Silence.)* Well?

**JADE**          Maybe.

**ROBBIE**        Don't.

**JADE**          Maybe I should.

**ROBBIE**        Don't do it.

**JADE**          Maybe I should keep my mystery. *(She stands,
begins the long painful walk to the door.)*

**CHRIS**         Suicide of course. You won't last the night. Get real
Jade. I need you to live on...

**JADE** *(stops at the door)* You need a sample?

**ROBBIE**        Walk away.

**CHRIS**         A part of you must live on. *(picks up a syringe.)*

**JADE**          Just one more prick?

**CHRIS**         I take your blood: your DNA lives forever.
*(Jade grabs the syringe from Chris.)* What – *(She spikes her
deepest wound.)* Not that way – it's tainted. I need a clean vein.
*(Jade presses the syringe of blood to Chris's neck)* ...you're
fucking with power beyond imagining –

**JADE**          So do doctors. With hard-ons.

**CHRIS**         Twisted sick SPASTIC –

**JADE**          Howell's Syndrome. Disease? Or Messiah? You
choose. *(She takes the syringe from Chris's neck and squirts the
blood all over him.)* Shit is made from bile. Bile from blood. And
bile is made from anger. Through blood, anger turns to shit...

Disease or messiah I'm worth more than this. (*She throws the empty syringe away.*) Come on.

**ROBBIE**   Where?

**JADE**   Wherever.

**ROBBIE**   We'll never make it.

**JADE**   Try. In order to be made whole –

**ROBBIE**   I'm… forgiven? (*Jade kisses Robbie on the lips.*) … phew… but… what about the Devil?

**JADE**   He means nothing. He doesn't exist. We're on our own. Follow me.

*Jade and Robbie exit. Chris is still dripping with Jade's blood.*

**CHRIS**   If heaven is what we love
hell is what we love
multiplied by infinity.

*Slow fade to darkness.*
*The end.*

**Peter Wolf**
Theatre: *Cargo Cult* (RSC), *The Last Crusade* (Kings Head), *Kill Devil Hills* (Elephant Theatre), *The Spirit of Jack Cade* (Edinburgh), *Beware the White Man* (Lilian Baylis Theatre), *Raising Mrs Rossetti* (Link Theatre), *Eisgeist (*Young Vic Theatre), *The Golem* (Bridewell Theatre), *Blood and Sperm* (Geilgud Theatre).

Radio: *Volcano* (runner-up Writers Guild Award), *The Man in the Elephant Mask, Death in Venice, City of the Mind, Strange meeting, The Blue Flower, The Prince, Ghost on the Moor, Crossing the Line.*

Libretto: *Silence and Poverty* (European tour/radio) *Silberkreuzung* (Klangspuren International Festival/radio.)

**<u>peeling</u>**

# peeling

I first learnt and used Sign-Supported English (SSE) in performance in 1987, when working as an actor with Grae*ae* Theatre Company. The urgent physicality of a spatial language delighted me; its fluidity made perfect sense to my then partially sighted vision.

Later, as my focus shifted to writing for performance, this interest developed. As a hearing writer, the notion of words, so apparently anchored with ink to the page, suddenly taking flight into three-dimensional language intoxicated me. I began working with Sign Dance Theatre and observed a transformation, where the literary text I had written became embodied; meaning sculpted in the air.

Eventually, my experimentation with form and the relationship between signed and spoken/written language led me back to Grae*ae* and Jenny Sealey. This collaboration was inevitable. Apart from her groundbreaking work with sign language in performance, it was Jenny who first introduced me to SSE in 1987 and set me off on this journey.

**peeling** is an experiment, an integrated collaboration between hearing and Deaf women theatre practitioners. The following text is the pre-rehearsal draft, a blueprint, which has not yet been tried and tested and will certainly change in production.

I'm aware that what we're trying to do, in form and content, may be provocative. Yet it is an attempt at total communication. We have taken certain devices such as sign interpretation and audio description (for blind or visually-impaired audience members) and woven them into the fabric of the text. It is an attempt to subvert but also explore the theatrical possibilities of these devices, whilst also making them central.

**Kaite O'Reilly**

# peeling

## Kaite O'Reilly

*This play is dedicated to Jenny Sealey*

First performed at The Door, Birmingham Repertory Theatre, on
14th February, 2002 with the following cast:

| CHARACTERS | CAST |
|---|---|
| **Alfa** | Caroline Parker |
| **Beaty** | Lisa Hammond |
| **Coral** | Sophie Partridge |

Directed and designed by Jenny Sealey.
Assistant Director Jamie Beddard.
Dramaturg Phillip Zarrilli.
Lighting Designer Ian Scott.
Sign Language consultants: Caroline Parker and Jéni Draper.

<u>*Notes:*</u>
*Three women, with outrageous, huge, gorgeous frocks, apparently
tied onto large chairs. They are part of the set design for a large
production, which is going on unseen elsewhere on stage. The
unseen parallel production is an epic visual piece about warfare
through the ages – 'The Trojan Women' updated and with
contemporary references. The three women have the occasional
moment when they are 'on' as tableaux-fodder and members of the
Chorus. Spotlight or floods signify these moments. The rest of the
time they are 'unlit', able to relax and chat in the shadows, or
comment on the scene before them. However, they are never
completely 'off' and they use the devices of the theatre (narration, a
form of audio-description, choral speaking, sign interpretation) even
when there is no apparent audience. They bicker, play, interrupt and
share the above devices – when one stops, another takes up that
role/device. They are constantly shifting and changing, sending each
other up, 'ruining' each other's 'moment', taking the piss, passing
easily between the formal 'roles' they play, i.e. – 'acting' (telling*

*stories, being a narrator/audio-describer etc) and 'being themselves' (the chat, heckling, etc). They obviously lie at times (for example in Scene 1, when Beaty & Coral pretend not to understand what sign language is, they are using SSE). As the play goes on, they change costume, simplifying, stripping down as the parallel unseen production becomes more modern and their stories become more personal and painful. By the end, they are peeled right down to simple underclothes: vests and pants.*
*(AD) denotes audio description*
*(SSE) denotes sign-supported English*
*(BSL) denotes British sign language*

<u>Characters:</u>
**Alfa**: *38, calls herself an actress. She is fiercely independent, eccentric and slightly puritanical. She is Deaf and uses sign language (both BSL and SSE).*
**Beaty**: *26, calls herself an actor. She is fierce, feisty, sexy and four feet tall.*
**Coral**: *30, calls herself a performer. She is small and looks very fragile, but has a ferocious, inquiring mind. She uses an electric wheelchair.*

**SCENE 1**
*Darkness. The stage is suddenly filled with floodlight. Three large mounds are visible – huge dresses, with women sticking out of the top. Two, Coral and Beaty, are in performance mode – poised, highly theatrical – the third dress is empty. As the two women realise there is a vacancy and begin to lose their focus, sudden blackout.*

*Five seconds pass. The stage is suddenly filled with floodlight. Three large mounds are visible – all three dresses are inhabited. Alfa, the latecomer, is slightly flustered. The women are static, artificial, poised in a series of tableaux. As Chorus in a strong post-modern production of 'The Trojan Women – Then and Now', they speak/sign to the unseen principles on stage (Hecuba and Andromache), as well as to the audience.*

*CHORUS:*

| | |
|---|---|
| **ALFA** | Raise your head from the dust. |
| **BEATY** | Lift up the throat. |
| **ALFA** | Sing. |
| **CORAL** | Hecuba: This is Troy, but Troy and we are perished. |

**BEATY** Woman: This is the world, for the verse of destruction you sing is known in other lands.

**ALFA** Are we not hurled down the whole length of disaster?

| | |
|---|---|
| **CORAL** | Throughout history, no change. |
| **BEATY** | Troy will be given to the flame to eat. |
| **CORAL** | Sad birds will sing for our lost young. |
| **BEATY** | The city will fall. |
| **ALFA** | A horse with its lurking death will come amongst us. |

**CORAL** Children will reach shivering hands to clutch at their mother's dresses.

| | |
|---|---|
| **BEATY** | War will stalk from his hiding place. |
| **CORAL** | We will be enslaved. |
| **ALFA** | We will die in our blood. |

**BEATY** The same, the same, through the long corridor of time. *(beat)*

**CORAL** Gone will be the shining pools where we bathed.

**BEATY** Our children will stand, clinging to the gates, crying through their tears. *(beat)*

**ALFA** Know nothing. Look for disaster. Lighten your heart. Go stunned with terror. *(beat)*

**CORAL** I lived, never thinking the baby in my womb was born for butchery…

*Long pause. A shift in style. The intensity of lights dip, denoting the women are 'off' and therefore 'themselves' – professional actors who have been performing the Chorus-characters.*

**BEATY** *(to Alfa)* So where were you? *(to Coral)* I turn round in the tableaux and there's an empty bloody dress beside me…!

**ALFA** I got stuck, having a fag in the loo. You know how far backstage it is.

**CORAL** No, I don't, actually. I have to cross my legs and hope for the best. Through the whole epic. All four hours of it.

**BEATY**        You must have very developed pelvic floor muscles,
   then.
**ALFA**        What?
**CORAL**        You gave me a right turn, the lights going up and
   you not there.
**ALFA**        How d'you think I felt? First time in my life I've
   missed a cue. I'm a professional. Things like that don't happen to
   me.
**CORAL**        They did this time.
**ALFA**        First and only.
**BEATY**        They'll dock your wages.
**ALFA**        So I'll speak to the Equity Dep.'
**BEATY** *(as self)* Director won't like it.
**ALFA**        It won't happen again. I'm sorry, all right? Beaty?
   Coral? *(BSL only)* Sorry. *(voiced)* It won't bloody happen again.
   *(beat)*
**BEATY**        Every night this play.
   Every bloody night this play.
   Every night this bloody play.
   It gives me a headache. *(Pause.)*

*The performers relax slightly, stretch in their cumbersome dresses.*
*Coral takes out a tartan flask and pours out a cup.*

**CORAL**        Hot chocolate, anyone?
**BEATY***(AD[1])* Coral offers us a drink from a tartan flask.
   *(as self)* No thanks.
**ALFA**        The wardrobe mistress 'll kill you if she catches you
   eating and drinking in costume. These frocks cost a fortune.

---

[1] *Where specified as being audio description (AD), the speaker clicks into a*
*different style of presentation – slightly more formal, neutral, muted BBC*
*announcer, perhaps. It should fit comfortably and seamlessly into the*
*dynamic of the dialogue/scene, but be done with attention to the audience.*
*Later, when used ironically by the women to comment rather than just*
*describe, it should be layered with meaning accordingly and have a less*
*neutral tone.*

CORAL          Though quite what significance they have to wars ancient and modern is beyond me.

BEATY          Oh, I dunno... Every day's a little battle... it helps if you face it correctly attired.

ALFA          And a bit of luxury can't do any harm. Life's hard enough as it is. I quite like a touch of sumptuous padding.

CORAL          I feel more like a clotheshorse than a commentator on war.

BEATY          It's probably meant to be ironic. *(She takes out a programme and studies it)* That's what they usually say when they bodge together classic texts with contemporary stuff. Postmodern and ironic.

ALFA *(AD)* Beaty refers to a theatre programme for 'The Trojan Women – Then and Now' which she handily has under her skirts.

BEATY *(reading)* Apparently, according to the director's notes, we've all been deconstructed.

ALFA          I thought I was being a metaphor.

CORAL          For what?

ALFA          I don't know. I didn't think to ask what the motivation of my metaphor was.

*They look at Alfa, then the stage before them. Pause.*

ALFA          Oh, here we go...

CORAL *(AD)* The extras and unseen chorus...

ALFA *(interjecting, BSL only)* That is, us...

CORAL *(AD)* ... stare at the stage and the performance going on before them.

*Several beats.*

BEATY          I hate this bit.

CORAL          Uummmmm.

BEATY          Pretty slow moving.

CORAL          Uuummmm.

ALFA          'Interesting' interpretation of Hecuba...

CORAL          Uuummmm.

*Several beats.*

| | |
|---|---|
| **BEATY** | Though she is very good. |
| **ALFA** | Yes, she is, she's very good. |
| **BEATY** | Marvellous. |
| **ALFA** | Really |
| **CORAL** | Uummm. *(beat)* |
| **BEATY** | Though I could do better |
| **ALFA** | Given the chance |
| **CORAL** | Given the chance... |
| **BEATY** | Given the chance I could definitely do better... |

*They sigh, attention begins to wane. Coral puts away her flask safely under her skirts.*

**CORAL**    They sit.

**BEATY**    They sit. *(beat)*

**ALFA**    My mother'd say this was money for old rope. Us sitting here. Though she doesn't quite understand how demanding it is. *(beat)*

**CORAL**    It can be taxing.*(beat)*

**ALFA**    To stay in the moment. Focused. Ready for the cue.

**BEATY** *(AD)* We look at her accusingly. Alfa flushes, recovers, continues.

**ALFA**    The chorus to the Trojan Women is central.

**BEATY**    Which is why they've left us, shoved at the back, unlit, onstage. *(beat)*

**ALFA**    It's a noble profession.

**BEATY**    I always wanted to go on the stage.

**CORAL**    And if we're going to be looked at, anyway, we might as well get paid for it.

**BEATY**    Did your mother tell you that?

**CORAL**    No. Did yours? *(beat)*

**ALFA** *(as storyteller)* Once... once... Once there was an ancient city...

**BEATY** *(interrupting)* She's off.

**ALFA**    ...Excuse me...? I'm rehearsing. *(As storyteller)* An ancient city set high...

**BEATY** *(interrupting)* ...She does this every night... Every bloody night, as if she doesn't know it by heart already...

**ALFA** *(as self)* It's called preparation, you know. And we are here to work. To do a job. For which we get paid. So whilst the principles are warbling on about their fate and the pity of war, I'm going to keep my mind on what I'm supposed to be doing here, thank you very much.

**CORAL** *(AD)* Beaty's eyes roll to the heavens.

**BEATY** *(mimicking Alfa)* "I'm a professional, how d'you do? Have a good look, I don't think you've met my kind before."

**CORAL** *(AD)* Despite the half-smiles, a cool, cruel glance passes between them. Alfa raises a finger.

**ALFA**　　　　Up yours, lady.

**BEATY**　　　　Ooooh. Will that be in the Sign Language dictionary?

**ALFA** *(stubbornly)* Once. Once there was an ancient city, high, set high among the olive groves.

**CORAL** *(as self)* And anyway it's terraces.

**ALFA**　　　　What?

**CORAL**　　　　Olive terraces. Set high, high among the olive terraces.

**ALFA**　　　　That's my line.

**CORAL**　　　　Well, they'll take it away from you unless you say it right.

**ALFA**　　　　Are you after my lines?

**CORAL**　　　　No. I've got my own. But if you can't remember them or get them right...

**ALFA** *(overlapping)* How do you know my part, anyway?

**BEATY** *(AD)* A glint of suspicion enters her eye

**CORAL**　　　　I've heard it a hundred times!

**ALFA**　　　　No you haven't!

**CORAL**　　　　Have!

**ALFA**　　　　Why are you learning my lines?

**CORAL**　　　　I'm not!

**ALFA**　　　　You're after my part! You're after –

**BEATY** *(AD)* A poison dart of a look whizzes past my ear – an arrow wwhhhissshhhh – embedding itself firmly into the forehead of Coral, the possible role stealer... The result? *(all pause, holding breath )* – sudden silence.

**ALFA**            Thank you. *(settles back into storytelling mode)* Set
high, high among the olive terraces and the almond orchards – an
ancient city of women –

**BEATY**            It'll have a bad end, wait and see. The ones with
women and children always do

**ALFA**            Ssh! An ancient city of women and children –
fatherless families – wandering...

*Coral sighs hugely, spoiling Alfa's moment.*

**BEATY** *(AD)* The most long-suffering sigh slides over Coral's
tongue, rubbing up against her cheeks, then out over the slightly
gappy, could really do with a scrape and polish, horse-like teeth
of –

**ALFA** *(interrupting firmly)* Fatherless families – wandering the
maze of narrow cobbled streets -

**CORAL**            Anyone seen *Eastenders* recently?

**ALFA**            Happy to be together

**BEATY** *(AD)* A nerve jumps in Alfa's cheek

**ALFA**            ...grateful that, so far, they had escaped the fate of
Troy...

**CORAL**            Boorrrriinnnggggg.....

**BEATY** *(AD)* Coral's eyes roll contemptuously to the heavens

**ALFA** *(to Coral)* WILL YOU STOP IT!!!!????

**BEATY** *(AD)* Flames blaze in angry eyes – Alfa's mouth scowls, the
lips pucker, *(as self)* really quite ugly, actually.

**ALFA** *(to Beaty)*  AND YOU!

**BEATY**            Sorry.

**ALFA**            Christ!

**BEATY**            I was just trying to...

*Coral takes over Beaty's describing role. The others, in intense
conversation, are oblivious to Coral.*

**CORAL** *(AD)* Her gaze drops, cheeks slightly aflame –

**ALFA**            Yes?

**BEATY**            I was trying to...

**CORAL** *(AD)* Beaty's teeth nip on her lower lip, pinching,
bloodless...

**ALFA**      What?

**BEATY**      Audio-describe it.

**CORAL** *(AD)* She hangs her head, awkward, uncomfortable.

**ALFA**      Audio –?

**CORAL**      DESCRIBE IT, idiot! *(To Beaty)* Bloody hell! She's away with the fairies, you know. Can't keep up. No brain – just mammaries on legs. *(immediately back, as though no interruption)* Audio describe it.

**ALFA**      And why would you do that?

**BEATY**      Makes it more interesting.

**ALFA**      Only if you can hear.

*Beaty and Coral continue, oblivious to Alfa.*

**CORAL**      I feel quite creative, actually.

**BEATY**      Yeah – I know what you mean.

**CORAL**      It's describing – innit?

**BEATY**      Yeah.

**CORAL**      Like – like painting the scene in visual images that the listener can absorb and internalise and – from spoken words – build that special visual world right inside their own head – in the heart of their imagination.

**ALFA**      Bollix to it, then. It's no bloody good to me.

**BEATY**      Yeah, but then you do all that lovely stuff.

**ALFA**      What?

**BEATY**      Y'know – all that lovely stuff - with your hands.

**ALFA** *(AD)* Beaty and Coral are sign-supporting bits of this as well as speaking. *(as self)* Sorry?

**CORAL**      Oh yeah – I know what you mean – it's lovely.

**BEATY**      Really...

**CORAL**      ...Yeah...

**BOTH**      ...Lovely!

**CORAL**      Lovely stuff when you wave them around – your hands – in the air – like... like...

**BEATY**      ...like disco dancing.

**CORAL**      Yeah...

**BEATY** *(starts singing and 1970's disco-dancing)* D.I.S.C.O

**CORAL**      D.I.S.C. –

**ALFA** *(BSL only)* Fuck off! Yes... true... Fuck off!

**CORAL** *(A.D. simultaneous with the above signing)* Alfa signs
    ferociously –
**BEATY** *(as self, interrupting)* Viciously –
**CORAL** *(AD)* Beaty and Coral try to translate.

*The following speech, is signed in BSL only, with no voice.*
*Simultaneously, Coral and Beaty try to understand what Alfa is*
*signing.*

**ALFA** *(BSL only)* …Fuck off. Fuck right off the pair of you. Cows.
    Moo. Go away and milk yourselves. Squeeze yourself dry of that
    cynicism and ignorance. Prats. Christ knows how I manage, stuck
    here with you two. I won't do it again.
**CORAL** *(translating simultaneously)* Slap hands… slap hands
    together…
**BEATY** *(simultaneous)* Fuck… fuck – fucking
**CORAL**        Cow… noise they make…
**BEATY/CORAL**  Moo… moo…
**CORAL**        Touch breast…
**BEATY**        Tit! Milk cow…
**CORAL**        Milk ourselves?
**BEATY**        Milk tit fucking…cow.
**CORAL**        Stupid!
**BEATY**        Milk tit fucking stupid cow.
**CORAL**        Fish!..shape hands make when…
**BEATY**        …No..no no never…
**CORAL**        …Not?

*Alfa has finished her signing.*

**ALFA**        Amateurs. Bloody amateurs.
**BEATY**        Did you know an avocado stone crushed and
    combined with yoghurt, makes an invigorating and exfoliating
    shower gel?
**CORAL**        Did you know courtesy is catching?
**ALFA**        Did you know we just had our lighting cue?

*Floods on. The women pose, high theatricality, then go into Chorus*
*performing mode.*

*CHORUS:*

**CORAL** Women of Troy, this is not just your story.

**BEATY** Hecuba and Andromache, this infamy has been well read.

**ALFA** It has been told and re-enacted, made flesh as the sword marries the bone.

**CORAL** in that city –

**BEATY** in that village –

**ALFA** in that settlement, high, up in the hills,

**CORAL** low in the valley,

**BEATY** out in the bush,

**ALFA** deep in the city,

**BEATY** women and children,

**CORAL** waiting... *(beat)* ...for that feared-for smoke on the horizon. A smudge at the point where earth meets sky,

**BEATY** like a swarm of locusts

**ALFA** choking the air

**BEATY** beating down between heaven and earth:

**ALFA** Fire

**BEATY** Smoke

**CORAL** Pestilence

**ALL** *(not without irony)* Men

**ALFA** Marching forward with their uniforms

**BEATY** and their machetes

**CORAL** and their orders:

**ALFA** To rape

**BEATY** To pillage

**CORAL** To conquer

**ALL** Destroy.

**BEATY** Slash and burn as they advance, burning the crops, killing the children.

**ALFA** Dismembering limbs,

**BEATY** detaching Achilles heels so the survivors can't run away, and so enabling the slaughter to continue, tomorrow.

**CORAL** Taking the women for

**ALFA** entertainment and pleasure

**BEATY** and preferably impregnate them and kill off the line.

**ALFA** Woman's body as battlefield. *(beat)*

**BEATY** Rape as a war tactic. *(beat)*

**ALFA**          Mutilation as a reminder... *(beat)*
**CORAL** *(sarcastic)*  Thank god that doesn't happen now.

*A brief silence.*

**CORAL**          In certain towns they chose to leave the dead where
they fell and kept them so as remembrance – a memorial of
scattered bodies... family members... neighbours... the school
master... midwife... *(beat.)*

*Beaty says the following as a chorus member telling a personal
testimony.*

**BEATY**          I had gone away that day, walking through the bush
to the medical centre. I went alone. My little brother cried to join
me, but I was a grown girl, on serious business. What use would
he be to me? I made him stay home. When I returned, our soldiers
stopped me from going to my village. They said there had been a
massacre. A rival tribe. There was one survivor. People were
hanging from the trees. Others lay in a pile of bodies in the
school-house, where they had been taken to be slaughtered. My
brother was in the schoolhouse. He was curled, on his knees,
covered by the body of my Mother who had tried to save him.
They had been butchered. The survivor was me.
**ALFA** *(AD)* The lights go down. Ladies and gentlemen, a brief
interlude.

*Pause. The lights go off. The women are 'off', now 'themselves'.*

**CORAL**          I don't think I like this play very much.
**BEATY** *(AD)* She shivers. Somewhere, big boots are walking over
her grave.
**CORAL**          Don't.
**ALFA** *(AD)* Alfa disappears from out of her dress.

*Alfa unstraps herself and disappears behind her dress*

**BEATY**          What's made you squeamish all of a sudden?

CORAL      Nothing, nothing, I – what!? Do you think something's different?

BEATY      No.

CORAL      Good, because there isn't. I'm just...

BEATY *(AD)* She shrugs, grimaces, runs a hand over her lined face.

CORAL      You know how sometimes when a show opens and it's been running a while and you get used to it and you go onto auto-pilot a bit...? *(pronounced pause)*
*(AD)* Beaty bites her lips, puffs her cheeks out a little, is reluctant to admit she knows what I'm talking about.

BEATY      Maybe...

CORAL      I know you're not supposed to go on auto-pilot, but... I've just crash-landed.

BEATY *(AD)* Coral struggles, pulls a face.

CORAL      ...I...

BEATY *(AD)* Her eyes hook into mine, urgent with meaning, but unfortunately I haven't got a bloody clue what she's talking about. *(as self)* What?

CORAL      I'm feeling it more. I've done it a hundred times, the mouth moving, words coming out, but I... I'm feeling it more... and I don't like it.

BEATY      Just don't let it get to you.

CORAL      But some of the stories, the modern ones, they're –

BEATY *(interrupting)* You think too much. Feel everything too much. Travel light. Go naked. Chill.

CORAL      Doesn't it get to you?

BEATY      No. 'Cause as an actress, I'm a carnivore – I like strong meat. So the stories are full-on... Would you rather be in music-theatre?

CORAL      No!

BEATY      Well then...

CORAL      ...but...

BEATY      What!?

CORAL      Well, I don't know... just sometimes... I'd like to do something... upbeat.

BEATY      Fantasy?

CORAL      No – positive. Uplifting. With a happy ending.

BEATY      Yeah. Fantasy.

ALFA      Who'd like some soup?

**BEATY** *(AD)* Alfa appears from behind her dress, with some carrots, a bowl, and her blender.

*In the following section, the women may unstrap themselves from their dresses and move around. Alfa will probably be very active in the making of her soup.*

**ALFA** I never go anywhere without this. *(She revs up her blender)* Hand-held, runs on batteries, hugely versatile… a lifesaver.

**BEATY** *(AD)* She begins making soup. *(Alfa does so)*

**ALFA** Well, while there's a lull in the action, we might as well make the most of it. And that useless stage manager isn't going to bring us any refreshments. He's terrified of me. I'm sure he thinks 'Deafness' is catching.

**BEATY** It is, if you're close to his ear and you shout loud enough.

*The following text in italics all done as Audio Description. Plain text is dialogue.*

**ALFA** *(AD)* *Alfa busies herself with grating carrots. As she is refusing to make eye contact, and is the main signer, that closes down that source of communication for a while – Beaty and Coral know this.*

**CORAL** *Coral squirms on her chair, takes out a half-deflated kiddie's rubber swimming ring with a duck's head and starts to blow it up.*

**BEATY** *Beaty takes out some risqué lingerie, sequins and a needle and thread. Coral notices Beaty's g-string–*

**CORAL** *largely because she's waving it around, some would say showing it off, generously displaying it's crotch-less nature…*

**BEATY** What can I say? Life's short. Enjoy…

**CORAL** Moonlighting, are we? I've heard you can earn oooh five quid an hour in some of the booths in Soho, if you're lucky.

**BEATY** Piss off, you're only jealous. *Smiling with anti-cipation, Beaty busies herself with choosing and sewing a sequin onto her evening attire.*

**CORAL** What's the occasion?

**BEATY**        I've a new boyfriend.
**CORAL**        Is he lush?
**BEATY**        Gorg'. You can see him yourself. He's picking me
up at the end of the show and I do so like customising what I wear
to bed.
**CORAL** *(AD)* *She continues with her adult-rated needlework.*
*Coral inflates the ring, then settles it under her skirts. She*
*wobbles onto it, sighs with contentment. (as self)* I'm a martyr to
haemorrhoids. *(She sits with great contentment, looking about*
*her, watching her industrious colleagues.)* Make do and mend.
*(New thought)* Preferably with cat gut. My body is criss-crossed
with scars like a railway track. Like Crewe station, seen from the
air: Single tracks, with no apparent destination; major interlock-
ing junctions, where intercity, sleepers and local lines all connect.
Puckering scar tissue, hand-sewn with careless, clumsy stitches. I
like to finger it, trace the journeys. That unborn skin: smooth,
intimate – the coral-pink colour of mice feet. It's beautiful. I love
it. Given the choice, I'd never have it any other way, now.*(Pause)*
Are you listening, Mother? *(Pause)*Do you hear me, Mother?

*Several beats. Alfa, still preparing her soup, uses her blender as*
*punctuation during the following:*

**ALFA**         Mine used to warn me about men. *(as her Mother)*
"You keep your hand on your ha'penny. You'll have to if you
want any kind of chance with a man. It's bad enough you being
damaged goods. He'll not want you if you're second-hand,
thumbed through and used already."
**CORAL**        Ouch!
**ALFA**         I didn't pay any attention, though. You wouldn't,
either, if you saw the cardigans she wore. … But bless… I love
my Mum…
**CORAL**        *(AD)* Beaty and Coral exchange a look of –
**BEATY/CORAL** *(AD)* Envy.
**BEATY** *(as her Mother)* "You have to entice; you have to beguile.
Put it all in the shop window Beatrice, though god knows you
have little enough. Put yourself on special offer, girl."
**CORAL**        Mothers… who'd be one, eh?
**BEATY**        They love to maim.

**ALFA**          But they think it's for our own good. Tough love.
They're trying to help.

**BEATY**          Absolutely. Because we don't want to get too big for
our boots, do we?

**CORAL**          And we mustn't aspire for other things… We have
to be kept in our places.

**BEATY** *(as her Mother)* "Keep your aim low and you'll never be
disappointed… You have a short shelf life, Beatrice."

**CORAL**          She's got a way with words, your mother.

**BEATY**          When they buried her, I had the greatest temptation
to laugh down into that hole they were putting her in: "So who
was it survived the longest, then?" She was convinced she'd see
me out.

**CORAL**          Was it sudden, then?

**BEATY**          For her, yes. Had no idea she was going. But I knew.
To the tick. It's a talent I have – I've been thoroughly trained in it
– to sense time passing and my old mate, the grim reaper, stalking
close behind. All my life, thanks to my Mum, I've felt the tip of
his scythe touching the nape of my neck. My Mother was so
focused on that, waiting for me to croak, she didn't notice the big
fingers come to snuff her out. So I buried her. There's not many
with "reduced life expectancy" can say that. It's an achievement.
There's not many like me can press the earth down on their
Mother's face. Stamp on the grave. Put a layer of concrete over so
she can't rise again. I joke of course.

**CORAL**          Of course.

**BEATY**          Though she was the joker in our family. She'd call
me into the bathroom and make me stare at her face. She was getting deep crow's feet around her eyes – she hated it – and the skin
around her jaw line was beginning to soften, sag a bit – her face
covered in fine hairs, like the fur of a peach. And she'd cradle her
face in her hands and stretch back the skin so the wrinkles would
disappear and she'd say, 'That's what I looked like when I was
sixteen. You're lucky, Beatrice. Just think, you'll never have lines
on your face like me – you'll never see your features blurring,
you'll never suffer from the ravages of age. You're so lucky,
Beatrice. You're so lucky you'll die when you're young. You're
so lucky you'll never live to be old.'

*Several beats*

| | |
|---|---|
| **ALFA** | Has anyone got any *Neurofen?* |
| **CORAL** | Are you starting? |
| **ALFA** | I'm in the most terrible pain. |
| **BEATY** | You look pretty crap. |
| **ALFA** | That's the pain. |
| **CORAL** | You want to eat bananas when you're on your |

period.

| | |
|---|---|
| **BEATY** | You do look crap. |
| **ALFA** | I can't help it. |
| **BEATY** | Ever heard of make-up? |
| **CORAL** | They're rich in potassium, which is exactly what you |

need.

| | |
|---|---|
| **ALFA** | I look crap even when I wear make-up. |
| **CORAL** | Or Evening Primrose Oil, that's good. |
| **BEATY** | You look crap. |
| **ALFA** | I look so crap because I'm in such pain. |
| **CORAL** | And star fruit. That's the new one. |
| **ALFA** | I have to have an operation. |
| **CORAL** | Yeah, well I'm on my period. |
| **ALFA** | And the pills I have to take... |
| **BEATY** | I shit pills. They shoot out like coins from a slot |

machine in Vegas. Just chug chug chug, all nudges and triples.
It's the amount of tablets I have to take. For my pain. When I
walk down the road I rattle.

| | |
|---|---|
| **ALFA** | You rattle? I'm like a broken washing machine. On |

spin.

| | |
|---|---|
| **CORAL** | Yeah, but at least you don't have your period. |
| **ALFA** | I am a wreck. In emotional and physical pain. I am |

embodied pain. I am the physical embodiment of emotional and
physical pain.

| | |
|---|---|
| **CORAL** | I get body cramps. Even my hair hurts when I'm |

having my period.

| | |
|---|---|
| **BEATY** | I lose my vision. |
| **ALFA** | I lose my hearing and I'm deaf. |
| **CORAL** | I'm on the toilet so much I might as well have it |

moved into the lounge so I can sit on it and watch the telly.

**ALFA**         Why don't you just go around with a bucket between
   your legs?
**BEATY**        I can't have children.
**CORAL**        I'm pregnant.
**ALFA**         What's that about being on your period, then?
**CORAL**        I was being nostalgic.

*Beaty and Alfa laugh. Coral doesn't. Beaty notices the lighting cue.*

**BEATY**        There's the lights – they're changing.
**ALFA**         I know it's only a brief interlude, but it gets briefer
   every night. I haven't had my soup, yet.
**CORAL** *(AD)* We swiftly put away our toys as Alfa climbs into her
   dress.
**ALFA**         I swear it's just so the crew can make last orders at
   the bar.
**BEATY**        Well, you have to get your priorities right.

*The women take a moment to prepare for the next scene – some
breathing, focus work, done seriously.*
*Floods come on. The women move into stylised tableaux, establish-
ing the change in dynamic for the 'parallel' play. Alfa continues as
storyteller, the story she was rehearsing earlier. The others follow,
as Chorus.*

*CHORUS:*
**ALFA**         Once, once there was an ancient city, high, set high
   among the olive terraces and the almond orchards – an ancient
   city of women and children, fatherless families – wandering the
   maze of narrow cobbled streets – happy to be together – grateful
   that, so far, they had escaped the fate of Troy.
**CORAL**        These women had lost their men to some fruitless
   battle over some unknown argument rooted centuries before…
**BEATY**        These women knew in which direction the world
   revolved and it was counter to them.
**ALFA**         They smelt the ash of a thousand burning bodies and
   sensed the military advance, watching the bruise of smoke deepen
   on the delicate flesh where the earth and the sky met.
**CORAL**        And these women knew the stories.

**BEATY**       Rape as a war tactic. Babies' heads split like conkers.

**CORAL**      And they knew what would happen. *(beat)*

**ALFA**       So they made a decision, those women with their children in the ancient city high in the hills, amongst the flowering almond blossom and the olive terraces: They taught their children to dance.

**BEATY**       Mamma's precious

**CORAL**      Future joy

**ALFA**       They taught their children to dance and, clasping hands, they danced up along the city gates

**BEATY**       as the bruise deepened on the horizon

**ALFA**       ...they danced out, along the city's upper walls, past the lookout

**CORAL**      where the armour of the approaching army was clearly visible, glinting in the light

**ALFA**       beyond the cobbled roads, where the path stumbled into rock and mud they danced, up along the steep incline, hands clasped, tiny feet stamping the rhythm

**BEATY**       Mamma's precious

**CORAL**      Future joy

**ALFA**       up towards the pinnacle

**BEATY**       as the soldiers grew closer

**ALFA**       where tiny feet faltered but were urged on, hands clasped, dancing, dragged

**CORAL**      Mothers' faces wet with tears

**ALFA**       feet dancing, on and on until there was no more land to dance on and their feet tripped on air and, hands clasped, dancing, dancing, they danced out and plummeted to their deaths.

*Beat. Floods off. The women still in chorus mode, but no longer 'on'.*

**BEATY** *(AD)* There is a pause in Alfa's signing hands – a hesitation before her fingers – the children and Mothers – descend. Descend.

**CORAL** *(AD)* Beaty's eyes fill with tears.

**BEATY**       No they don't.

**ALFA** *(AD)* She stares at Coral viciously.

**BEATY**       They don't.

**CORAL**      Okay.

**BEATY**      Say it.

**CORAL** *(AD)* Beaty's eyes do not fill with tears. *(A beat)*

**BEATY** *(as self)* Thank you. *(As storyteller)* Some versions claim that heavenly creatures swooped and caught the fragile bodies before they smashed into the rocks below. Spared pain, delivered to safety, a happy ending, stopping our minds from imagining the broken, mangled bodies – bones splintering on impact, childrens' screams as they realise Mamma isn't to be trusted, after all –

**CORAL**      Versions that save us from the horrific contemplation of the Mothers' decisions and those last terrible moments... *(She can't say it. Finally Beaty does for her)*

**BEATY**      ...killing your own child.

**ALFA**      As you've probably gathered, this is not one of those versions.

**BEATY**      But we don't believe in the pretty stories, the 'being spared all that' – the lies. We believe in knowing the full picture so you can prepare yourself for the worst

**CORAL**      but also – why not? – hope for the future...?

**ALFA**      Finished?

**BEATY**      Yes. Thanks.

**CORAL**      I told you, I'd already heard it.

*Blackout.*

**SCENE 2**

*Alfa is knitting, Beaty reading an up-market gossip magazine and Coral making changes with her costume. Beaty's magazine-related lines should be up-to-date, show-biz gossip taken from the week of performance. *Stars names should be changed to the latest flavour of the month.*

**ALFA**      I sometimes think my entire life is spent behind screens – at the hospital, here at the theatre, and when I'm sign-interpreting, I'm always kept apart, away from the action.

**CORAL**      In a performance, when it's happening, do you –

**BEATY** *(cutting Coral off)* I think there's something really sinister about Chris Evans* and Billie Piper.*

**CORAL**      What?!

ALFA      Even at the hospital I've a bit part – *(as nurse)* 'pop
     your clothes off and the doctor will be with you in a moment' –
     all the drama and interesting shenanigans happen the other side of
     the screen to me.
BEATY *(of magazine)* I like her hair colour. D'you think it'd suit
     me?
CORAL     What?!
ALFA      But it's even worse here –  I'm an actor – I should
     be full of action rather than the passive recounter of doom.
BEATY *(of magazine)* Jesus, she's really put on weight.
CORAL     Beaty, d'you mind putting down the magazine and
     giving me a hand with the costume-change?
BEATY     I'm busy.
CORAL     Please?
ALFA      The done-to, that's me.
CORAL     Pretty please?
ALFA      I'm never the doer.
CORAL     Alfa?
BEATY     She's busy knitting.
CORAL     Well, piss off, the lot of you, then.
BEATY     Ooooh... madam...
ALFA      Is she getting a strop on?
BEATY     Yeah.
ALFA      She does that.
BEATY     Yes, she does do that
ALFA      get a strop on
BEATY     I know.
ALFA      Terrible.
BEATY     Not enough sex
ALFA      or chocolate
BEATY     or both
ALFA/BEATY at the same time.
ALFA      Oh – she didn't like that.
BEATY     No – she didn't like that.
ALFA *(AD)* Alfa admires Coral's disapproving little pout...
CORAL     I haven't got a disapproving little pout.
ALFA *(AD)* Coral's pinching facial expression tells otherwise.
CORAL     That's not fair. You're describing me all wrong.

**BEATY** *(AD)* Her face shrivels with indignation, becoming mean, ugly and malignant like a tumour.

**CORAL**          Oh great – insult by audio-description.

**BEATY** *(AD)* Her lips pucker; her nostrils flare self-righteously.

**CORAL**          They did not do that! I couldn't do that if I tried!

**ALFA** *(AD)* Coral tries to be the indignant ingenue, but is unfortunately too old to play that part.

**CORAL**          You're not telling the truth!

**ALFA**          You're in a war play, dearie. Surely you know in a war play, the first casualty is truth? *(Pause)*

**ALFA**          Remember that time we were appearing in 'Metamorphosis' in Watford and there was a fire? *(as Deputy Stage Manager)* "Mr Sun is in the building…" and they evacuated the theatre, but left us beetled-up on stage? She got stroppy then, as well.

**CORAL**          I wasn't a dung beetle. I was playing a black widow spider, stuck upside down in some kind of web.

**BEATY**          Yeah, I remember – that giant rope ladder from the Army and Navy stores.

**ALFA**          None of it adequately fire-proofed. We could have fried.

**CORAL**          Us and the wheelies abandoned in the front row. Just as well it was a false alarm.

**ALFA**          And after, when they realised they'd left us, that bloody theatre manager running round screaming:

**CORAL** *(hijacking story)* "And this is why 'handicaps' are a health and safety risk."

**BEATY**          Prick.

**ALFA**          There was cause, then, to be judgemental, to get a strop on. That was justified.

**BEATY** *(flicking through her magazine)* Now, Michael Douglas*…I wouldn't touch him with a bloody barge pole.

**ALFA**          I wouldn't touch anyone. I'm more a unicycle than a tandem these days, if you get my meaning. Unless you want a family, or you've met the love of your life – which I think is a myth – why bother? Life's complicated enough as it is.
Did you know that women over thirty in New York are more likely to develop cancer *and* be a victim of violent crime than have a lasting monogamous relationship with a straight man?

**BEATY**     Did you know when you mix avocado and garlic and lemon juice, you get guacamole?

**ALFA**     Did you know the end of the world is nigh?

**CORAL**     Did you know the most famous disabled woman is Helen bloody Keller?

**BEATY**     Is that her name? Helen Bloody-Keller? As in double-barrelled.

**CORAL**     But to people she's the Marvellous Helen Bloody-Keller, a sort of superspas'.

**ALFA**     "Disabled people are the heroes of our time." Peter Brook said that.

**CORAL**     Heroes for whom?

**ALFA**     Exactly.

**BEATY**     Peter Brook as in 'The Man Who Mistook his Wife for a Hat'?

**CORAL**     No. Peter Brook as in 'The Director who mistook exploitation for disability politics'.

**BEATY** *(AD)* Beaty checks her watch, then reluctantly puts away her magazine. *(as self)* Get out the canary, we're back to the coal-face....

**CORAL**     We're not on for a while, yet.

**BEATY**     So where are we, then?

**CORAL**     Towards the end of Act Two: The fall of Troy and the slaughter of the innocents

**ALFA**     Oh, I like that bit... *(AD)* The extras – i.e. us – stare, with varying levels of involve-ment, at the dramatic scene going on before them. *(They do so)*

**CORAL** *(as self)* In a performance, when it's happening, do you–?

**BEATY/ALFA** ...Sssssh.

**CORAL** *(AD)* Beaty and Alfa are enthralled, lip-syncing the actors, up-staging them, in the dark *(as self)* like they do in this scene, every bloody night.

**BEATY**     I'd love to play Andromache. I could do it better than her. *(She refers to the 'unseen' performer on stage)* *(As Andromache)* I nursed for nothing. In vain the labour pains and long sickness

**ALFA**     Oh, bless.

**BEATY** *(as Andromache)* I have no strength to save my children from execution. Nor the children of other mothers –

**ALFA/BEATY** – who are suffering no less than me.
**CORAL** *(as self)* In a performance, when it's happening, do you –
**ALFA/BEATY** Ssssh...
**BEATY** *(as self)* I love this bit...
**CORAL** *(AD)* In synchronicity, they shift, heads moving, following
the action about the stage.

*They do so for some time, Alfa and Beaty creating the illusion of
watching an emotional scene in the unseen parallel play. This
continues under the following text.*

**ALFA** *(as self)* They're going to kill her little boy...
*(BSL only)* Beautiful.

*Alfa makes another happy, heartfelt sigh, reacting to what's
happening 'on-stage.'*

**CORAL** *(AD)* Coral's attention wanders.
**ALFA**               ...so poignant... I wish someone would let me do a
scene like that.
**ALFA/BEATY**  Oh!
**ALFA** *(as Andromache)* Child, your fingers clutch my dress.
What use, to nestle like a young bird under the mother's wings?
*(quietly, as self)* ...Fantastic...
**ALFA/BEATY** *(as Andromache)* I cannot help you.
**ALFA** *(as Andromache)* My voice is hoarse from shouting, but no-
one hears... *(as self)*They're stuffed. No power, no hope, just the
boys marching in and –
**BEATY** *(as self)* I can't look at this bit when they take the baby.
Have they taken him yet? Have they taken her baby?
**ALFA** *(as self)* Well, that's fate, when you're Hector's child...
You've got to be sacrificed... they can't keep alive a dead hero's
son...
**BEATY**          Bastards.
**ALFA**            They're just following orders.
**BEATY**          Killing off the line...
**CORAL** *(AD)* Coral's attention continues to wander, further out into
the auditorium *(as self)* In a performance, when it's happening, do
you –

**ALFA/BEATY** Ssssh...

**CORAL** *(AD)* They are engrossed. Eyes on stalks.

**ALFA**          They'll never see each other again...

**BEATY**        I can't... (look)

**CORAL** *(AD)* Their attention is pinned to the action like an
Amazonian butterfly onto a dusty baize presentation board.

**ALFA** *(whispered, to unseen players)* Just... yes... hold... hold...

**CORAL** *(AD)* Alfa, unseen, conducts the actors on stage.

**ALFA**          ..that's it...yeees....hooollld...hooollldd...

**BEATY**        ...two... three...

**ALFA**          and releeeaaassse....

**ALFA/BEATY** There!

**CORAL** *(AD)* Alfa and Beaty smile satisfied and strangely self-
congratulatory at each other.

**ALFA**          That timing!

**BEATY**        That was really good.

**ALFA**          Her discipline!

**BEATY**        Well, eight years doing psychophysical work....

**ALFA**          ...Exactly! I mean....

**CORAL** *(AD)* They nod. Reminiscent of those little toy dogs that
were put in the back window of cars in the 70's. *(they nod)* But
not our car, because we couldn't afford a car.

**ALFA**          I love seeing good work. Makes it all worthwhile.

**BEATY**        They did that scene really well... Let's hope the rest
of the show doesn't suffer because of it...

**CORAL** *(AD)* Coral looks at the action, then out towards the
audience. *(as self)* In a performance, when it's happening, do you
ever watch the audience watching the show?

**ALFA**          No.

**CORAL**        You just sit there and ignore what's going on in front
of you!?

**ALFA**          Yes. D'you want a hand with your costume change?

**CORAL**        Please.

**BEATY** *(AD)* The performers help each other out of their big flashy
dresses revealing yet another frock underneath.

*The performers help each other out of their big dresses, revealing
another underneath. Alfa makes an audio description of the actual
costumes used in performance, then:*

**CORAL**        Is this a posh war, or what? Red silk dresses...

**ALFA**          Don't knock it. I'm hoping to keep mine, afterwards.

**CORAL**        It doesn't feel right.

**ALFA**          What do you want? A horse-hair shirt?

**CORAL**        I thought we'd be in khaki.

**ALFA**          We're the Chorus of a war play, not Kate bloody Adie. And the costume designer did train with Jean-Paul Gaultier...

**BEATY**        We could have ended up with conical tits! Imagine: us lifted, separated and strategically aimed...

**ALFA**          I'd rather that than some worthy interpretation. The Furies or Fates. Or the bloody Graeae sisters, with an eye and tooth shared between them...

**CORAL**        And, god forbid, if we were them, we might be meaningful and have to be taken seriously – given some status instead of bit parts, in the shadows. You know, it's a shame your wonderful costume designer didn't just build us into the scenery, so they could have done away with our bodies and contribution altogether. *(beat)*

**BEATY**        What's bitten you?

**ALFA**          Oh don't complain to anyone about the dresses... please don't take away my one little luxury... life's hard, please, please don't put us in khaki...

**CORAL**        ...You're right, I see that now. If we were dressed in khaki, that might suggest reality and make the audience think about us and what we're saying rather than the quality and texture of what we're wearing on our backs... Don't look at me like that. *(AD)* Pensive, calculating – their mouths shrewish, eyes narrowed. *(as self)* It wasn't me acting along with the principles, ready to sell my soul for a decent part... It wasn't me lip-syncing Andromache ... *(beat)* Don't you get tired of being the decoration... the mute mime show... the right-on extras stuck at the back whilst the real actors continue with the real play?

**ALFA**          I'm tired of sign interpreting a performance but never getting the chance to perform it properly.

**CORAL**        Well, I've had it with bath chairs. I'm not doing a period piece again. And my agent... if he ever puts me up again for a casting for 'Aliens'...

**ALFA** *(emphatically interrupting)* Don't. Go. There.

**BEATY** *(AD)* Beaty has been watching all this, silently, her teeth
   lightly catching on the ulcer growing on the inside of her mouth.
   *(as self)* Well, if I get a job, it's down completely to my talent.
**CORAL**         Yeah, the talent to be the ticked box on an equal
   opportunities monitoring form.
**BEATY**         My, aren't we bitter and twisted?
**CORAL**         No, even when we're ideal for the part we don't get
   it.
**BEATY**         Look, I know you would have been a brilliant Hedda
   Gabler and you were born to play Joan of Arc, but disappoint-
   ments happen and you just have to –
**CORAL** *(interrupting)* You know what I mean..
**BEATY**         …No. Don't use excuses and don't include me in
   your resumé of failure.
**CORAL**         Excuses!

*The following dialogue overlaps, all speak/sign quickly and simult-
aneously – creating a moment of chaos and poor communication.*

**BEATY**         It's a tough business.
**CORAL**         Even when it's a disabled character, they give it to a
   walkie-talkie.
**BEATY**         No-one said it would be easy.
**ALFA**          Cripping up. The twenty-first century's answer to
   blacking up.
**BEATY**         If you can't run with the big dogs, stay on the bloody
   porch.
**CORAL**         My agent was telling me there's talk of doing a bio-
   pic about Tamara Detreaux.

*Overlap ends as though it never happened*

**ALFA**          Tamara…?
**CORAL**         A bio-pic about Tamara Detreaux. You know, the
   Hollywood actress who played E.T?
**BEATY**         Really?
**CORAL**         Yeah.
**BEATY**         They're casting?
**CORAL**         Apparently.

**BEATY**        When!? I'd be perfect! I'd be absolutely perfect for–

**CORAL**        …They're gonna cast either Angelina Jolie* or Penelope Cruz*, then digitally shrink her down to size.

**BEATY**        You Are Joking.

**CORAL**        Nope. Computer generation. It's the future.

**ALFA**          So then – d'you think they could film you two, then blow you up to size?

**BEATY**        I am 'to size', thank you, fuck-face.

**ALFA**          You have such a problem with aggression.

**BEATY**        No – I have such a problem with you being a fuckwit.

**ALFA**          And your language! I really don't like it. I don't like signing all those fucks, you know.

**CORAL** *(AD)* Alfa signs fuck repeatedly and with violence. It is not a pretty sight.

**ALFA**          Fuckfuckfuckfuckfuckfuckfuckfuckfuck *(pause)*

**CORAL**        Do you think we all end up just like our mothers? If we had kids, would we make the same mistakes?

**ALFA**          Where did that come from?

**CORAL**        Nowhere… just… *(to Beaty)* In a performance, when it's happening, do you ever watch the audience watching the show?

**BEATY**        Yes. I make a mental note of who yawned and who forgot to switch off their mobile phone, then I have a contract taken out on them.

**ALFA**          The magic of theatre. Live performance as a collaborative act, the dynamic created by the relationship between the spectacle and the spectators. That's why no two performances are the same. It's symbiotic.

**BEATY**        Exactly. And if the audience don't respect that, they're asking for their legs to be broken… *(AD)* We look out at the audience expectantly.

*Several beats as they stare at the audience expectantly.*

**BEATY** *(AD)* Slowly the expectation turns to boredom and disappointment. Only Coral remains staring.

**CORAL**        I watch them – the audience – their heads sleek in the dark – furtive – secretive, with their little habits, tics, inappropriate coughs, gaze. I watch them – but it's transgressive – I'm to be stared at, not them. But I look and I want to ask who are you? why are you here? what do you think of me? As you sit there in your rows in the dark rubbing shoulders with strangers, looking, listening – what do you think of me? Am I just another performer? What am I? My Mother could never find the exact word for me – even though she's still searching – *(as Mother)* 'What are you like Coral? I'll tell you what you're like: A disappointment. A let-down. And after all my sacrifices....' *(To audience as self)* I'm watching you. *(beat)*

**BEATY**      We're on.

*The performers possibly go into a series of tableaux denoting battle and warfare. If so, each image should be audio described.*

| | |
|---|---|
| **CORAL** | And as the battle commenced and the |
| **BEATY** | heat-seeking missiles |
| **ALFA** | arrows |
| **BEATY** | bayonettes |
| **CORAL** | stones found their mark and as the |
| **ALFA** | soldiers |
| **CORAL** | mercenaries |
| **BEATY** | widow-makers |
| **CORAL** | serial killers |
| **ALFA** | former-neighbours advanced |
| **ALL** | on both sides |
| **CORAL** | and as the mortar |
| **ALFA** | shrapnel |
| **BEATY** | boiling oil |
| **CORAL** | poured down, |
| **ALFA** | we sat in the ruins and laughed: |
| **ALL** | Haven't we been here, before? |
| **CORAL** | And as the radio blared |
| **ALFA** | and the spider shuttled back and forth into the corner |
| **BEATY** | and the children were taught marching songs in the |
| courtyard | |
| **ALFA** | we signed their death warrants |
| **CORAL** | by not saying |
| **ALL** | no. |

**ALFA**        Child – I should have taken your nursery pillow and suffocated you myself rather than leave you to bleed dry on nomansland.

**BEATY**       I should have crushed you in the womb – folded you back inside myself rather than let you die by suicide bomb in a crowded discotheque.

**CORAL**       Her hope is that he died, dancing

**BEATY**       Mama's precious

**ALFA**        Future joy

**BEATY**       hands clasped, dancing, dancing.....

*Alfa signs a version of the 'dance of death' as at the end of scene one.*

**CORAL** *(AD)* Alfa's fingers dance, dancing, dance down the deaths... *(beat)*

*The moment is slowed, completed. Floods go off. A beat.*

**CORAL**       I'm pregnant. *(beat)*

**ALFA** *(to Beaty)* She's pregnant.

**BEATY**       How?

**CORAL**       Immaculate conception second time round. How d'you think?

**ALFA**        She shagged somebody. A man. Shagged him.

**CORAL**       And this is doing my head in... This play is – help me.

**BEATY**       What?

**CORAL**       Help me by telling me

**BEATY**       What d' you want me to say?

**CORAL**       That it'll be alright. That... that earth's an okay place to take a baby... That... I'd be a good mum... That...

**BEATY**       But we don't know that, do we?

**CORAL**       What?

**BEATY**       Any of it. We don't know any of it.

**CORAL**       But tell me.

**BEATY**       I can't answer that. I don't know.

**CORAL**       Please...

**BEATY**       You want me to lie? *(beat)*

**ALFA** *(AD)* Coral looks at Beaty, who doesn't speak. Alfa takes out her knitting.

**BEATY** *(AD)* Beaty sets up her mirror, takes out her wig and prepares for the next scene. *(They do as described)*

**CORAL**    Please.

**ALFA** *(AD)* A painful pause. *(A painful pause, then as self)* How about the dad?

**CORAL**    Gone. Not worth it anyway. Better off without him.

**BEATY**    Why'd you get pregnant if you didn't want to get pregnant?

**CORAL**    It wasn't planned.

**ALFA**    Were you taken by force?

**CORAL**    No... It seemed a good idea at the time.

**BEATY**    I've a really nice recipe for sweet potatoes. You put them in olive oil and in the oven and when they come out, they're all really nice and soft.

**ALFA**    Is there a low fat version?

**CORAL**    It'd be irresponsible for me to have a baby I don't really want.

**BEATY**    Exactly. Story over. Move on.

**ALFA**    Sod it, I've dropped a stitch.

**CORAL** *(to Beaty)* Are things always so black and white to you?

**BEATY**    Yeah.

**ALFA** *(to Beaty)* You know – that wig really suits your skin colour.

**CORAL**    But it doesn't stop me from thinking about it. It's real. It could happen. I could have... I could... If things were different, I'd have it. I'd like to look after it in a family – what's that stupid word? Nuclear? Nuclear family. Only I'd have mum, dad, baby and fucking personal assistant. I wouldn't do that, subjecting a baby to that. No privacy. Every Tom Dick or Harriet sticking their noses in and the mood of the day dependent on some mardy P.A. 'Why, you've really fucked me up and over today, how very caring of you...' A baby couldn't grow up in that. All those people... passed around, one pair of stranger's hands to another. Not knowing whose arms are holding you. Watching mummy be patronised, treated as an incompetent; some kind of Frankenstein with her new-born baby. I couldn't put a child through that. I couldn't. Never mind everything else – how unsafe the world is... how suddenly filled with sharp edges and...

**BEATY** *(rudely interrupting)* Great. Decision made. End of
conversation.

**CORAL**  No! I was still speaking, I was…

**BEATY**  Shit, or get off the pot.

**CORAL**  What?!

**BEATY**  You're going on and on and on. Make the decision.
Or if you're going to whinge, be a bit more entertaining, would
you?

**CORAL**  What's wrong with you?

**BEATY**  You wittering on about this frigging baby.

**ALFA**  It's not a baby. It's a collection of cells. A blood
clot. Little more than a minor thrombosis and nothing you say
will convince me otherwise. *(beat)*

**CORAL**  Well, thank you, both. This is probably the most
important decision I'll ever make in my life. I thought you'd
understand, help me think it through, but no. Who was I kidding?
Just forget it. Just forget I ever said anything.

**BEATY**  Ooooh. Little Miss Tantrum…

**CORAL**  Conversation closed.

**BEATY**  Don't take it out on us that the one time you shag in
your life you get caught.

**CORAL**  Dialogue finito.

**BEATY**  Wasn't us that put you up the duff off the rag and in
the family way.

**CORAL**  Just leave it.

**BEATY**  Why?

**CORAL**  Just…

**BEATY**  Why?

**CORAL**  Because you wouldn't know a helpful, sympathetic
thing to say if it jumped up and bit you in the arse. Because you
don't understand.

**BEATY** *(interjecting)* No?

**CORAL**  Because you're so lacking in the milk of human
kindness, you've gone rancid. Because you haven't the slightest
idea…

**BEATY** *(interrupting)* I've had to make the same decision. *(beat)*
I've had a child. But I've not been a mother. I've had a child. But
it's not the same.

**CORAL**  Isn't it?

**BEATY**  It doesn't count. I had all the biology… the physical sensations – that new life moving under my hand…

**ALFA** *(BSL only)* Fish under ice

**BEATY**  ..stirring inside...

**ALFA** *(BSL only)* night swimming

**BEATY**  waking me in the night…

**CORAL**  But you haven't mothered?

**BEATY**  No.

**ALFA**  And it's not the same.

**BEATY** *(to Alfa)* And you'd know about that, would you?

**ALFA**  I know a sad woman when I see one.

**BEATY**  Know all about babies? About carrying them and giving birth?

**ALFA**  Ugly and sad. It's there, in your mouth.

**CORAL** *(AD)* Alfa's hand shapes the air.

**ALFA**  I can see it. *(AD)* Sorrow. The lips pulling down, mouth sunken with its weight.

**BEATY**  I don't want to hear this.

**ALFA**  You can always tell who got rid of their baby.

**BEATY** *(overlapping)* Enough, that's enough.

**ALFA**  In a room full of people, or walking down a crowded road, you can always tell…

**BEATY**  I'm not listening.

**ALFA** *(continuing, oblivious)* It leaves its traces – an ugliness, a sorrow, a –

**BEATY**  I've stopped listening to you. Oi! Deafie! *(She sticks two fingers up at Alfa)*

**CORAL** *(AD)* Beaty sticks two fingers up in a very un-Churchill like kind of way.

**BEATY** *(waving her fingers)* Sign language everyone can understand.

**ALFA**  Only if you can see.

**BEATY**  Just leave it – shut the fuck up, okay?

**ALFA**  I hate being in the Chorus with you. You're an ugly person, Beaty, did you know that?

**BEATY**  I'm ugly?

**ALFA**  I'm not talking appearance; I'm talking inside. Ugly ugly ugly

**BEATY**  Watch it.

**ALFA**          Ugly ugly ugly

**BEATY**          You're so ugly, your Mother didn't give birth to you. She shat you.

**ALFA**          You're so ugly, when you were born, the midwife slapped your mother.

**BEATY**          I'm so ugly, I had the baby and she was taken away from me. Yeah… Because I'm what's ill-advisably known as a 'handicap', a 'retard', a 'special person with special needs' and because I'm 'special', apparently I'm especially incapable of grasping the concept of contraception or looking after a baby. Or so the experts said. And because I'm a freaky damaged sick chick and because I have an interesting and increasingly rare genetic conjunction, it's best to tie the tubes – no, better still to slice them – as we don't want the special egg meeting with the sperm again, do we? We don't want any more special babies born because they're expensive, a drain on limited welfare resources and, let's face it, they don't really do much, do they? And while we're on the subject, let's be frank, 'normal' society finds 'special' scary and would much rather have them put down… did I say that, oops I meant sterilise the fuckers, stop their depraved genes in their tracks, stop that freaky evolution, we don't like special, we want all to be the same and so during the caesarean when my apparently normal not at all special baby was delivered, this special mum received a special operation, without consent or knowledge, to ensure no further specials were conceived. And it took me years to find out as they didn't think it important to inform me I was made sterile.

**CORAL**          But they can't do that!

**BEATY**          No?

*Long pause.*

**CORAL**          I'm sorry.

**BEATY**          Not as much as I am.
          *(aggressively, in the style of Chorus)*
          The last of my line.
          A full stop.
          The blank page following the final chapter in a book.

**CORAL**        And the baby? *(beat)* What happened to the baby? Did the baby survive?

**BEATY**        Yes.

**CORAL**        Was the baby adopted? Beaty? Was the baby adop –

**BEATY**        By a nice non-disabled family with a life expectancy much longer than the biological mother's. And that's all I'm gonna say about it.

**CORAL**        But –?

**BEATY**        It's none of your fucking business.

**CORAL**        But we've just…

**BEATY**        …I work with you, you're not my best friend and just because we've both had a bun in the oven doesn't mean we're sisters under the skin.

**CORAL**        Beaty you just told me –

**BEATY** *(interrupting)* We haven't shared anything significant, just an unfortunate coincidence.

**CORAL**        …but the baby, the…

**BEATY**        If you put a slice of brown bread with garlic and some parsley into the microwave for less than a minute, then eat it up quickly before it goes hard – you'll have a nice something for when you're in from work, feeling tired and wanting a snack. And the parsley's great as it gets rid of the garlic smell…

**CORAL**        Stop it! Just chit chat chit fucking chit chat.

**BEATY**        Don't you like chit chat?

**CORAL**        No, I don't fucking like chit chat and I don't like garlic on brown fucking sliced bread.

**BEATY**        What about ciabatta? Seeded bread rolls, rye bread? How about thinly sliced white bleached processed bread…?

**ALFA** *(to Beaty)* I like that German one. What is it? Pumpernickel?

**CORAL**        Don't you ever take anything seriously?

**BEATY**        No. Because life's too short – or apparently in my case not as short as my Mother or the medical profession led me to believe… I lost my little girl. Every day I think of her. Every day I think I could have been with her, whilst I'm living *now* and they said I'd be rotting in my grave. After that, I never want to take anything seriously again. So good old Coral… good on you, having a bun in the oven. A little loaf. Your yeasty high-riser. What kind is it, eh? Irish soda bread – was the daddy a paddy? Or petit pain – maybe he was French…?

**CORAL**        Beaty…

**BEATY**        Or a Scottish griddle cake….

**ALFA** *(AD)* Beaty has gone off in a world of her own.

**BEATY**        …maybe Italian Focaccia….

**ALFA** *(AD)* Beaty lists all the bread she can remember.

**BEATY**        ….Well, there's always the American Wonder loaf;

**ALFA** *(AD)* As she does so, Alfa signs a story in BSL – the story she wants to tell.

**BEATY**        …sweet zucchini bread…

**ALFA** *(AD)* A terrible one, about warfare and eugenics …

*Alfa signs her story using BSL, but with no voice, whilst Beaty very slowly lists the breads. It may take some time, finishing just slightly before Alfa's signed story ends.*

**BEATY**        Sour dough balls, baguette, Walnut pavé, organic sundried tomato and basil plait, *Hovis, Sunblest, Nimble,* wholemeal bloomer, cholla, oaty tin, cheese and onion bread, panini, garlic and coriander naan, chapatis, pitta bread, poppyseed rolls, floury baps, warburtons, scofa, Irish boxty, poppadums, French stick, wheatgerm...

*The following is a spoken English language précis of what Alfa will sign in performance, using BSL only and no voice. It is reproduced here in this version solely for the purposes of the published text. Another version of this speech occurs in scene 3, with a translation of BSL into spoken English.*

**ALFA** *(all in BSL, only. No voice)* A story starting a long time ago, in the war. A woman. Her community was uprooted and replanted in alien soil. She saw many things. The cruelty of men and women. A baby's nose gnawed away by a rat. Men and women starved so their ribs showed. This way the laboratories. This way the crematoriums. Many had not survived. She was taken the experimental route, along with the others – those who were blind, or had polio, and a plethora of other conditions and disabilities, including her own, which was to be deaf. She survived, along with others with an invisible sensory disability – who could almost 'pass'. She was useful. Could work. She was 'allowed' to

survive – but with one amendment. They made her the last in her
line – they sterilised all the men and women. After... she was
repatriated to England – and lived in a small flat on the outskirts
of London. She was grateful. She avoided her relatives. She found
a companion, a quiet, troubled man who had been in a similar situation as she. They didn't speak of it. They didn't speak at all.
They married. They had no children. People asked : why don't
you have children? Why can't you have children? Are you sterile,
then? Mule. Is that what you are, then, a sterile mule?' They were
silent. They did not speak about it. The war was over – 10, 20, 40
years and she was silent – he was silent – waiting for the knock
on the door, the butt of a revolver against the skull, the bludgeon-
ing hammer to fall. She lived daily with fear of violence, should
she tell what happened to her in the camps. She was one of
hundreds, perhaps thousands... subjects of former experiments,
trapped behind their net curtains, caught in a binding agreement
not to tell – never to tell. All stuck. All silent. Our story.
*(with voice)* Schtump. *(Alfa's signing of the story and Beaty's
naming of bread come to an end. A pause. Coral looks at Alfa
expectantly.)*

**ALFA** *(with voice)* I'm not going to voice-over for you so don't look
at me expecting an interpretation.

**CORAL**      But... I... but... but you...

**ALFA**      It's not a secret language. It's in the public domain.

**CORAL**      But... I –

**ALFA**      I'm not going to cheapen my exquisite signing with
your words.

**CORAL**      But.you... but, but...

**ALFA** *(BSL only)* Jawjawjawjaw, bloody talkies, always eating air.
*(With voice)* Learn it yourself.

*Several beats. The floods come on – Beaty moves downstage, caught
in a spotlight for the parallel play.*

*CHORUS:*
**BEATY**      All men know children mean more than life.
Which is why they kill them.

*Blackout.*

**SCENE 3**

*A huge wall of sound – loud music with explosions, sirens and gunfire beneath. When the lights come up, the women are out of their silk dresses, wearing worn clothes. The sounds continue intermittently throughout the start of the scene. The women do not react to them, except as a brief silence, then continuing with their speech / actions. The women are involved in small, slowed activities. Coral removing her costume, Beaty sewing a small white (as yet unrecognisable) garment. Alfa is heating the soup she was making, earlier, with a travel electrical element.*

*Later, she passes around bowls and they eat. They speak a 'Non-Chorus' at the opening, i.e. they are no longer the Chorus, although they still assume the form. They speak in their usual voices, everyday, tired, with no performance mode. Even the Audio Description (AD) is closer to their usual voices and lacks the presentation of before. There are no floods.*

*Non-Chorus.*

| | |
|---|---|
| **ALFA** | And as the trumpets |
| **BEATY** | wailing |
| **CORAL** | all-clear sounded, the women came forward to harvest their fallen fruit. Fields ripe with a strange crop: |
| **ALFA** | Limbs |
| **BEATY** | torsos |
| **ALFA** | arms |
| **CORAL** | heads |
| **ALL** | plucked |
| **CORAL** | ready to be gathered. |
| **BEATY** | Here a hand relaxed, palm open, lying as it did so frequently in life. |
| **CORAL** | Here a body, soft, almost in repose |
| **BEATY** | faces twisted |
| **CORAL** | teeth bared |
| **ALFA** | eyes rolled back |
| **ALL** | dead. |
| **CORAL** | All dead. |

**ALFA**     They claim them, the living, crawling across the
rubble
**BEATY**     seeking the familiar known faces
**ALFA**     remembered hands
**CORAL**     half-forgotten birthmarks
**BEATY**     flesh that when new was bathed, kissed, patted dry,
powdered –
**ALFA**     sung over
**BEATY**     lullabyed
**ALFA**     Mama's precious
**CORAL**     future joy
**BEATY**     now rank
**ALFA**     sullied
**BEATY**     gone forever.
**ALL**     Child – Child. *(beat)*
**CORAL**     They've forgotten about us. *(beat)*
**ALFA** *(to Coral)* Soup?
**CORAL** *(to Alfa)* Yes, please.
**ALFA** *(AD)* Alfa finds a soup bowl for Coral. *(as self)* It's awfully
quiet. Can you see the other side of the screen?
**BEATY**     No.
**ALFA**     I hate being behind a screen. I seem to spend my life
behind a screen. I –
**CORAL**     – Is anyone else feeling the heat? Have they
switched off the air-conditioning?
**ALFA** *(to Beaty)* Soup?
**BEATY**     Yes.
**CORAL** *(AD)* Coral loosens her clothing. She sees everybody's face
is beaded with sweat.
**ALFA** *(AD)* They eat.

*Several beats as they eat.*

**CORAL**     Once... Once there was a Trojan horse wheeled in
through the gates of the city, with death hidden in its belly.
An intelligent betrayal. Violence contained. Death controlled.
Now it just falls from the sky. It has no boundaries. It's invisible.
War without frontiers. Or states. Or –
**ALFA**     Has anybody got any painkillers?

CORAL — identification. It's faceless.

BEATY I can do you *Codeine, Ibuprofen, Benelin, Night-nurse or Aspro.*

ALFA Nothing stronger?

BEATY *Quaaludes* and *Cipro?*

CORAL We sit eating oven-ready dinners on our laps in front of the telly, the volume turned low, whilst food parcels are dropped in the middle of minefields.

ALFA I can't remember that speech from the play.

CORAL The food we eat is poisoned. There are more wars raging now than in previous centuries put together.

ALFA Is she rehearsing a new scene?

CORAL As the ice caps melt, the land will be submerged. The planet is dying. We inject it with cancers and yet we still procreate, we still continue the old dance, covering our eyes, feet stamping the rhythm, mama's precious, future joy –

BEATY I think her hormones are fucking her over. Gone tired and emotional, have we? A bit weepy?

CORAL Fuck You.

BEATY That oestrogen's a right bastard. Just chill. Have some more nice soup and borrow my mobile, call your boyfriend and give him the good news.

CORAL Don't Patronise Me. *(beat)*

ALFA It's really quiet. *(AD)* Alfa stares out into the darkness before her. Why can't we see out? Have they brought the fire curtain down? Has everybody been sent home? It really has gone awfully quiet.

BEATY And you'd be able to tell the difference?

CORAL Don't start.

ALFA Is it over? *(beat)* Did anyone hear the applause? *(beat)* Was everyone sent home? *(beat)* Didn't the audience come back after the third interval?

CORAL It's an epic, alright.

ALFA I've no idea what Act I'm in. Where am I? Where was I?

CORAL Women. Children. Variations on a theme.

BEATY Men.

CORAL Yeah, men. Women. Children. War. Women being strong.

| | |
|---|---|
| **BEATY** | Killing their babies. *(AD)* Alfa flinches. |
| **ALFA** | I don't think I like this play very much. |
| **BEATY** | So when did you have your abortion? |

*A shocked silence.*

**CORAL** *(AD)* Alfa closes her eyes, cutting out all communication.

*Alfa speaks/signs the following at breakneck speed, without punctuation.*

**ALFA**      It was supposed to be the ideal perfect punctuation two people who love each other plus baby full stop baby made up from each other as though we could disassemble ourselves then reinvent two as three and it was perfect right from the start we felt we were doing more than making love we really were making life and I knew even before the pregnancy test I could feel it like there was a fizzing in my blood a secret I shared with my tissues and bones the fleshy matter that made up me and the father moved in and we booked the registry office and I *(slower)* arranged for an amniocentesis test ...

**CORAL** *(AD/storyteller)* Alfa opens her eyes. She shrugs, drops her eloquent hands. They lie in her lap, palms up, as though unable – or unwilling – to shape the words to come.

**ALFA**      What destroyed us was trying to decide where to put the blame. These two making three... when the sums don't add up – when the calculations are faulty – when the perfect multiplication comes out wrong. Who made the mistake? Whose was the rogue gene? Who brought the unwanted guest to the intimate family dinner? We discovered a hierarchy of acceptability. He didn't mind a sensory disability, he didn't mind me being deaf...

**BEATY**      That's really big of him.

**CORAL**      Ssssh.

**ALFA**      But when it came to that missing chromosome... I know what I'm *supposed* to think, I know what's right-on, I know what I'm supposed to do, but... I couldn't do it. The effort – the work involved – the never-ending dedication that was required having a rewarding but exhausting child, forever and ever. I couldn't do it. Okay? I couldn't fucking do it. And then I realised

nobody needed to know. I could keep my political correctness and
my disability awareness and my halo still shining. I could remain
holier than thou and get rid of it, flush it away, throw the blood-
clot in the bin. So I did. And I asked the father to return my keys,
pack his toothbrush and go off and worship some other flawed
goddess, because I didn't deserve love – I needed to be punished.
And I'm still serving time. So do you have a problem with that?

**BEATY** *(AD)* She looks at me, then out towards the auditorium.

**ALFA**          Have they forgotten about us? Have they all gone
home?

**BEATY** *(AD)* Beaty takes Alfa's bag of knitting and empties it of
finished garments. She begins laying the clothing on the floor,
adding her own contribution – tiny white matinee jackets, a new-
born baby's vest, booties…

*She does so, covering the floor with the baby clothing, including the*
*white garment she had been sewing – a baby's vest. Alfa joins her.*
*They continue the action through the following.*
*A shift again in style and place. When they make a statement about*
*war, the women speak slowly with dignity, low-key.*

**BEATY**          They rounded up all the men and male children and
brought them to the stadium. The grass now grows over them.

**CORAL**          They bombed the people in the bread queue, then
shot those trying to comfort the dying.

**BEATY**          They killed all the boys a moment before their
fathers, so the men could see their hopes destroyed.

**CORAL**          Yesterday, four pupils were killed at their desks at
school.

**BEATY**          There was an explosion in the market place. People
lay scattered. Blood flowered on a woman's face.

*Alfa repeats a version of the BSL eugenics speech of Scene 2, this*
*time without sign language, but vocalising BSL. Instructions in*
*italics are placement.*

**ALFA**          Happen war past. People force move strange place
Woman there watch watch. See bad things like what? Baby rat
crawl up baby gnaw. People cruel. Men women food nothing go

thin ribs. Strange place have what? *(point left)* Science test.
*(point right)* House fire bury people queue pile in burnt. Woman
in where? *(point left)* Science test. Many people them have what?
Disability blind weak the shakes the limp. Some see, some
hidden. Woman *(point index)* she what? Deaf. She get away.
Many people die. Bith finish. She not. She useful. Work. She
live-win can. Allowed. But *(point left)* happen what? Men penis
cut. Woman insert cut. Birth children stop. Finish. Many many
die. Many live-win not. She live-win. War finish woman go
where? England. Live London outside. She relief-thankful.
Woman meet meet family? no. Woman *(point right)* man *(point
left)* meet partner marry join. Children have p-hho. People ask p-
hho children why? Problem what? Insert cut bin both? You yaah
damage? You yaah destroy? Sterile you? Stomach suck out bin?
She tell past no. He tell past no. Couple schtum always discuss
nothing schtump. Life progress 10, 20, 40 years progress. She
continue silent. Why? continue wait for what? Soldier guns door
bash bash bam beat. Bin told before 'you let know bin insert cut
we you punish suffer suffer more hup'. She every day continue
live how? Schtump. Why? If tell, punish. Frighten frighten. Life
danger. She alone no. Many many same. All over house house
house house people people people people stuck stuck stuck stuck.
Fix forget never say nothing fear inside body schtump want
release mouth not allowed zip mouth. Our story. Schtump. All
schtump.

*Pause.*

**BEATY**     Have the baby.

*A change back.*

**BEATY**     Have the bloody baby. *(beat)* To make up for those
we've lost.
**ALFA** *(AD)* We glance sideways at each other, eyes swivelling,
avoiding direct contact.
**CORAL**     Oh yeah, right – let's all go out and have babies as
some response to the holocaust. Or if not that atrocity, some other

war; there's plenty to choose from. And if the baby isn't disabled, what do we do then? Get rid of it?

**ALFA** *(AD)* Temperature rising – a rush of blood to my face.

**CORAL** 'Cause we want the 'whacky' genes, the 'impairments', right?

**ALFA** *(AD)* A nervous tic beneath my right eye – morse code tapping out all is not well.

**CORAL** Let's go procreate to ensure in the future there's still an excluded underclass. Let's fill the day centres and institutions with another generation undervalued by the rest of the country. Let's have children so they'll suffer the pain we can hardly bear; let them continue with the same struggle for basic human rights; the numbing round of political and social campaign. Sure, let's patent our genes so no multinational pharmaceutical company can wipe us out, as we have such high quality of life we want more to experience it.

**BEATY** You talk such bullshit.

**CORAL** No. I know what I'm *supposed* to think – what is right-on to say – but this isn't a political theory, this is my life and I'm not convinced I want another poor bastard to go through everything I have.

*Several beats. The women reflect. They go into performance Chorus mode – no floods – this is their own version. They begin to remove and discard the remains of their costumes.*

**ALFA** So they made a decision, those women with their phantom children,

**BEATY** These women who knew in which direction the world revolved: counter to them.

**ALFA** They smelt the ash of a thousand burning bodies, watching the bruise deepen on the delicate flesh where the earth and the sky met.

**CORAL** And these women knew the stories and they knew what would happen.

**ALFA** So they taught their children to dance

**BEATY** Mamma's precious

**CORAL** Future joy

**ALFA**　　　　They taught their children to dance and, clasping
hands, they danced up along the city gates
**BEATY**　　　　as the bruise deepened on the horizon
**ALFA**　　　　they danced out, along the city's upper walls, past
the lookout
**BEATY**　　　　Mother's faces wet with tears
**ALFA**　　　　beyond the cobbled roads, where the path stumbled
into rock and mud they danced, up along the steep incline,
**BEATY**　　　　hands clasped, tiny feet stamping the rhythm
**ALFA**　　　　Mamma's precious
**CORAL**　　　　Future joy. *(They stop. A beat.)*
**ALFA** *(to Coral)* Did you know you can make oranges less messy to
eat by putting them in the freezer for half an hour before peeling
them?
**CORAL**　　　　Just fucking get on with it!
**ALFA**　　　　With –? *(Pause.)*
**BEATY** *(AD)* They are silent. They do not move. *(A beat.)*
**CORAL**　　　　I think I'm bleeding.

*Immediate blackout.*
*The end.*

### Kaite (Caitlin) O'Reilly

She is an award-winning playwright. *Yard* won the 1998 Peggy
Ramsay Award and was subsequently produced at the Maxim Gorki
Theatre, Berlin. *Belonging* opened at Birmingham Rep's The Door in
2000. *Lives Out of Step* in 2001, was commissioned by BBC Radio 3
as part of the experimental radio drama strand, *The Wire*. Future
commissions include: Sgript Cymru and Contact Theatre,
Manchester. She is working on her first feature film.

# GRAE*ae* since 1980

1980    **SIDESHOW** Grae*ae*'s premier production, devised by Richard Tomlinson and the company.

1981    **3D** Devised by Richard Tomlinson and the company. Directed by Nic Fine.
**BBC 2 ARENA** Documentary on the work of the company.

1982    **M3 JUNCTION 4** Co-directed by Richard Tomlinson and Nic Fine.
**PEOPLE'S MINDS** Channel 4 documentary about the making of the show.

1983    **THE ENDLESS VARIETY SHOW** a show for children by Chris Speyer. Directed by Geoff Armstrong.
**NOT TOO MUCH TO ASK** by Patsy Rodenburg. Directed by Caroline Noh.
**CASTING OUT** Written and directed by Nigel Jamieson.

1984    **COCKTAIL CABARET** Devised by the company. Directed by Caroline Noh.

1985    **PRACTICALLY PERFECT** by Ashley Grey. Directed by Geoff Armstrong.
**CHOICES** Central TV Programme about the Theatre In Education work of the company.

1986    **WORKING HEARTS** by Noel Grieg. Directed by Maggie Ford.

1987    **EQUALITY STREET** Theatre In Education show. Devised by Ashley Grey and Geoff Armstrong.
**PRIVATE VIEW** by Tasha Fairbanks. Directed by Anna Furse. Grae*ae*'s first women's project. National and international tour.

1988    **THE CORNFLAKE BOX** by Elspeth Morrison. Grae*ae*'s first community play.

1989    **WHY** by Geoff Armstrong and Yvonne Lynch. Directed by Ewan Marshall. Theatre In Education show.

1990    **WHY** (As above.) Adapted for a national tour.

1991    **CHANCES ARE** by Jo Verrant. Directed by Annie Smoll. Theatre In Education national tour.

1992    **HOUND** by Maria Oshodi. Directed by Ewan Marshall. National 10th anniversary tour.
**A KIND OF IMMIGRANT** by Firdaus Kanga. Directed by Ewan Marshall. National tour.

1993    **SOFT VENGEANCE** Adapted from the book by Albie

Sachs, by April De Angelis. Directed by Ewan Marshall. National and international tour.

1994    **PLAYBACK**  Forum T.I.E. Programme.
        **UBU**  by Alfred Jarry. Adapted by Trevor Lloyd.

1995/6  **PLAYBACK 2 U**  Forum Theatre Programme.

1996    **FLESH FLY**  Adapted from Ben Jonson's *Volpone* by Trevor Lloyd. Directed by Ewan Marshall.
        **SYMPATHY FOR THE DEVIL**  written and directed by Ray Harrison Graham. A co-production with Basic Theatre Co.

1997    **WHAT THE BUTLER SAW**  by Joe Orton. Directed by Ewan Marshall.

1998    **TWO** by Jim Cartwright. Directed by Jenny Sealey.
        **ALICE** A free adaptation by Noel Greig of *Alice in Wonderland*. Directed by Jenny Sealey and Geoff Bullen. A co-production with Nottingham Playhouse and Nottingham Roundabout TIE.

1999    **A LOVELY SUNDAY FOR CREVE COEUR** by Tennessee Williams. Directed by Jenny Sealey. National Tour.
        **FITTINGS: THE LAST FREAK SHOW** by Mike Kenny. Co-directed by Jenny Sealey and Garry Robson. A co-production with Fittings Multi Media Arts. National tour.

2000    **THE FALL OF THE HOUSE OF USHER** by Steven Berkoff. Directed by Jenny Sealey. National Tour.
        **WOYZECK** by Georg Buchner. Directed by Philip Osment. Performed by graduates of The Missing Piece One Training Course. London Tour.
        **MESSAGE IN A BOTTLE** by Michelle Taylor. Directed by Peter Rumney. Performed by graduates of The Missing Piece One Training Course. London Tour.

2001    **INTO THE MYSTIC** by Peter Wolf. Directed by Jenny Sealey. National Tour
        **BLOOD WEDDING** by Federico Garcia Lorca. Directed by Philip Osment. Missing Piece Two Training Course. North West Tour.
        **THE CHANGELING** by Middleton and Rowley, adapted by Clare McIntyre. Directed by Jenny Sealey. National Tour.

2002    **PEELING** by Kaite O' Reilly. Directed by Jenny Sealey. National Tour.
        **BENT** by Martin Sherman. Directed by Jenny Sealey. National tour.

# GRAE*ae* THEATRE COMPANY

*'Graeae has a thought-provoking line in outrageousness'*
The Independent

Established in 1980 by Nabil Shaban and Richard Tomlinson, Grae*ae* is Britain's leading theatre company of people with physical and sensory impairments.

Funded by the Arts Council of England, London Arts and the Association of London Government, Grae*ae* tours nationally and internationally twice a year with imaginative and exciting productions of both classic and newly-commissioned theatre.

Grae*ae*'s aim is to redress the exclusion of people with physical and sensory impairments from performance and is concerned with developing high quality, genuinely pioneering theatre in both its aesthetic and content.

As well as touring, the company has a strong commitment to training disabled people in performance and other production skills, and to young people's theatre, outreach and education.

*Staff Team*
Artistic Director Jenny Sealey
Executive Producer Roger Nelson
Administrator Annette Cumper
Access Officer Claire Saddleton
(Arts Council of England)
Asst. Director Jamie Beddard

*Board of Directors*
Steve Mannix (Chair)
Vicky Featherstone
Dinah Lloyd
Andy Morgan
Ben Payne
Rena Sodhi
Theresa Veith

Hampstead Town Hall
213 Haverstock Hill
London, NW3 4QP
T 020 7681 4755
F 020 7681 4756
M 020 7681 4757
email **info@graeae.org**
**www.graeae.org**